D1083821

FRAMES OF MEANING

FRAMES OF MEANING
The social construction of extraordinary science

H.M.Collins and T.J. Pinch
School of Humanities and Social Sciences, University of Bath

ROUTLEDGE & KEGAN PAUL LIMITED
London, Boston and Henley

First published in 1982
by Routledge & Kegan Paul Ltd   c . 2
39 Store Street, London WC1E 7DD,
9 Park Street, Boston, Mass. 02108, USA and
Broadway House, Newtown Road,
Henley-on-Thames, Oxon RG9 1EN
Printed in Great Britain by
St Edmundsbury Press, Suffolk

Library of Congress Cataloging in Publication Data

Collins, H.M. (Harry M.), 1943-
Frames of meaning.
Bibliography: p.
Includes index.
1. Psychical research. 2. Knowledge, Theory of.
3. Knowledge, Sociology of. I. Pinch, T.J. (Trevor J.)
II. Title.
BF1040.C53   133.8   81-13990

ISBN 0-7100-9011-0   AACR2

CONTENTS

v

PREFACE

This book reports the findings of an extended piece of research. Its origins lie in an invitation to the senior author to participate in a series of experiments on children who claimed they could bend metal by paranormal means. It soon became apparent that this area had many of the characteristics of 'revolutionary science' and that the experiments on 'spoon-bending' would provide an opportunity for the first contemporaneous study of a potential revolution in science. The experiments on child spoon-benders started in the spring of 1975, and a first report on this work was published in 'Nature' in September of that year. A grant from the British Social Science Research Council enabled the other author to join the project in the autumn of 1975, and made it possible to continue the research with the help of some of the physicists then engaged in work on spoon-bending.

In the book we address, not only the problems of science, but also the wider issues of the 'rationality debate'. The theoretical discussions and résumés of this problem which are found in philosophy and the social sciences invariably rely for their empirical grounding on one or two classic reports of rituals practised by primitive tribes. Since this is the first contemporaneous empirical study of a major discontinuity in what counts as rational action, it should fill a gap in the literature.

The material covered ranges from issues of sociology, philosophy and epistemology, through esoteric aspects of science, such as quantum theory, to some of the more bizarre aspects of paranormal research. Though some parts of the text may be difficult, or unfamiliar, we hope that with an appropriate introduction undergraduates in their later years of study will find the book useful. Scientists and others interested in the paranormal, or in events surrounding the emergence of Uri Geller, may also find much of interest in the text. The prime aim of our book is, however, to make a contribution to current concerns in sociology, history and philosophy.

We would like to thank all those scientists and others who gave up their time to talk to us. Nearly always this time was given whole-heartedly with friendship and hospitality. Because of this our research was a pleasure as well as a job of work. Over the years the authors have spoken to some hundreds of respondents, whose views have helped us to form the ideas we present. These include: Cleve Backster; Eduardo Balanovski; Ted Bastin; John Beloff; David Bohm; Eldon Byrd; Fritjof Capra; Bernard Carr; John Clauser; O. Costa de Beauregard; Henry Dakin; David

Davies; Douglas Dean; Philippe Eberhard; Arthur Ellison; Chris Evans; William Fairbank; Gerald Feinberg; Harvey Flowers; Stuart Freedman; Martin Gardner; Robert Gasteiger; Joe Hanlon; John Hasted; Arthur Hastings; Ron Hawke; Nick Herbert; Chuck Honorton; Bascom Jones; Brian Josephson; George King; John Kmetz; Ed May; Jeffrey Mishlove; Robert Morris; Philip Morrison; Thelma Moss; Brendan O'Regan; Brian Pamplin; Adrian Parker; David Parkin; Andrija Puharich; Hal Puthoff; James Randi; Elizabeth Rauscher; Theodore Rockwell; Jack Sarfatti; Gertrude Schmeidler; Helmut Schmidt; Saul-Paul Sirag; Ingo Swann; Russell Targ; Charlie Tart; John Taylor; Melanie Toyofuku; Marcello Truzzi; Evan Harris Walker; Paul Werbos; Fred Wolf.

We are grateful to our young spoon-bending subjects without whom it would not have been possible to write chapters 5 and 6. They spent hours in our laboratory for, regrettably, very little reward. The experiments would not have been able to go ahead without the technical assistance of Mark Price and Megan Patel and hours of patient voluntary help from Bob Draper. Helen Weinreich-Haste facilitated our use of the psychology laboratory at the University of Bath in every way possible. Without Brian Pamplin there would have been no experiments. We are also in the debt of the Society for Psychical Research for a small grant (about £30) toward experimental expenses.

Finally, we would like to thank those colleagues who have read and commented on parts of the manuscript. Naturally any mistakes or infelicities remain the responsibility of the authors. Isobel Osborne, Elizabeth Sherrard and June Davison helped us with tape transcription and typing, working cheerfully and helpfully through large amounts of difficult material.

Our research was supported by the Social Science Research Council (UK), grant number HR 3453/1.

Harry Collins
Trevor Pinch
University of Bath

INTRODUCTION

The rationality debate - science as a good location for work on the rationality problem - radical interpretation of Kuhn - spoonbending as the case study - description of each chapter - Appendix: the study and the respondents

SCIENCE AND THE PROBLEM OF RATIONALITY

Let the reader consider any argument that would utterly demolish all Zande claims for the power of the oracle. If it were translated into Zande modes of thought it would serve to support their entire structure on belief (Evans-Pritchard, quoted by Winch, 1964).

A scientist engaged in a piece of research, say in physics, can attack his problem straight away. He can go at once to the heart of the matter: that is, to the heart of an organized structure. For a structure of scientific doctrines is already in existence; and with it, a generally accepted problem situation (Sir Karl Popper, 'The Logic of Scientific Discovery', 1934).

A young Israeli named Yuri Geller put on a strange demonstration in a London hotel. . . . His principal claim is that he can affect material objects by will power. . . . He has agreed to be tested under rigorous scientific conditions at a United States scientific institute this month ('Ariadne', 'New Scientist', November 1972).

. . . imagine certain very general facts of nature to be different from what we are used to, and the formation of concepts different from the usual ones will become intelligible . . . (Ludwig Wittgenstein, 'Philosophical Investigations', 1953).

This book is about the relationship between different cultures, an area of concern normally referred to as the problem of rationality. To study this problem we have looked at cultures within modern science. We have looked at physicists as they have tried to work in an area which is not a 'generally accepted problem situation in physics', an area where the 'general facts of nature' seem to be 'different from what we are used to'. This is the area which has to do with the effect of mind over matter. That rash of phenomena associated with Uri Geller, which came to public and scientific attention in the early and middle 1970s, is the particular object of attention for the case study.

Philosophers, historians and sociologists have carried on a debate about the problem of rationality which shows little sign of reaching a conclusive outcome. The debate concerns the relationship between the categories of thought pertaining to widely separated cultures, or to historical epochs within the same culture. The debate has more than purely academic importance. If modern ideas are seen as continuous with primitive rationality, and can therefore be shown to be 'more advanced', then a modernising attitude to backward societies is more easily justified. If primitive rationality is merely different from modern rationality, each having its own self-contained order of categories which are mutually translatable, then our view as to the advanced nature of our ways of thought should not be expected to be widely appreciated. On a narrower canvas, the debate is relevant to arguments concerning developments within modern society. It lies at the root of arguments about the superiority of scientific reasoning over 'common sense', for instance, in the question of the development of nuclear power. A solution to the rationality debate would not entail a solution to problems of modernisation or nuclear power but it would help to delimit the ground upon which each of these debates should be held and to clarify the basis of legitimate scientific authority.

The more narrowly intellectual importance of the rationality debate is that a proper understanding of the notion of rationality is fundamental to sociological and historical explanation. Most contemporary sociologists and historians would agree that a proper explanation of the actions of members or groups within a society must rest upon some understanding of the categories of thought pertaining to that society. If cultures and their constituent categories of thought are continuous across large societal and historical distances, then this understanding presents no special problem. If, however, different cultures and historical epochs are so divided from us as to render their ideas untranslatable into ours, then substantial methodological and conceptual problems are presented to the sociologist and historian. At best we will not know how to gather 'data' about a strange society. At worst, there will be no hope of explaining action in such a society.

The sociology of knowledge is presented with the opposite problem. If what counts as rationality is continuous across societies, then it would not be sensible to try to give a sociological explanation to rational knowledge. Those elements of knowledge that remained invariant across all possible present and future social and historical transformations would be better explained in terms of some innate human propensity to reason in a certain way. In these circumstances the sociologist of knowledge would need to be clear about the area of invariance before he or she could embark with confidence on a full-blooded sociological explanation of the residue.[1] If rationality is discontinuous across cultures, and across time, so that invariant properties which place restrictions of substance on human thought are not to be found, then the sociology of knowledge can proceed with unabashed vigour.

One handicap to argument in the rationality debate is the inaccessibility of examples of self-contained systems of rationality. The ways of thought pertaining to cultures are difficult to grasp for mundane, as well as philosophical, reasons. Firstly, modern cultures are large, diffuse things which are hard to pin down. Those which are less large and diffuse present difficulties of access because they are historically distant or simply because they are inaccessible for logistical reasons. In recent years, the debate has taken as its exemplary case the rationality of the Azande oracle, yet it is doubtful whether any of the recent debaters have ever visited the Azande, or poisoned a chicken. This is not only a problem of geographical distance, it is also a problem of language, and the very strangeness of the culture which is under debate. A field trip of several years would seem to be a minimum requirement for anyone who wanted to get first-hand experience of what the poisoned oracle means to the Azande.

Of course, to suggest that lack of empirical access is a handicap is to make an assumption about the nature of the debate. The assumption is that it is a debate upon which evidence has some bearing, and not a purely formal exercise. This does indeed seem to be the case, since the experience of anthropologists is frequently brought up in order to make one point or another within the debate, and the details and meaning of oracular procedures are often a point of reference. If some easier way of handling the problem of rationality were to be found, philosophers, and others engaged in the debate, would surely be interested.

We do think that we have found a class of cases of rationality difference which yield more easily to empirical analysis. These empirically accessible cases are cases within science. The idea that radical differences in 'world view' pertain to 'epochs' within the history of science in the same way as they may pertain to epochs within history as a whole has come to the fore since the mid-1960s, largely as a result of the work of the historian of science, T.S. Kuhn. If a certain interpretation of this view is correct, it makes possible new and better empirical research on the general problem of rationality through studies of its particular manifestation within science. This is because science is a peculiarly accessible social institution.

On the whole, science is done in 'controlled conditions'. It is done in laboratories, conferences, journals, books, universities, and, of course, it is done here and now. Thus while it is certainly not true that every influence upon scientific development is transparent, most of what happens in science today is associated with a visible and investigable 'outcrop'. The claim made here is that the social study of science offers a new way of looking at the old problems of cultural discontinuity.[2]

The ideas of Kuhn only have special significance for this study when they are given a radical interpretation. Kuhn has now retreated from the position he seemed to set out in his book, 'The Structure of Scientific Revolutions' (Kuhn, 1962), and it may be

that radical interpretations of that work were mistaken ones.[3]
These broadly radical interpretations arise out of a reading of
the work informed by certain Wittgensteinian, phenomenological
or Collingwoodian views.[4] For example, the notion of 'paradigm'
found in Kuhn (1962) is closely related to concepts such as
'language game', 'form-of-life', 'taken-for-granted reality' and
'set of absolute presuppositions', but only when it is given a
radical interpretation. Only then does the Kuhnian analysis have
relevance for the socio-cognitive discontinuities perceived by
some philosophers, sociologists, anthropologists and historians.
It is the radical interpretation that we adopt throughout and which
we explain more fully in chapter 1.

THE CASE STUDY AND ITS BEARING ON PARADIGM CONFLICT

Most of the material present in this book stems from the study of
an apparent collision of scientific paradigms. This grew out of
the attempts by scientists, in the early and mid-1970s, to research the strange phenomena associated with the Israeli showman
Uri Geller. The best-known example of his purported abilities
was 'spoon-bending', or to give it a scientific name, Paranormal
Metal Bending (PMB). The bizarre activity of bending spoons and
other items of metal by allegedly paranormal means occupied
pages in the press and hours of television coverage, spawned at
least one film, some half-dozen books, and many magazine and
journal articles. 'Geller' became a household word in the mid-1970s.
Of more immediate relevance, the phenomenon came to occupy the
attention of a number of established physicists working at universities and other research institutions (see chapter 2). These
physicists attempted to experiment with, and devise esoteric
theoretical explanations for, the phenomena produced by Geller
and the host of imitators who came forward claiming similar powers
(chapter 4). They began to build up the paraphysics of mind-
over-metal.

The literally extraordinary activities of these physicists, and
of those others who were opposed to their ideas, are examined in
detail in the chapters that follow. In chapter 1 we examine some
of the terms associated with Kuhn's elaboration of the idea of
paradigm conflict and the philosophical and methodological difficulties involved in an empirical examination of such a conflict.
We conclude that potential revolutions can be found in science
and that they may be examined as the locations of differently
developing types of social actions. The term 'action' is used to
signify the inextricable nature of ideas and social life. Though
different parts of the book are devoted to examination of the
cognitive and social aspects of the debate about paranormal metal
bending, an overall aim is to show the inadequacy of such a
separate conception.

In chapter 2 we present a brief history of the emergence of
Geller into Western scientific circles and the development of scien-

tific research on the phenomena and the opposition to the research. The research on paranormal metal bending is placed in
the wider context of the history of parapsychological research,
and the ambivalent relationship between the wider community
and the new physicist entrants is discussed. Some evidence of
the extent of covert, as well as overt, research on Geller phenomena in the mid-1970s is presented. The rumours and counter-
rumours surrounding the area are discussed along with the
emergence of a dedicated opposition, which we describe as a scientific vigilante group.

In chapters 3 and 4 we show the inadequacy of any conception
of major scientific disagreement in purely cognitive terms such
as logical incompatibility. Deductive arguments and contradiction
do not seem to provide a definitive way of settling the relationship
between the paranormal and orthodox paradigms. Even the attempts
to bring to bear theories of modern physics, such as quantum
theory, do not enable the logical relationship between the two
paradigms to be settled.

The lack of constraint in cognitive argument draws attention
to the need to look at practical activity - in science this means
experimentation. Thus two chapters of the book (5 and 6) are
devoted to a detailed analysis of experimental activity. The experiments we describe are ones to which we had privileged access.
This is because we ourselves acted as experimenters, in collaboration with physicist colleagues. The experiments on paranormal
metal bending which were performed as part of this project led
to a publication which seems to have had a significant effect on
developments in the area. This does seem to be the first time
participation has been carried so far in the sociology of science.[5]
Using material gathered during the 'participant observation'
phase of the project we are able to show how it is that a set of
experiments cannot provide a definitive means of deciding between
the two scientific world views. Experimental activity or what
might be called the rules of inductive reasoning are shown to be
construed in different ways within the two rival paradigms. Nevertheless, although experimental action cannot settle the issue, it
can give the appearance of providing a definitive answer. This
apparent paradox is explained in chapters 5 and 6.

In chapter 7 we extend the examination beyond the sub-set of
experiments with which we were involved. We look at the actions
of a wider group of respondent scientists as they attempted to
develop new ways of scientific life within the emerging world view.
Here the organic relationship between the active and the cognitive
in scientific development is shown by the pragmatic approach to
theoretical difficulty which allows physicists to proceed with their
research in the face of an apparent impasse.

In chapter 8 we concentrate on the changes in the world view
of scientists whose work belongs in the new paradigm, changes
which become visible as changes in their social lives within the
scientific community. Changes which seem to be typical of the
transitory stage of the revolution include the growth of antagon-

istic and vituperative relations with colleagues, a concentration on problems of replicability at the expense of detailed technical and theoretical development, and an increase in the likelihood that the actions of colleagues will be thought of as inauthentic. In the final part of chapter 8 we look into the future and, by extrapolating our observations on new ways of acting in parapsychology, we try to describe what scientific social life would be like if paranormal phenomena were to form the basis of a scientific revolution.

Our overall aim is to make a contribution to the rationality debate by showing that it is possible to investigate such questions in an empirical fashion, by studying science. Inevitably, other themes are touched on through the book. The work as a whole should help to explain why it is that speedy resolutions of scientific controversies are not to be found in 'rigorous experimental tests'. Controversies, it will be seen, are settled in science as they are settled in other walks of life - by negotiation, not revelation. Chapters 3 and 4 may help to show how the appearance of a deductive solution to paradigm debates could be 'socially negotiated', and chapters 5 and 6 show how inductive certainty is apparently arrived at. We would hope that the detailed first-hand material presented in chapters 5 and 6, including as it does some tape-recorded material, would be of special interest to ethnomethodologists and to those interested in how scientific accounts and scientific papers are constructed. We would stress, however, that the detailed analysis of individual scientific incidents, or even of individual scientific laboratories, cannot go very far in explaining scientific discovery. The minimum unit of inquiry is the network of laboratories and the network of argument and negotiation between them.[6]

Another theme which reappears throughout the text is attention to the effect of the passage of time. Since a major conclusion of the book is that it is possible for something to appear true at one time and place and false at another time and place, it was vital that the authors remained self-conscious of the time and place they occupied as they wrote various sections of the book. Finally, we hope that our experience in doing this study, and the explicit methodological notes scattered throughout the chapters, will prove helpful to those who would want to do similar work and share our aim of leaving the Azande in peace.

APPENDIX: THE STUDY AND THE RESPONDENTS

One author, Collins, has been engaged in fieldwork on parapsychology since 1971 (e.g. see Collins, 1976). In the autumn of 1972, while conducting interviews at Stanford University, Collins first heard of Geller and the associated work. Interest in the specific area reported in this work first arose out of an account, heard at that time, of seemingly paranormal events associated with the Stanford 'quark detector' (see chapter 7). In this con-

nection Collins interviewed Russell Targ of the Stanford Research Institute in 1972, though little could be discovered (see chapter 2).
The impact of Geller was subsequently watched with some interest, as the veil of secrecy was lifted after 1972. In the spring of 1975 Collins started to co-operate on some experiments (see chapter 6) with child spoon-benders. The initiative for these experiments came from Dr Brian Pamplin of the Department of Physics, University of Bath. The idea of treating spoon-bending research as exhibiting paradigm incommensurability with respect to orthodox science emerged soon after these experiments were begun. The field was monitored in a more systematic way from about the late spring of 1975. Some results of the spoon-bending experiments were published in September 1975 (see chapter 5 for details).
Pinch joined the project in October 1975. In the same month Collins, while completing fieldwork in America on an earlier project, was able to conduct a few interviews which established contact with respondents and 'set the scene' for later work in the USA. Contact with British respondents began to be explored in the winter of 1975 (though Collins had met Professor John Taylor in September of that year through a TV programme (see chapter 6). Interviews with British respondents were conducted during 1975, 1976 and 1977. Most interviews were carried out by Collins and Pinch together, Pinch supplying in particular the necessary quantum physics expertise. Interviews were carried out with scientists and others on the East Coast of the USA in the autumn of 1976 by Collins alone. Both researchers carried out a set of interviews on the West Coast of the USA in the spring of 1977.
Experimental work on spoon-bending children continued through to the end of 1977. Several of these experiments were done in co-operation with respondents including Professor Taylor, Professor Hasted and, on one occasion, the 'Amazing' Randi. Written, photographed, tape-recorded and videotaped records were made of most of these experiments.
Sources of knowledge and understanding of the field come then from participation, including publication, in the field; from experimental co-operation with scientists on a number of occasions; and from (frequently tape-recorded) interviews/discussions/meetings with other scientists, magicians and parapsychologists in circumstances where more than one contact either took place or might be expected to take place. Descriptions of these latter respondents as 'interviewees' would be misleading. It would be more appropriate to think of the researchers as temporary members of a very loose network. Interviews were also conducted with some thirty other respondents (mainly American) in circumstances where the termination of the interview would normally be expected to be the termination of contact (mainly because of geographical/logistic considerations). However, even here, the attempt was made to foster as informal a situation as possible, so that in one or two cases interviewing contacts were maintained over a period

of days. In these cases, for short periods, we felt ourselves to
be temporary members of the small communities of scientists, believers and sceptics on the West and East coasts of the USA.
These respondents comprised the majority of those scientists and
commentators who had (or had had) interests in the field of spoon-
bending in particular and a large number who were interested in
parapsychology in general from a positive or negative point of
view. They include, then, the proponents, the more-or-less
active sceptics, vigilantes and a group of quantum theoreticians
and experimentalists whose work impinged more or less directly
on the attempts to explain psychokinesis through quantum
physics.

In addition, of course, data were gathered from the literature,
conferences, talks, newspapers, the media and so forth.

A first draft of this manuscript was presented as a final report
to the Social Science Research Council in June 1978. Subsequent
re-drafts have involved matters of style and organisation rather
than substance or interpretation.

1 THE IDEA OF SOCIO-COGNITIVE DISCONTINUITY AND ITS PROBLEMS

*Understanding and the universality of rational categories –
paradigm incommensurability – its organic quality – idea of
paradigm – idea of incommensurability – Kuhn's terminology –
problem of progress – problem of relativism – neither problem
substantial – methodological considerations – identification of
revolutions – revolutions can be studied contemporaneously if an
idea of an unsuccessful revolution in science be accepted –
paranormal metal bending a suitable area – problem of access
to ideas of communities with different rational categories –
participation as a solution – evidence of success in understanding*

THEORETICAL CONSIDERATIONS

Arguments about the appropriate way to understand primitive
cultures are of long standing (see, for example, the collections
of Wilson (1970) and Horton and Finnegan (1973)). The same sort
of problem has given rise to a debate over our ability to understand ways of thought pertaining to past epochs (see, for example,
Collingwood, 1939, 1967; Krausz, 1972, 1973). At the root of
both these sets of debates is the question whether the ways of
thought that seem rational to us are appropriate categories for
understanding primitive or past ways of thinking and acting. If
we believe that our ways of thinking are universal, in other
words, that rationality remains constant through social change,
then we may be entitled to consider certain actions of unfamiliar
peoples irrational, where these actions do not seem to make
rational sense to us. It is likely that we will choose to explain
irrational actions differently from rational actions (MacIntyre,
1962; Laudan, 1977). On the other hand, if we believe that each
society's form of life is self-contained and cannot necessarily be
understood through categories pertaining to another society, we
may have to accept that we will never understand certain strange
actions – or at least never be able to translate them into our
categories. This does not mean that we are entitled to label these
actions 'irrational' (Winch, 1964). In this case, the explanation of
action would not differ according to its apparent rationality.

This study takes seriously the idea that the categories which
inform social action are self-contained and may not be mutually
translatable. The study deals with a contemporaneous 'conceptual
discontinuity' such that the researchers had access to members

whose actions belonged, apparently, to two such 'incommensurable' sets. What is more, in the area studied, the actors were
themselves confronted with problems of conceptual change. Rather
than being in the isolated position of members of primitive tribes,
both sets of actors lived and worked within the institutions of
Western natural science. However, they worked in an area, and
at a time, of schism.

Of course, the suggestion that the notion of self-contained
socio-cognitive systems can be taken seriously throws into question the very possibility of an empirical investigation. How can
investigators, let alone readers, understand a self-contained
system that is not their own? The answer would seem to be a
negative one, but the authors have taken their cue from scientist
respondents and got on with the research in a pragmatic frame
of mind. As will be seen, our claim is that we did achieve this
understanding. The reader must find the proof of the pudding,
or otherwise, in the eating.

Conceptual discontinuities are to be found in the contemporary
and accessible world if it is true that periods within the development of science exhibit similar discontinuities as those between
ourselves and primitive societies or between epochs within history
as a whole. If this is true, then science is an excellent location
for research on the problem of culture. The suggestion that this
is indeed the case has arisen with greatest vigour out of the work
of the historian of science, T.S. Kuhn (1962). Kuhn's ideas about
the history of science contrast strikingly with the cumulative
progressive model which underlies the usual brand of scientific
education. Textbooks suggest that current knowledge has been
built up by successive additions, one upon another, until the
present edifice was constructed. According to this model a full
understanding of the conceptual history of science would be gained
best from the contemporary vantage point, where it is easy to
separate the chaff of mistakes and blind alleys from the wheat of
genuine contributions to current true knowledge. In contrast,
according to Kuhn's model the history of science exhibits periods
of 'normal' science characterised by progress along the lines of
the canonical model, but these are separated by periods of 'revolutionary' science during which the whole conceptual basis of
science is turned over. Thus the ensuing period of normal science
cannot easily be related to the previous one through the idea of
cumulativeness. The new science is a different animal. In some
respects it may seem to be more powerful, but an elephant is not
made by accumulating ants. Within the Kuhnian model, understanding the history of science requires that the concepts pertaining to each scientific epoch be understood in their own terms,
not in the terms of modern science.

PARADIGM INCOMMENSURABILITY

In developing his picture of science Kuhn used two words which
have caused great controversy. He spoke of each period of normal science as being based on a 'paradigm' and he spoke of the
relationship between paradigms as being one of 'incommensurability'. Subsequently, both of these words, particularly the
former, have been used in a variety of different ways in a variety
of different contexts. This has happened because the words were
not carefully defined in terms of more readily available concepts.
Most commentators (e.g. Masterman, 1970) find this irritating
and Kuhn, latterly disavowing the more radical interpretations
of his ideas, seems prepared to accept their criticisms in his
later writings (Kuhn, 1970a, 1970b; Pinch, 1979a). Thus, Kuhn
(1970a, p. 175) wrote of his earlier usage:

. . . the term paradigm is used in two [undistinguished] different senses. On the one hand, it stands for the entire constellation of beliefs, values, techniques, and so on shared by
the members of a given [scientific] community. On the other,
it denotes one sort of element in that constellation, the concrete puzzle-solutions which, employed as models or examples,
can replace explicit rules as a basis for the solution of the
remaining puzzles of normal science.

Some sociologists have also adopted an analytic approach in
their prescriptions for the proper application of the new model
of the history of science in sociological research. Whitley (1975),
for example, separates out five components of scientific activity,
ranging from 'research practice' to 'metaphysical assumptions'.
His examples suggest that these may be looked at separately in
practice. Within this type of approach similar research practices
may be underpinned by different metaphysical assumptions.
Applied to the study of primitive societies, this approach would
make it sensible to search for tribes who used the same techniques
for poisoning chickens as the Azande (Evans-Pritchard, 1976),
but did not share the Zande concern with magic and oracles.[1]
   In contrast to this analytic approach, our understanding of
the notion of paradigm is a radical interpretation of Kuhn's 1962
(unrevised) text. Our reading is informed by Winchian/Wittgen-
steinian ideas about the integral nature of the practical and cognitive aspects of social activity.[2] This integral nature is captured
in Winch's description of the development of the germ theory of
disease. In his book, 'The Idea of a Social Science' (Winch, 1958,
p. 122), he wrote that this development

involved the adoption of new ways of doing things by people
involved, in one way or another, in medical practice. An
account of the way in which social relations in the medical pro-
fession had been influenced by this new concept would include
an account of what that concept was. Conversely, the concept

itself is unintelligible apart from its relation to medical practice.

This quotation will be repeated throughout the text. We can read the following comment, typical of Kuhn's early work, in the same vein. Kuhn wrote (1962, p. 47):

the process of learning a theory depends upon the study of applications, including practice problem-solving both with a pencil and paper and with instruments in the laboratory. If, for example, the student of Newtonian dynamics ever discovers the meaning of terms like 'force', 'mass', 'space', and 'time', he does so less from the incomplete though sometimes helpful definitions in his text than by observing and participating in the application of these concepts to problem-solution.

It is the mixture of the practical and the conceptual that gives the notion of paradigm its special appeal. When it is taken to imply that concepts are not separable from action - in this case, experiments - then the notion of paradigm is the equivalent within science of the Wittgensteinian idea of 'form-of-life'. It is this reading that lends Kuhn's version of self-contained socio-cognitive communities its sociological and philosophical excitement and sympathy. This is why it falls naturally alongside the equivalent ideas pertaining to primitive cultures and to past epochs. To analyse the notion into its constituent parts is to lose the combination of concept and practice that makes the term so useful.

Incommensurability is another problematic idea. A dictionary definition is 'having no common measure'.[3] A clear application of the term concerns the relationship between the side and the diagonal of a square. It can be shown by a simple proof that the length relationship between the side and the diagonal cannot be expressed as a fraction, that is, as one finite sequence of digits divided by another. That is equivalent to saying that there is no way of constructing a ruler so that if the length of the side is an exact number of divisions of the ruler, the length of the diagonal can be an exact number too. Literally, the side and the diagonal cannot be measured (exactly) with the same systems of measurement - they are incommensurable.

In 'The Structure of Scientific Revolutions' Kuhn seems to use the term figuratively, to refer to the relationship between whole paradigms, the forms-of-life which define different epochs within science. However, most commentators seem to have thought about incommensurability as 'incomparability' or some kind of logical 'incompatibility'. This emphasis on the logical use of the term, an emphasis which Kuhn himself was later to endorse (Kuhn, 1977, p. xxii; Pinch, 1979a), again wastes the opportunity of adding a word to the sociological vocabulary which draws its usefulness from its synthesis of conceptual and behavioural life. Incommensurability refers to a relationship between sets of actions, and there is a shortage of such words in sociology.

Incommensurability describes a relationship between two social groups such that no actor can do actions appropriate to both groups at the same time. This inability is not like not being able to run and stand still at the same time. It is less purely logical than that. Nor is it like not being able to play ice hockey and perform brain surgery at the same time. It is not only a question of lack of dexterity. One could imagine an extremely dextrous brain surgeon/ice hockey player who continues with operations during the game with the aid of an operating table on skates! But one cannot imagine that the acquisition of even the most bizarre social and intellectual skills would enable an actor to partake of the life of two different paradigms at once. What we suggest, *pace* Kuhn, is that 'incommensurability' and 'paradigm' are best interpreted as belonging to a vocabulary that refers to social actions, not to thought or behaviour alone. When thus interpreted they remain outstandingly useful.

That said, no empirical work informed by the new notions can be undertaken unless one has some idea of what to look for in situations of paradigm incommensurability. Kuhn's book (1962) offers the following formulations regarding the relationship between succeeding paradigms, the consequences of this relationship, and certain concomitant properties of the relationship. These formulations will guide the analysis in this work as a whole.

On page 7 of 'The Structure of Scientific Revolutions' the professional community is said to re-evaluate traditional experimental procedures, alter its conception of entities with which it has long been familiar, and shift the network of theory through which it deals with the world, when the commitments of normal science change. Later it is suggested that 'Like the choice between competing political institutions, that between competing paradigms proves to be a choice between incompatible modes of community life' (p. 94). Differences between paradigms are said to be irreconcilable (p. 103) and 'not only incompatible but often actually incommensurable'. It also is suggested that there is a sense in which paradigms transform the world (p. 106).

As a result of these changes, laboratory procedures change, in so far as certain measurements become irrelevant and new ones relevant (p. 129); also, old manipulations in new roles may be indices of quite different natural regularities, or may even yield new concrete results (p. 130), though much of the scientist's language and most of his laboratory instruments remain the same. In such situations, scientists belonging to different paradigm communities can be seen as 'responding to different worlds' (p. 111), as disagreeing about problems as well as results (p. 148), and as inevitably talking through each other (p. 109). Communication will inevitably be partial, for the same terms, concepts and experiments will assume different relations with one another (p. 149).

These problems cannot be settled by recourse to any extra-paradigmatic observation language (p. 114), nor do scientists have freedom to compare paradigms by switching from one to the other like the subject of a gestalt switch (p. 85). What is more,

the changeover to a new paradigm (like a gestalt switch) cannot
be done a step at a time; it has to be accepted all of a piece (p.
150). These qualities of involuntariness and wholeness are
stressed by the setting up of a distinction between accepting,
but not internalising, the correctness of a new paradigm as a
result of persuasion and being converted in the sense of 'going
native' (pp. 203-4).

AN INFLUENTIAL BUT MISTAKEN OBJECTION TO THE IDEA OF PARADIGM INCOMMENSURABILITY

The last phrase in the preceding section draws attention once
again to the similarity between Kuhn's suggestions about the
relationship between paradigms and discussions pertaining to the
relationship between societies as a whole, especially between
Western and primitive societies. Several writers have discussed
the philosophical problems of the notion of paradigm change
alongside the problems of understanding primitive societies (e.g.
Giddens, 1976; Trigg, 1973). These writers are concerned, above
all, with the problem of relativism which is seemingly precipitated
by any notion of radical cultural discontinuity. In the case of
scientific paradigms the relativistic consequences of the notion
grow out of Kuhn's suggestions that there is a sense in which
paradigms 'transform the world' so that scientists belonging to
different paradigm communities can be seen as 'responding to
different worlds' and will inevitably talk through each other; that
their disagreements cannot be settled by recourse to any extra-
paradigmatic language; and that conversion to a new paradigm has
to be accepted 'all of a piece'. From this it follows that there is
no way of standing outside a debate between proponents of
two paradigms and finding 'rational' arguments which would show
the correctness of one picture of the world and the incorrectness
of any picture that conflicts with it. Nor can members of different
paradigm groups 'refer to the world outside' in order to settle
their differences, for they will see different worlds.

The 'familiar and banal' objection to this viewpoint is put by
Giddens (1976, p. 145), who points out that to claim that 'all
knowledge is relative' is to make a universal claim the possibility
of which is precisely what is denied by the claim itself. It seems
then that all such claims are 'self-negating'. Giddens also suggests
that in any case the problem of cultural discontinuity has been
overstated (p. 144). However, evidence is not brought to support
this latter claim. In any case, it is at best an empirical claim so
it cannot rule out the notion of radical cultural discontinuity a
priori.

More extended criticisms of Kuhn's position have been made,
for example, by Roger Trigg (1973) and Israel Scheffler (1967).
Both of these authors argue that the relationship which Kuhn
claims to hold between paradigms cannot hold; that is, that incommensurability could not be the relationship between periods of

scientific history. Thus Scheffler (1967) writes 'I cannot myself
believe that this bleak picture representing an extravagant idealism is true. In fact it seems to me a *reductio ad absurdum* of the
reasonings from which it flows.' And Trigg finds a host of incompatible consequences flowing from Kuhn's ideas, among which is
the consequence of a notion of scientific progress which is not
progress towards the truth (1973, p. 116):

> . . . a more fundamental question . . . is what possible grounds
> Kuhn could have had for talking about 'progress' once he scraps
> talk about progress towards the truth? . . . Kuhn seems to
> think it is possible to have progress even when it is not 'pro-
> gress' in any direction. This is absurd.

Part of the reason why these authors find Kuhn's position not
only distasteful but also absurd is that they consider, with
Giddens, that any full-bloodedly relativist position is unacceptable.
Kuhn lends weight to their arguments when he attempts to defend
himself while retreating from the radical interpretation of his ideas.
For example, in the Postscript to the second edition of 'The Structure of Scientific Revolutions' (1970a, p. 206), he suggests that
progress in science is recognisable by succeeding paradigms by
such criteria as:

> [increasing] accuracy of prediction, particularly of quantitative
> prediction; the balance between esoteric and everyday subject
> matter; and the number of different problems solved. . . .
> [Also but less important] such values as simplicity, scope, and
> compatibility with other specialities.

It is easy to understand the frustration of commentators when
presented with bland assertions such as that the predictive power
of successive theories increases over time, while at the same time
those theories may belong to members who inhabit different worlds
and whose predictions therefore, one would imagine, could not be
compared for relative power. Kuhn must be mistaken if he believes
that particular assertion to be unproblematically reconcilable with
the rest of his position.

Nevertheless, it does not follow that the radical interpretation
of Kuhn's ideas is similarly flawed. Elsewhere it has been argued
that the apparent power of the 'logical argument' as mounted by
Giddens is illusory, depending as it does on universal acceptance
of the logic in which it is cast (Collins and Cox, 1976). In any
case, even if valid, the argument does not disqualify most knowledge from being relative so that there is nothing within it to stop
the sociologist assuming, say, all scientific knowledge to be relative
and proceeding accordingly (Collins and Cox, 1976, pp. 431-2).
Indeed it was argued in the same place (and in Collins and Cox,
1977) that such an assumption is desirable, if not essential, for
the sociology of scientific knowledge. As for the apparent *reductios*
produced by Scheffler and Trigg, they depend for their power on

preconceived notions of the rational quality of scientific debate.
In spite of the manifest evidence that scientists use every available resource of rhetoric; that people may be persuaded to believe
in the most 'unlikely' things by means of propaganda, weight of
numbers, accidents (location) of birth and upbringing, promise
of financial gain or increase of status; in spite of the fact that
people may change their minds about things simply because, for
example, they get bored with an old and tired set of ideas, the
suspicion seems to lurk that scientists reserve their final commitment to new ideas until they are forced to accept them by logic,
or experiment.[4] Scheffler (1967, p. 88) asks the question: 'What
compelling reasons have we been offered for denying objectivity
to the processes by which scientific theories are critically evalu-
ated?' He should ask: 'What evidence is there for accepting the
objectivity of these processes?' The latter question requires an
empirical answer, not an a priori logical exercise. It is an empirical
approach to these questions that we adopt here.[5]

METHODOLOGICAL CONSIDERATIONS

Given the ambitious project of looking at contemporary revolutionary change, a problem immediately presents itself. Though paradigm changes in science may be relatively frequent and relatively
well documented, they are not easy to recognise with certainty.
Of episodes drawn from the history of science Kuhn himself has
remarked (1970b, p. 251): 'I am repeatedly asked whether such
and such a development was "normal" or "revolutionary", and I
usually have to answer that I do not know.' It is, then, even
more difficult to identify with certainty a contemporary revolutionary episode.
    Revolutions, whether in political or scientific life, can only be
identified as revolutions, if they can ever be so identified, after
sufficient time has elapsed for them to have proved fruitful or
otherwise. However, in the case of political life it makes some
sense to talk of a category of attempted revolutionary acts, which
fail to result in the desired revolution. Such a category might be
defined by reference to the revolutionary intentions of the actors,
or by the short-term success of what becomes long-term failure.[6]
A sociologist might be able to find a 'group of political revolution-
aries' to study, and in principle might be able to watch and participate in an attempted political revolution. It is not immediately
clear that the possibility exists for doing the same in respect of
scientific life.
    One problem in recognising an attempted scientific revolution
arises because the native members do not themselves have the
category of scientific revolution - not yet, or at least not in any
large numbers - so that the search for actors with deliberately
scientific revolutionary intentions would be fruitless.[7] What is
more, the category of failed or attempted revolution does not seem
viable in Kuhn's writings. Though Kuhn wishes to talk of scientific

revolutions as being like political revolutions, he seems to think in terms of an immanently deterministic progressive model, rather like vulgar interpretations of Marxism. Somehow, though revolutionary choices have to be made by actors, those revolutions that do occur must occur and no others could occur. Now, assuming that the sociologist is not gifted with prescience, that is, assuming that he cannot foresee the future content of scientific knowledge better than the scientist, this leaves hindsight as the sole judge of what constitutes even revolutionary activity, because all properly revolutionary activity, for Kuhn, must end in successful revolution and scientific progress. Without prescience, contemporary activities cannot be classified.

What follows from this is that, even if the sociologist could discover the scientific community's equivalent of a group with revolutionary intentions, he would not know how to treat them until he understood whether or not they had been successful. For instance, if they were unsuccessful the appropriate sociological treatment would be similar to that usually reserved for religious cults, or mass hysterical movements, whereby large numbers of people mysteriously come to believe false ideas.[8] Coming to believe false ideas is essentially different from participating in scientific paradigm change if Kuhn's non-relativistic stance is correct.

If, then, what come to be seen as true and false beliefs are taken to be different types of social phenomena requiring different techniques of analysis, there is only a chance possibility of using the right technique for the analysis of any contemporary, as yet unfulfilled, development. As most radical developments probably fail, the likelihood of being lucky enough to stumble upon what turns out to be some successful development, and analysing it appropriately, is quite remote. From this point of view the only reasonable data source for a study of scientific revolutions is history.[9]

There is no satisfactory solution to this problem if it is genuine. However, it is a problem that only arises out of the point of view that successful and unsuccessful revolutions are different sorts of phenomenon, needing to be analysed in the terms appropriate to rational and non-rational action respectively. As has been mentioned, a premise of this work is that a viewpoint which distinguishes the type of explanation required according to the rationality of the action is profoundly mistaken, and has been shown to be so in the work of Barnes (1974), Bloor (1976) and others (e.g. Collins and Cox, 1976; Collins, 1975, 1976). From the relativistic point of view adopted within the project the distinction between 'true' and 'false' beliefs, or 'rational' and 'non-rational' beliefs, cannot figure in social explanation.[10] Rather, the way this distinction is applied by society is something to be explained in each particular case by reference to factors outside of these categories.

To make this point clear the argument of the last few paragraphs will be reiterated. There is a logical distinction between revolution and revolutionary acts which are sterile. Only with hindsight is

it possible to distinguish between sterile revolutionary acts and
acts which are part of successful revolutions. If it is believed
that sterile and successful revolutionary acts require different
sorts of explanation and different approaches to their sociological
investigation, then revolutionary acts proper can only be studied
with hindsight. Certain of Kuhn's views seem to lead in this
direction. If, on the other hand, it is assumed, as it is assumed
here, that revolutionary acts are essentially similar whether or
not they issue in successful revolutions, then it makes sense to
study revolutionary acts contemporaneously.

Given licence to investigate the contemporary world, how does
one make the case that a group of scientists might be the social
location of potentially revolutionary ideas? At least two precondi-
tions must be met. Firstly the group's ideas must be in conflict
with those of orthodox science. Although, as Mulkay (1975)
argues,[11] conflict may not be the invariable accompaniment of rapid
development and change in science, conflict at the level of ideas,
if not at the level of personal interaction, must accompany anything that is to 'turn over' what went before.
  A second, truistic, precondition for a 'scientific' revolution
must be that the revolutionary group engage themselves with
orthodox science, and that their ideas are in some sense 'scientific'.
There are many sets of ideas and groups of people who are in conflict with science but who one would not think of as the seed-bed
of a potential scientific revolution. In one sense members of certain
environmental movements are in conflict with science. In another
sense, so are newspaper astrologists, believers in orgone energy,
and even Velikovskyites. None of these – the last arguably –
could conceivably affect the fabric of science culture sufficiently
to engender a revolution. For the most part they are simply
ignored by scientists and the scientific journals.
  The area of science chosen for our empirical focus in this study
was 'Paranormal Metal Bending' (PMB). It will be described in
detail in the next chapter. It is treated by many as a part of
parapsychology, and this has been described by one authority in
the area, John Beloff (1974, p. 1), as follows: 'Parapsychology
means the scientific study of the "paranormal", that is, of phenomena which in one or more respects conflict with accepted scientific
opinion as to what is physically possible.' Further, PMB has
generated publications in the legitimate scientific press – what we
have elsewhere referred to as part of the 'constitutive forum'
(Collins and Pinch, 1979). Added to this, the authors' own native
scientific competences and experiences of parapsychology seemed
to indicate that PMB would be an appropriate area.
  Though parapsychology seems to be an area of genuinely
scientific endeavour which does conflict with established scientific
belief, it has a long history itself, and because it has not spawned
any scientific revolution during the course of a hundred years or
so, it might be thought to be unsuitable as an area for study. It
has settled down, as it were, to a kind of steady institutionalised

conflict relationship with orthodox science. There are now several
parapsychology journals and several institutions in the United
States devoted solely to the study of parapsychology. Many of its
best-known investigators lead a rather mundane 'nine-to-five'
scientific life, no longer expecting an immediate breakthrough
which will elevate the discipline to a central position in the scientific world. In this sense the body of parapsychological work
should not be expected to manifest all the characteristics of
excitement and change of a potential revolution. However, the
sudden growth of interest in paranormal metal bending by physicists with little previous knowledge of parapsychological work
seems to provide a case to study which is not disqualified on
these grounds. Indeed, as will be shown in chapter 2, nearly all
those who took the new phenomenon seriously had had little
previous contact with professional psychical research.

One more question needs to be asked about the suitability of
this group, for though they were fresh, scientific, and in relationship of conflict with orthodox science, these are only necessary,
not sufficient, conditions of revolutionary potential. (Remember
the term 'revolutionary potential' is not supposed to imply successful revolutionary potential – this would be a bonus but only recognisable with hindsight). One may imagine groups in apparent
conflict, whose ideas become absorbed into the body of scientific
knowledge without any great adjustment to orthodoxy. Indeed it
was found that some respondents believed that just such a process
of peaceful absorption could take place with regard to certain
aspects of the paranormal were these to be explained by reference
to accepted scientific phenomena such as electromagnetic radiation
or the more exotic quantum effects. However, by referring to the
experiences and problems of experienced parapsychologists, and
by extrapolating these to the area of PMB, the revolutionary
possibilities can be seen[12] (for discussion, see chapters 7 and 8).

Given a potential paradigm change, methodological problems at
another level can be discussed. At some stage what must be looked
for are socio-cognitive changes associated with a change in meaning frame. Winch (1958, p. 122), it will be recalled, says of the
development of the germ theory of disease that it

> involved the adoption of new ways of doing things by people
> involved, in one way or another, in medical practice. An account
> of the way in which social relations in the medical profession
> had been influenced by this new concept would include an
> account of what that concept was. Conversely, the concept
> itself is unintelligible apart from its relation to medical practice.

Now Winch's account is designed to rule out behavioural approaches
to research in the social sciences, but though Kuhn does not share
Winch's underlying programme, the potential failure of any purely
behavioural approach to the investigation of paradigm change is
inherent in his work also. In Kuhn's account, it will be remembered,
different paradigms embody 'incompatible modes of community life',

though much of the scientist's language and most of his laboratory instruments remain the same. What is more, in the case of paradigm change new natural regularities may be revealed by old manipulations. Thus, much scientific behaviour will represent different actions. Hence, in many respects purely external appearances will give no clue to underlying changes.

In chapter 7 the point will be made concretely by presenting examples where the same experiment, with the same results, is perceived as demonstrating the existence of quite different regularities in nature. The research problem that is precipitated is that of gaining access to, and developing sufficient understanding of, the esoteric culture of the sciences, in order to recognise the type of alternative perception discussed above.

Now, Winch, addressing himself to describing the task of the social scientist, writes (1958, p. 87) that

> whereas in the case of the natural scientist we have to deal with only one set of rules, namely those governing the scientist's investigation itself, here [in the social sciences] what the sociologist is studying, as well as his study of it, is a human activity and is therefore carried out according to rules. And it is these rules rather than those which govern the sociologist's investigation, which specify what is to count as 'doing the same type of thing' in relation to that kind of activity.

In the case of the sociologist of science we can see that it is precisely those rules 'governing the scientist's investigation itself' which are those rules 'which specify what is to count as "doing the same type of thing"'. Understanding the actor's frame of meaning thus seems to require the development of competences which the scientist has taken many years of training and professional experience to accomplish, a level equivalent not so much to the Ph.D. qualification as to active research engagement in the narrow scientific field being studied.

Such a demand carries two sorts of what will be called a 'complementarity principle' in its wake. Firstly, there is the purely practical difficulty that both sociological and scientific research are full-time jobs with their own specific prerequisite academic and professional careers - the more adequate one is in one field, the less adequate one is likely to be in the other. Secondly, there is the familiar theoretical difficulty that while the sociologist remains a sociologist he is not a proper native member (unless he is studying the sociological community) and this may prevent him from understanding native members both by virtue of his untypical array of competences and by virtue of his position as sociologist/ outsider with regard to the native community - again, the more he wishes to be a sociologist, the less can he be a native. Both these problems were evident in this study in the investigators' relationship with the parapsychologists, though here the investigators came as near as possible to overcoming the practical difficulty, by virtue of parapsychology's special status.

Parapsychology is a 'special-case' science in many ways (see chapter 2). Apart from its cognitive relationship with orthodox science, which makes it particularly suitable for the wider purposes essayed, it is also special in that the depth of esoteric knowledge required in order to be able to participate at the research level in most branches of the subject is not great. In most branches of the subject, previous training in some other scientific or social scientific field will put one in a position to master the literature relevant to research in a matter of months, rather than years. (That is not to say that assiduous study of the literature, potential pitfalls, etc. is not required, as many beginning parapsychologists have found to their cost.) Thus it seems easier to research and publish findings in the parapsychological journals than in other professional journals, and far easier to publish something that will be noticed.

These elements of 'special-case quality' on the one hand must render extrapolations from experience in the parapsychological field suspect, but on the other hand they allowed the investigators to enter a relationship with the field which was close to the ideal theoretically attainable position. It enabled the investigators to become participators. However, in spite of this apparent success, the first complementarity is manifested in that the ideal has been attained only in an untypical case.

Against the experiences of interaction with scientists whose professional community life was shared to a small extent can be judged the experience of interactions where far less has been shared. For instance, 'straight' quantum physicists, orthodox physicists in their capacity as physicists not as parapsychologists, and sceptics from a variety of disciplines were all interviewed. Also both researchers had experience of interviewing and otherwise interacting with 'straight' scientists in connection with other research projects (Collins, 1974, 1975; Collins and Harrison, 1975; Pinch, 1977). There is no objective external index of success in understanding to which the researcher can appeal in order to construct a scale of comparison. The authors can only say that the experience of talking to orthodox scientists has been broadly similar to that of talking to parapsychologists. It seemed possible to interact successfully - to ask sensible and sometimes thought-provoking questions, to elicit favourable and thoughtful comments and to hold comprehensible conversation - with nearly all respondents. Comments from respondents such as 'I hadn't thought of that' or 'Yes, we did try that' or 'That's a possibility' or 'no, we found that that doesn't work', etc., acted as indicators of mutual understanding within a technical discussion.

We should add here that Collins has some thirteen hours of tape-recorded interviews of discussions with physicists working on a theory of amorphous semi-conductors which he is quite certain he does not understand, in spite of the knowledge of technical terms and acquaintanceship with the literature which were developed over such a long period of interaction. This knowledge of what mutual incomprehension is like, ironically, lends confidence to ther judgments regarding mutual comprehension – every cloud . . .!

Regarding the second 'complementarity', due to the inevitable marginality and untypicality of the experiences of the sociologists, the investigators' experiences with the parapsychological community need qualifying in several ways. One factor which must have strained relationships to some extent is the general defensiveness toward outsiders of scientists working in a field which has special connotations of 'crankiness'. The authors were known to be sociologists as well as parapsychologists, and sometimes they had the impression that scientists were acting in a particularly defensive manner toward them. Secondly, Collins and Pinch did not partake fully in the life of a parapsychological investigator, in that at times of risk to themselves they were able to slip easily into the sociologist-participant identity. We soon learned to do this when under threat by journalists, academic colleagues, the Social Science Research Council and so forth. Thus the degree of professional risk and the threat of ridicule was far less in the case of Collins and Pinch than it would be for a fully authentic researcher in the field. Nevertheless, the large number of occasions on which they were forced into this process of rapid re-identification and the frequency with which they experienced such threats is not untypical of the experiences of researchers in the field.

A third and related point concerns a further element of flexibility in the authors' position. Most of our respondents could be fairly unequivocally identified as either 'believers' or 'sceptics' for at least limited periods, and at one time or another most had committed themselves openly to one side or the other. Perhaps because of Collins and Pinch's peculiar route into the research, and our continued peculiar introspective relationship with it, we neither felt prolonged intense commitment to one side or the other nor did we commit ourselves openly. The authors, if pressed, would say that they felt distaste for the activities of the (most extreme, activist) 'sceptics' more frequently than for the activities of the 'believers'. On the other hand, the published report of Collins and Pamplin's experiment (see chapter 6) told of the discovery that most young subjects who came to the laboratory claiming to be able to bend spoons by paranormal means had cheated, and this report was read by the sceptics as demonstrating Collins and Pinch's scepticism. However, Collins and Pamplin included a qualification on all possible occasions. For instance on the day of publication, Collins, invited to 'confront' Professor John Taylor on the 'Nationwide' programme, stressed heavily the open-endedness of the report. Subsequently, in interviews with 'believers' the authors would lay great stress on the qualification, whereas in interviews with sceptics the authors would tend to say nothing, but bask in the friendly atmosphere of apparent common causes.

Thus, Collins and Pinch had three identities available to them – parapsychological experimenter, sceptic and sociologist – and tried, with some success where only short-term contact was involved, to slip between them as seemed appropriate and necessary for the purpose at hand. The relative ease of availability of these identities might seem to make the experience described untypical, though on the other hand many practitioners try to achieve something similar; 'disinterested scientist with no preconceived ideas and delighted to be proved wrong' is an identity which most parapsychologists have learned to assume with some facility at times of danger, and to that extent the experience is not untypical. Apart from this assumed public face, and various 'hardnosed' strategies which are adopted by scientists, many respondents perforce changed their personae as they moved between the close world of the paranormal and their lives within orthodox physics departments.[13]

Finally, as Collins and Pinch spent time with respondents of various persuasions we came to find their arguments not only comprehensible but, until again exposed to an opposite view, often compelling, and this too suggests a depth of understanding. Also it draws attention to the central paradox of the whole research design that has already been hinted at. The authors claim to be investigating and understanding alternative perceptions drawn from orthodox and potentially revolutionary scientific communities. If these claims are correct and the alternative paradigms stand in a relationship of incommensurability with one another, this should make it impossible to see both sides at the same time! In Kuhn's terms, 'the scientist does not preserve the gestalt subject's freedom to switch back and forth between ways of seeing' (Kuhn, 1962, p. 85). In the face of this, it can only be stated that both investigators did experience changes in their beliefs in both directions. However, it would still be true to say that we were not able to change our beliefs 'voluntarily', at least not in a certain sense. Our beliefs tended to change as a function of the nature of the latest period of prolonged exposure to scientists. Long exposure to critics made their point of view seem to be the only sensible one, and seemed to make the believers appear hopeless cranks and even charlatans. On the other hand, prolonged exposure to believers - for instance, in the remarkable cultural climate of the West Coast of the USA - made paranormal phenomena seem to be an obvious fact of everyday experience which only the most pig-headed could fail to perceive. In the latter circumstances it was the sceptics who looked like dense, dishonest and antediluvian conspirators battling tenaciously for a lost cause. Thus, we could change our beliefs and perceptions by exposing ourselves to the appropriate influence for long enough, but not while sitting in our offices.

This claim is not disingenuous. We really did experience changes in the content of what we took for granted as a matter of course, and this did change our views on how experimental manipulations should be interpreted - whether, for example, some manifestation should be taken as evidence of a poorly controlled experiment or as evidence of psi effects. Thus there have been several occasions over the last two years when the investigators found the phenomenon of, for example, retroactive psychokinesis (mind over matter acting backwards in time) not only acceptable, but also a necessary phenomenon in the world of ideas inhabited at the time. This memory is of a feeling that cannot be recaptured at the time of writing, and the embarrassing uneasiness that the memory engenders, and will perhaps engender in the reader, is perhaps the best indicator that is available of the adequacy of past internalisation of a strange culture.

2 PARANORMAL METAL BENDING RESEARCH:
Its background and its growth

The subject matter of parapsychology described – the extent and style of parapsychological research in Britain and the United States – resistance to paranormal findings – ambivalent reaction of parapsychologists to research on metal-bending phenomenon – emergence of Geller and metal bending – route into field of first researchers and their backgrounds – most researchers from physical sciences and new to paranormal area – sketch of paranormal metal-bending research – the mini-Gellers – early publications – early conference programme – scientific vigilantes – myths and rumours about paranormal research – believers and sceptics

THE PARAPSYCHOLOGICAL BACKGROUND

Paranormal metal bending, the particular subject of attention in this book, is often seen as one area of interest within the field of parapsychology. Parapsychology itself, as we have noted, has been defined as follows: 'Parapsychology means the scientific study of the "paranormal", that is, of phenomena which in one or more respects conflict with accepted scientific opinion as to what is physically possible' (Beloff, 1974, p. 1). The phenomena which have actually been studied by parapsychologists include telepathy, clairvoyance and precognition, which are collectively referred to as 'extra-sensory perception' (ESP), and the ability of mind to affect matter, or 'psychokinesis' (PK). Spoon-bending and its associated manifestations are a subclass of PK phenomena. The whole range of ESP and PK effects are referred to collectively as 'psi' phenomena.

The name 'parapsychology' reflects the fact that the majority of scientific researchers into the paranormal are psychologists by training. More recently physicists have moved into the field in greater numbers. Some of these researchers prefer to call the subject 'paraphysics' so as to stress differences in emphasis in the methods of investigation used. In particular, some paraphysicists are impatient with the traditional statistical methods employed by the majority of parapsychologists.

A typical statistical experiment in, say, telepathy might involve a 'sender', a 'receiver' and a pack of cards with symbols printed on them. The order of the cards is randomised by reference to carefully prepared random numbers, and the pack is presented to the sender. The sender is physically isolated from the receiver –

in a separate, shielded room, or even in another country. The
sender then looks at each card in turn while the receiver guesses
(or uses extra-sensory perception to judge) the symbols on the
cards. The order of symbols in the randomised pack is then
compared with the receiver's claims. Typically, the receiver will
have guessed wrongly in the large majority of cases, but if a
sufficiently large number of guesses are made (the number must
be decided on before the experiment commences, of course), the
receiver need only guess correctly slightly more frequently than
prior probability calculations would suggest to score significantly
overall.

In general, then, such experiments are long, boring and produce no dramatically obvious results but may be shown to yield
statistically significant results after the appropriate calculations
have been done. These experiments can be done in different ways.
Various parameters, such as the physical separation of the sender
and receiver, the symbols on the cards or other artifacts which
are 'transmitted', the personality profiles of the subjects and the
personality profiles of the experimenters, can be controlled and
changed. Over the years a large body of work has been produced
which tries to show how such parameters correlate with success
at ESP. The majority of orthodox scientists would still dispute
that the existence of psi phenomena has been properly demonstrated by any of these experiments, let alone the claimed correlations with other parameters.

Other psi phenomena can be investigated in a similar way to
the experiment just described. For instance, in a psychokinesis
experiment the 'psychic' subject could attempt to affect the order
of the cards, perhaps by influencing the operation of the device
that produced the random numbers used to determine their order
in the first place (see chapter 7 for a description of a related
experiment). In practice, most PK work has been done directly
on random mechanical systems such as shaken dice. For example,
the subject might try to produce a statistically significant pre-
ponderance of sixes with a die that is repeatedly shaken and
thrown by some automated means. Again, in general, the results
would show a small, undramatic, 'above-chance' effect only after
a large number of 'runs'.

PK can be done in a more dramatic way. There are films which
seem to show subjects moving objects such as matchboxes and so
forth across tables without obvious physical contact. Such phenomena are rare, and most such exhibitions are open to accusations
of trickery.

Sudden surges of interest in new parapsychological phenomena
do not seem untypical occurrences in the history of the field.
Perhaps sociologists of other persuasions might be interested in
paranormal metal bending as a typical example of a new fad within
parapsychology, revealing characteristics of this, and perhaps
other 'fringe' sciences. We intend, however, to ignore the remote
history of the field. Like many of our respondents, we are going
to treat the growth of PMB research as a unique and original

occurrence; the conceivable scientific legacy of which should not
be diluted or debunked by comparison with earlier periods of
excitement that were to prove – in the long term – to be without
substance. Nevertheless we cannot ignore completely the pre-
existing social and cognitive milieu of parapsychology, for even
PMB researchers who had no prior knowledge or interest in parapsychology (the majority) found that it soon took an interest
in them.

A number of studies of parapsychology have been made from a
sociological or historical point of view.[1] Most commentators divide
the history of parapsychology into periods, taking the modern,
or scientific, period as beginning around the time of the Second
World War with the growing widespread acceptance of J.B. Rhine's
statistical methods in parapsychological research. Indeed, several
commentators have been tempted to describe this period as characterised by a Rhinean 'paradigm' (McVaugh and Mauskopf, 1976,
1980; Nilsson, 1975, 1976). This seems reasonable if 'paradigm'
is construed in the restricted sense of experimental 'exemplar'
or series of exemplars. There seems no particular reason to suppose, however, that Rhine's work marked a watershed in the
'world view' of parapsychology researchers. Allison (1973, p. 62)
characterises the period since 1947 as 'normal science or puzzle
solving' and also suggests that research has become more inwardly
directed, toward other professionals in the field. At all events,
in the mid-1970s in the United States there were some half-dozen
institutions of fairly long standing which supported full-time
professional researchers in parapsychology – usually about two
or three each – and maintained what one might call a 'nine-to-five'
atmosphere. The University of California at Santa Barbara had a
full-time member of staff (externally funded) employed to teach
parapsychology courses and several American colleges offered
'minor' courses in parapsychology. In addition there were a number of smaller institutions, mostly around the San Francisco Bay
area, which had less of an air of permanence and 'nine-to-five'
routine yet supported full-time research. Many of these latter grew
up in association with the 'consciousness movement'.

Britain has the Society for Psychical Research, which has permanent staff at its administrative headquarters, but no full-time
researchers (there was one in the past). Otherwise, there is a
parapsychology-associated chair at Surrey University (set up
very recently); a number of members of different disciplinary
communities and other educational institutions at universities
around the country who actively pursue or are at least interested
in parapsychology research; and a number of students working
for higher degrees in parapsychology or parapsychology-related
subjects in four (or more?) British universities. Finally, there
are two or three rather 'fringe' parapsychological laboratories
and research centres.[2]

Progress over recent years could perhaps be best described as
'steady state', illuminated by the occasional development of techniques which have, for a time, seemed to promise more rapid pro-

gress. Examples of these developments include the discovery of
the 'sheep-goat' effect, which apparently shows a clear correlation
between psi ability and belief in psi phenomena (Schmeidler and
McConnell, 1958); the growth in the use of quantum random-number generators, pioneered by Schmidt (e.g. 1969a, 1973), which
has made randomisation processes much more reliable and convenient and led to the design of new automated equipment; and
growth of work with rodents rather than humans, which seemed
to promise unprecedented reliability and repeatability. This last
development was nipped in the bud by the discovery that its
major proponent had cheated in producing some of his results
(see Collins and Pinch, 1979).

In recent years, American parapsychology has produced all of
these new developments and has attracted a number of grants
from government agencies, though the amounts involved are small
compared with the funds distributed by private benefactors.
Allison lists six awards given to the parapsychologists by offices
such as the US National Institute for the Study of Mental Health
and the Office of Naval Research, between 1950 and 1973. These
probably did not total more than $100,000 but he points out that
the resources of the parapsychological foundations must run into
several millions of dollars. Since the growth of interest in Geller
other government grants have been attracted to the relevant
American parapsychological effort, but here too private sources
have been important in keeping the work going. Irrespective of
the small amount of government funding, it has a disproportion-
ately large symbolic function, serving to bestow a kind of publicly
recognised respectability on the field (see Collins and Pinch, 1979:
also Allison, 1973). In 1969 the American 'Parapsychological
Association' was admitted to the American Association for the
Advancement of Science, a goal which had eluded them when they
tried on three previous occasions[3] (see Dean, 1969, for details).

British parapsychology has not attracted any government money.
(As far as we know, our own project, described in chapter 5,
represents the first award to a parapsychology-connected subject
and this connection is somewhat tangential.) Indeed, there is
speculation that money was withdrawn from one research project
because, though dressed in orthodox garb, it may well have
included parapsychological research (Hanlon, 1975). One of our
respondents claimed that when he had suggested to a high-ranking
officer in the Science Research Council that parapsychology projects should attract government support, the reply was 'But suppose questions were asked in the House?' British parapsychology
has a much 'cosier' atmosphere than its American counterpart.
The headquarters and library of the Society for Psychical Research
in Kensington is staffed by helpful, friendly assistants. There
one is likely to overhear a joke about the appropriate subscription
for members who have passed over, but less likely to hear details
of the latest computer programme for analysis of results. The
atmosphere of British parapsychology is perhaps a cross between
Victorian correctness and Mittel-European warmth. Few results

have been forthcoming of recent years, far fewer that the Americans have produced. Probably the British parapsychological establishment would consider that the care used to eliminate normal explanations in British work accounted for at least some of the non-reproducibility of some American effects in Britain. Publication of findings is easily available on both sides of the Atlantic in the parapsychology journals provided that the appropriate (high) professional standards are achieved. There are three long-standing refereed journals, similar in appearance to other disciplines' professional outlets, and a number of others of less immaculate pedigree. There are also regular series of meetings and conferences and occasional publications of sets of conference papers. All in all, outlets within the field are probably somewhat more easily available in parapsychology than in other disciplines.

However, publication in orthodox scientific journals had eluded both communities of parapsychologists up till 1974 except for very rare exceptions. One small survey of the orthodox journals found that such publications as there were, were biased toward reporting negative results (Billig, 1972). Positive publications tend to be followed by strings of critical letters or disclaiming editorials (see Collins and Pinch, 1979, for discussion of a recent case). An editor of a respected journal told us that the refereeing system has virtually broken down in respect of parapsychology papers, for the argument had become so polemicised that the reports of referees could be predicted.

Certainly parapsychology arouses strong passions in some whom one would expect to be otherwise disinterested scientists. One extraordinary statement, located by Allison and made by an eminent physicist, Condon, puts extra-sensory perception and psychokinesis into the class of pseudo-sciences of which the publishers and teachers 'should, on being found guilty [of claiming them to be absolute truth], be publicly horsewhipped, and forever banned from further activity in these usually honorable professions' (Condon, 1969, p. 6). Other scientists have devoted long periods to the most painstaking research in order to show that parapsychologists' claims could be explained by 'normal' means. Mark Hansel, Professor of Psychology at Swansea University, has written a whole book dedicated to showing that all so-called paranormal feats could have been produced by one trick or another (Hansel, 1966). Immense efforts have been put into the re analysis of the Soal-Goldney experiments (an important and relatively early (1941-3) series - see Scott and Haskell (1973) and Scott and Haskell (1974)). This is the sort of energy that one would expect to be expended only by scientists trying to establish some fascinating new natural truth rather than elucidating a negative thesis (see chapter 2 for further discussion; and Pinch, 1979b).

This negative energy and perpetual conflict is now frequently interpreted by the parapsychologists by applying Kuhn's picture of scientific development to the field as a whole. The Kuhnian thesis was seized upon in parapsychological circles with perhaps even more avidity than was manifested in sociological circles. Allison conducted a postal survey of members of the American Parapsychological Association in 1972 and found that 57 per cent of his sample 'agreed strongly' with the statement that a satisfactory explanation of psi would require a revolutionary change in some sciences. He also found that several parapsychological 'authorities' had expressed the view in their published work that they were engaged in revolutionary activity, although, as Allison pointed out (1973), the view that parapsychological findings are incompatible with orthodox science is one which pre-dates Kuhn.

This 'thumb-nail sketch' is intended to show the parapsychological milieu into which the Geller affair was injected. It was a milieu of a rejected science modelling its internal structure on orthodox disciplines and struggling continuously for an internal scientific breakthrough and external recognition – struggles which the most dedicated might think were slowly bearing the fruit of a far-distant revolution in our understanding of the world. Some of the tactics used in this struggle have been described elsewhere (Collins and Pinch, 1979) but we must note here that an important element in the attacks of critics has been their attempt to associate scientific parapsychology with manifestly 'unscientific' areas such as occultism, astrology, spiritualism and so forth. Thus, far from embracing any new fad that comes along, professional parapsychologists have been careful not to endorse any phenomenon that does not have a good pedigree. It must be realised, then, that the reaction of professional parapsychologists to Geller, with his associations of showmanship, was ambivalent. It was ambivalent also to the initial reports of Geller's scientific successes, where these came from members of the physics community who had no professional training in parapsychology. As one esteemed American parapsychologist wrote to us, referring to physical scientists:

> I regard the work by X and the group at Z [two of the leading groups of physicists] to be both naive and sloppy. . . .
> I am convinced that the major problem facing orthodox scientists entering this area is that they are simply not familiar with the methods and findings of serious parapsychological research during the last forty years. There is a certain arrogance on the part of certain physical scientists, to totally disregard the large body of rigorous experimental work done in this field.

And similar sentiments were expressed in a letter to the 'New Scientist' by A.J. Ellison, Professor of Electrical Engineering at City University London and, at the time of writing, president of the British Society for Psychical Research (SPR): 'I fully agree that physical scientists can be exceedingly naive outside their own fields. . . . It is sad to see recently "converted" physical scientists trying to investigate parapsychological matters outside their field of experience' (Ellison, 1974).

THE EMERGENCE OF PARANORMAL METAL BENDING

Reports of 'psychokinesis' are not new. Some typical results have been described above. However, PMB was unique in two ways. Firstly, it added a most unlikely and gross manifestation to the (relatively) familiar psychokinetic repertoire. Secondly, it was, apparently, more reliably reproducible than other effects and therefore held the promise of the possibility of convincing laboratory verification. On the whole, other effects either were seemingly difficult to reproduce in the laboratory or, where they emerged only after statistical calculations, were short of rhetorical impact on the conservative scientific community.

It seems that tales of Geller's abilities first impinged upon the Western scientific community at a conference in New York in 1969. This 'International Life Energies' conference brought together scientists (including Columbia University physicist Gerald Feinberg, inventor of the 'Tachyon', and British physicist Ted Bastin) and some parapsychologists and 'subjects' who were interested in the scientific verification of psychic phenomena. At this conference an Israeli scientist, Dr Bentov, reported on rumours of Geller's abilities. Dr Andrija Puharich was delegated to travel to Israel to investigate his seemingly remarkable feats and report on their suitability for scientific investigation.

Puharich is an M.D. with medical and electronic patents to his name. He also has a long-standing interest in psychic phenomena. Of recent years this interest has, however, been of a sort which would be likely to encourage professional parapsychologists to keep their distance. Thus, a review (White, 1974) in the 'Journal of the American Society for Psychical Research' of the published proceedings of a conference held in 1971 said this of Puharich's contribution:

> I must confess that I am unable to extract any meaning from this paper, nor can I grasp just how the author has made out a case for the relevance of his exotic theoretical ruminations . . . for an understanding of psi. (In passing, it is interesting to note that out of more than a hundred bibliographic references, only three cite material which has anything to do with parapsychology - and two of these works are by Puharich himself!) . . . in the opinion of this reviewer, [the paper did not merit publication in the proceedings or] anywhere else.

Again, in his book 'Uri', published in 1974, Puharich described a history of his contacts with extra-terrestrial beings. Further, he is currently sponsoring research designed to show that paranormal metal bending is a manifestation of the attention of higher-order beings.

Puharich went to Israel in August 1971 and stayed for some time observing Geller's impressive performances on stage and in private, and experiencing various momentous happenings himself. In mid-1972, Puharich set about organising the scientific investigation

of Geller. He wrote that he formed a 'Theory Group' whose leader-
ship 'was eventually assumed by Dr Ted Bastin of Cambridge
University' (Puharich, 1974, p. 171), though this 'group' does
not appear to have developed any lasting social substance.

Dr Bastin is a physicist and editor of 'Theoria to Theory', a
broadly based interdisciplinary journal orientated toward the
philosophy of religion and science. At one time he held an academic post at Cambridge University, and now works with the
so-called 'Language Research Unit' which produces the journal,
but is not part of the university proper. (Several well-known
Cambridge philosophers are associated with it, however.) Bastin's
main interests and field of research have been in the foundations
of relativity and quantum theory and he edited the conference
proceedings, 'Quantum Theory and Beyond' (Bastin, 1971).

Also in mid-1972, a research proposal was submitted, in co-
operation with the 'Theory Group', to the American National
Science Foundation. According to Puharich, personal strings were
pulled by Ed Mitchell amongst others. (Mitchell is the astronaut
famous for attempting an ESP experiment while on a flight to the
moon in 1971; he is now an important fund-raiser for the parapsychological community.) This research proposal met with no
success.

Mitchell also attempted to arrange for scientific research on
Geller to be carried out at Kent State University under Dr Wilbur
Franklin but here too they failed through problems of funds and
'other resources' (Puharich, 1974, p. 172). Franklin is chairman
of the Department of Physics, Graduate Division, at Kent State
and has written on the Geller phenomenon (Panati, 1976). He
appears to have been brought into the investigation in the first
place by Mitchell.

Eventually, through the intercession of Puharich (1974, p. 172)
it was agreed that Geller would be looked at by Dr Harold Puthoff
and Russell Targ. They were successful in arranging for the research on Geller and others to be carried out at the prestigious
Stanford Research Institute (SRI) with Mitchell as the sponsor.
Targ and Puthoff are both scientists with a background in laser
physics. Puthoff is co-author of a book, 'Fundamentals of Quantum Electronics' (Pantell and Puthoff, 1969), and had only a
casual interest in parapsychology before the research project at
SRI began. Targ worked on the development of the gas transport
laser and is the author of many articles on laser physics. His
interest in parapsychology is long-standing, and he had published
work in the parapsychology field before the SRI experiments commenced. Their research on Geller was to start in earnest in
November 1972.

At the end of August 1972 Geller paid his first visit to the United
States and informally demonstrated his powers to Professor Gerald
Feinberg and 'many others' (Puharich, 1974, p. 173) including
Mitchell, Wilbur Franklin and Werner von Braun. Geller then re-
turned to Germany where he was touring with his stage show.

On 30 October 1972 Puharich brought Geller to England for the first time and, at the Royal Garden Hotel, London, he showed his powers to a group of interested scientists. These included Bastin and some journalists. This meeting precipitated the first report of Geller's powers in the British science news press, but it would have taken an unusually alert reader to have seen the significance of the rather 'throw-away' comments of 'Ariadne' on the last page (p. 360) of the 'New Scientist' of 9 November 1972 (see quotations on p. 1).

Geller eventually reached California on 11 November 1972, after a week in the New York area, and commenced experiments at SRI. These experiments were conducted in secrecy, except that a privileged group of scientists were given demonstrations of Geller's abilities. By coincidence Collins was in the Stanford area around 20 November, when he first heard of Geller from a physicist at Stanford University who was a respondent in another study (Collins, 1975). Collins was told about 'subject' Ingo Swann's seemingly paranormal effect on a 'superconducting magnetometer' at the university (see Targ and Puthoff, 1977, for details and also chapter 7). Collins was told about the Geller demonstration and later was able to interview Russell Targ, but Targ would not talk about Geller or his abilities. The atmosphere surrounding the work seemed to be one of almost paranoiac secrecy masking a suppressed excitement and certainty that something big was going to emerge from the research – something that would lead to a publication in the orthodox physics journals of such a nature as to create an unprecedented impact. (Later, it became clear that the excitement, if this had centred on Geller's psychokinetic abilities, was not to be maintained, for the publications which did eventually emerge from SRI were concerned with other paranormal effects.)

The first public announcement of the SRI work did not appear until 9 March 1973 at a specially arranged symposium at Columbia University. On 12 March 'Time' magazine ran an extremely hostile story about the SRI work, citing Ray Hyman, a psychologist and Department of Defence consultant, who claimed to have observed Targ and Puthoff's work and found it to be 'incredibly sloppy'. Targ and Puthoff (e.g. 1977) were later to deny that Hyman had witnessed any of their controlled experiments – rather he had seen and conducted some informal tests.

The Columbia conference was reported in the British 'New Scientist' on 22 March by Peter Gwynne, who was science editor of 'Newsweek'. Gwynne's report was generally favourable: 'With a cautious approach of this nature, it could be that parapsychology will finally undergo a genuinely disinterested study of its validity' (Gwynne, 1973, p. 677). These conflicting reports, coming from the two American news weeklies, set the scene for a continued disagreement between them over the value of the Stanford work. Charles Panati, editor of 'The Geller Papers' (1976), an uncritical collection of scientists' eyewitness reports of Geller's activities, was a former science editor of 'Newsweek'. John L. Wilhelm, author of 'The Search for Superman' (1976), a volume that most would

perceive as highly critical of the SRI work, was a former staff
writer for 'Time'. More significant than the sides taken by these
magazines is the extent of their interest, and their attempts to
assess the validity of the work carried out at a major scientific
institution. It represents the entry 'with a vengeance' of what
has elsewhere been called the 'contingent forum'[14] (Collins and
Pinch, 1979) into activities which are constitutive of scientific
knowledge.

The next report in the British science press was by Brendan
O'Regan in 'New Scientist' of 12 July 1973. O'Regan was later to
become research director of Edgar Mitchell's organisation for
scientific funding, the Institute for Noetic Sciences, at Menlo
Park, a few blocks from SRI. O'Regan's report was a favourable
survey of Targ and Puthoff's research to date.

In August 1973, Bastin was reported as having spoken at a
conference on religion and science held under the auspices of the
Modern Churchman's Union. Bastin's account of his observations
of Geller's powers was said by Bernard Dixon ('New Scientist'
Editor) to have been greeted with 'healthy scepticism' (Dixon,
1973).

It was not until 23 November 1973 that Geller became widely
known in Britain. On that day he appeared on the David Dimbleby
'Talk-In' television programme with John Taylor, Professor of
Mathematics at King's College, London. Taylor was to represent
the 'scientific' viewpoint, replacing Chris Evans who was originally
to appear. On this programme Geller bent metal objects and Taylor,
on witnessing this, proclaimed that the effect could not be explained by science. The newspapers reported the events widely,
and several newspaper science correspondents and other reporters
claimed to have been first-hand witnesses of further Geller events
in the following days. At this point the wave of young children
who claimed to be able to perform similar feats began to emerge,
seemingly catalysed by Geller's performance. Doubtless, this
episode itself would have made an interesting study in social
epidemiology.

During 1974 Geller visited England on at least four occasions
and did experiments at Birkbeck College, University of London,
in the presence of, amongst others, David Bohm and John Hasted
– both professors of physics at Birkbeck – and Bastin and O'Regan.
The connection between Bohm and Hasted, and Geller was through
scientific visitors to Birkbeck's physics department, notably Jack
Sarfatti and Fred Wolf. Sarfatti and Wolf, who were at one time
professors of physics at San Diego State University, were attracted
by Bohm's famous and heterodox interpretations of quantum
theory (Bohm, 1952; Jammer, 1974; Pinch, 1977). Together with
Bob Toben, they were authors of a speculative and illustrated
adventure beyond the frontiers of physics ('Space, Time and
Beyond', 1975). They knew of Geller through their associations
with Brendan O'Regan, West Coast fringe science, and the 'consciousness movement' in general. It seems that these tests at
Birkbeck were not intended to be sensationalised, but were in

fact widely reported because of an indiscretion on the part of
Sarfatti. During 1974, and continuing up to the time of writing,
both Taylor and Hasted experimented on the host of young
'subjects' who were coming forward. They also worked with Geller
whenever the opportunity arose. By this time, the phenomenon
was so widely known as to render pointless any further attempt
to delineate its emergence into the scientific world.

The only major scientific publishing events to take place up
to this time occurred in the middle of October 1974 when Targ
and Puthoff (1974a) finally succeeded in publishing the first report of their work in the prestigious scientific journal, 'Nature'.
This report did not contain any positive report of paranormal
metal bending, however, but was concerned in the main with
telepathy, clairvoyance and 'remote viewing' experiments. Almost
simultaneously (by design not accident - see Collins and Pinch,
1978a) 'New Scientist' carried a long and scathing article on the
SRI work by Joseph Hanlon (see below and chapter 7). The
responses to Hanlon's article, in the form of letters to the 'New
Scientist', revealed the extent of continuing positive interest in
Geller among British scientists such as Bohm, Hasted, Taylor,
Bastin and Ellison. On 31 October 1974 the 'Guardian' quoted
Professor Taylor as saying:

> Our basic problem now is not to ask whether the phenomenon
> can occur but how it occurs. It is a very important phenomenon
> - it will tell us new things about human beings. The problem
> of understanding it will be one of the most exciting pieces of
> research of the next few years.

Professor Hasted is quoted in the same piece, 'It is time that
scientists stood up to be counted on this issue.'

It can now be seen that the only figure at centre stage in the
development of research on Geller, who was at the time strongly
tied in with professional parapsychology, was Russell Targ. Targ
had published an article in the 'Parapsychology Review' (Targ and
Hunt, 1972), and had another submitted at the time of Collins's
interview with him in November 1972. Also, Targ, on the evidence
of that interview, was connected, in the sociometric sense, with
figures such as Charlie Tart, Gertrude Schmeidler and Charles
Honorton, all well-known in the American parapsychological scene.
He would regularly talk to them on the telephone, visit them and
meet them at conferences. However, Puthoff, his colleague, was
a newcomer; Puharich, the instigator, was a maverick; and the
research took place in a new setting for parapsychology (SRI)
with funds from outside the usual sources, or at least directed
through an unusual channel. Mitchell, the sponsor, wrote that he
became interested in psychical research in 1967, but of course
remained an amateur until in late 1972 he retired from the Navy
and his work as an astronaut. In a book which he edited in 1974
he made clear that he did not accept the scientific limitations of
the subject as seen by Rhine and he deliberately talked of 'psychic

research' rather than parapsychology (Mitchell, 1974b, p. 40). What is more, the intention of the SRI group seemed to be to break away from run-of-the-mill statistical parapsychological research. Targ suggested that he could do more in a month at SRI than could be done in a year in a typical parapsychological laboratory (interview 1972). As regards publication, the intention was definitely to avoid publication in the parapsychology journals but to open the way into the physics journals for reports of paranormal phenomena. As Puthoff told us in a 1977 interview, 'I feel if what we do cannot make it in the hard science journals then it is not worth doing.' Even for Targ, the SRI research was to be a fresh start in parapsychology backed by the resources of hard science.

In Britain, Ted Bastin had a tangential relationship with the field. Though he had published results of telepathy experiments conducted in 1953 in the 'Journal of Parapsychology', he had not kept up with the literature of the field, and his more recent connection with it had developed through interests in the philosophy of religion, meditation, and their connection with physical theory. In this way he had come to attend conferences where such inter-relationships were discussed, including the Life Energies Conference in New York.

Taylor had dabbled with some ideas pertaining to parapsychology in a popular book on the brain which he had published in 1971 but this was the full extent of his previous connection with the field. His contact with Geller arose through his connections with the BBC. They had used him as a 'scientific personality' on previous occasions, most notably in a programme on Black Holes. Neither Hasted or Bohm had any previous connections with the field, and their contact with Geller came through yet another independent route - Wolf and Sarfatti. Ellison, who became president of the SPR in 1976, did not play a great role in the early days of research, taking part in a newspaper-sponsored trans-atlantic telepathy test with Geller - which failed - and witnessing certain effects produced by young subjects in their homes which could not be reproduced in his laboratory. Pamplin, our colleague who originated our participant observation experiments at Bath, became interested as a result of seeing the Dimbleby show on television. He collected a series of young local spoon-benders through astute use of local newspapers and without help from other researchers. He had no previous connections with the para-psychology field. He probably typifies the route into interest in PMB of those who became interested after the 1973/74 outbreak of publicity. (Our experiments started in early 1975.)

Thus, PMB research originated largely outside the cultural and cognitive milieu of professional parapsychology in a relation-ship, where any existed, of ambivalence, even antagonism.

A SKETCH OF PMB RESEARCH

Though it is difficult to obtain direct and certain knowledge of the sources and size of financial support for PMB research, it is clear that the Stanford work was lavishly funded by parapsychology standards, and that work in Britain has been done on a shoe-string budget. The SRI project has had to support the salaries of two full-time researchers in the middle of their careers, provide fairly handsome 'retainers' for the 'subjects' over periods of months and cover overheads. Presumably 'six-figure' dollar sums are involved. The sources of this money are the subject of a great deal of rumour (see below).

In Britain researchers have had to make do with small sums from the Society for Psychical Research and whatever could be 'bootlegged' from departmental funds. Journalist Joseph Hanlon has reported that in 1974-5 Professor Taylor was deliberately prevented from using part of a Department of Defence contract for PMB research by 'unusually' precise control of the project (Hanlon, 1975). The project did not continue. (Professor Taylor denies that the parapsychology connection was the reason for the discontinuance of the project.)

The only government money coming directly into PMB research has been £200 from the Social Science Research Council allowed for the cost of the experiments at Bath University (described in chapter 5), as pieces of participant observation within the larger sociological project. Of this allowance, some £90 was actually spent, largely on the travel expenses of the researchers and subjects.[5]

The research atmosphere in Britain was one of either 'string-and-sealing-wax' ingenuity or ingenuity directed at begging and borrowing sophisticated apparatus when this was required. Both of these approaches were exemplified in experiments done in collaboration with the authors, the former by Professor Hasted's invention of a cork-and-water suspension for a sensitive rotating psychokinesis detector and the latter by Professor Taylor's hurried carrying out of a series of experiments in the short time during which he could borrow a sensitive electromagnetic radiation frequency analyser.

The American scene has not been characterised by the emergence of large numbers of 'mini-Gellers', the name given to the swarm of children who came forward claiming similar powers to those of Geller following the initial publicity. No children have performed at SRI or seemingly any other major American PMB centre, though rumours have suggested that a few such children emerged in California. In Britain research time with Geller himself has been hard to come by, and the mini-Gellers have provided the great majority of research opportunities. However, the mini-Gellers have not proved to be reliable subjects. The large number in the early years has rapidly fallen to single figures with only one or two 'stars', whose powers appear to wax and wane rather disconcertingly. Most of the children find that they work best when

Geller himself is either present or at least performing simultaneously on TV. With the passing of the publicity band-wagon such subjects find it more difficult to produce the effect. Some have tried to recapture the atmosphere of the early days with posters of Geller and with his long-playing record. Some certainly treasure photographs of him, especially where they appear with him. A collection of such Geller gewgaws decorated the sitting-room of one of our subjects.

One difficulty with the PMB field is that there is no point which marks an unambiguous beginning to the debate amongst scientists because there is no refereed publication in an orthodox scientific journal claiming verification of paranormal metal bending. Papers were submitted to 'Nature' on this topic but were not accepted. The only publications are, then, in the parapsychology journals, and these do not reach the attention of anything but a very small proportion of the scientific community; in popular and semi-popular books such as Puharich's exotic account, 'Uri', and Taylor's glossy 'Superminds'; in articles, reports and letters in the scientific news press such as 'New Scientist'; and in the few comments which have appeared in the non-refereed sections of 'Nature'. The responses of the critics have to a large extent been directed at the newspaper and television coverage of Geller's performance, and at the comments of scientists in the same media.

In Britain the most important critical article of the early years was the one written by Joseph Hanlon, covering sixteen pages of the 'New Scientist' of 17 October 1974. This followed Geller's eventual failure to submit to a panel test of his abilities arranged by 'New Scientist' after his appearance on the Dimbleby 'Talk-In' in November 1973. ('New Scientist' reports that Geller initially accepted the invitation in writing on 3 December 1973.) The major thrust of Hanlon's criticism, as has been pointed out, was directed at the paper published almost simultaneously in 'Nature' (Targ and Puthoff, 1974a). This, however, dealt hardly at all with metal bending. Hanlon devoted six-and-a-half pages to the 'Nature' article and the SRI research. Only one-quarter of one of these pages (p. 180) was taken up with PMB at SRI. This quarter-page referred, firstly, to Targ and Puthoff's declaration that they were unable to capture metal-bending phenomena under sufficiently controlled conditions to enable them to 'obtain data sufficient to support the paranormal hypothesis' and, secondly, to an SRI videotape of Geller's metal-bending attempts that Hanlon had been allowed to view.

The rest of the article included criticism of Geller's performances based on witnesses' descriptions of the following:

(i)   Tests at the Institute of Noetic Sciences, California
(ii)   Events in a taxi on the way to London airport (25 November 1973)
(iii)   Events at Bell Laboratories, N.J. (8 June 1973)
(iv)   A performance on the Mike Douglas TV show in Canada (29 October, 1973)

(v)   A reported case of teleportation of a camera case from
           New York to Israel
(vi)   A so-called paranormal stopping and starting of a cable
           car in Germany (June 1972)
(vii)   Events around a TV programme in New York
(viii)   Events connected with a Thames TV film made in New
           York (December 1973)
(ix)   A performance on the Merv Griffin TV show in the USA
(x)   A performance on the Johnny Carson 'Tonight' TV show
           in the USA (August 1973)
(xi)   Geller's attempts to stop a lift in a New York store
(xii)   A Thames TV performance (15 January 1974)
(xiii)   Ray Hyman's visit to SRI in December 1972
(xiv)   A performance in the offices of 'Time' (March 1973)
(xv)   A report which appeared in several places including the
           'News of the World' (2 December 1973)
(xvi)   A transatlantic telepathy test conducted by the 'Sunday
           Mirror' (10 December 1973), at which Hanlon was present
(xvii)   An informal test with Hanlon and Bernard Dixon (editor
           of 'New Scientist') at the Montcalm Hotel, London (19
           June 1974)
(xviii)   Tests at Birkbeck College in June 1974 (Hanlon here
           used evidence from an unpublished report)

Hanlon's article provides a fair indication of the type of evidence
that was publicly available to the wider scientific community at
the time it was written, in October 1974. As will be seen, only
three out of eighteen events discussed took place in front of
scientists in scientific laboratories. The responses to Hanlon's
article will be discussed in chapter 7.

To complete this historical sketch of the early development of
the field and to indicate the scope of the unpublished scientific
interest, we present below the programme of a conference on 'The
Physics of the Paranormal' held in Tarrytown, N.Y., on 21-23
February 1975. A great deal of secrecy surrounded this conference and it was difficult to find out much about it. No proceedings
have ever been published, and neither author has been able to
see any of the papers. From the comments of our respondents it
seems that some contributors felt themselves able to discuss findings in a manner less guarded than would have been necessary if
the conference had not been secret. In the circumstances of
confidentiality these scientists did not fear the public ridicule
that might have greeted some of their more extravagant reports.

The programme for the conference was as follows:

21 February
  9.00 - 10 p.m.   Opening remarks: Brendan O'Regan,
                       Programme Chairman; Dr Harold Puthoff,
                       Stanford Research Institute: A discussion
                       of over one hundred experiments involv-

	ing effects on magnetometers and laser-pendulum systems with research subjects Patrick Price and Ingo Swann.
10.00 - 10.30 p.m.	Dr Ronald Hawke, Lawrence Livermore Radiation Laboratories: A discussion of some experiments.

22 February

9.00 - 9.45 a.m.	Dr Ronald Hawke: A discussion on some experiments on magnetically sensitive systems with research subject,
10.00 - 11.00 a.m.	Dr Helmut Schmidt, Mind Science Foundation, San Antonio, Texas: Statistical PK effects: are they basically different from macroscopic PK?
11.00 - 11.30 a.m.	Dr Edward G. Bastin, 'Theoria to Theory', Cambridge, England: A comment.
2.00 - 3.00 p.m.	Dr John Taylor, King's College, University of London: Metal bending - the general nature of the phenomenon. Studies with Uri Geller and several child subjects in England.
3.15 - 4.15 p.m.	Dr John Hasted, Birkbeck College, University of London: Disappearance/appearance phenomena and quantum theory.
4.15 - 5.30 p.m.	Dr Harold Puthoff and Russell Targ: Film and videotape of metal-bending and PK with Uri Geller. Recent results in remote viewing research.
8.00 - 8.45 p.m.	Dr Wilbur Franklin, Kent State University, Ohio: Scanning electron microscope observation of fracture surfaces.
8.45 - 9.30 p.m.	Eldon Byrd, Naval Surface Weapons Center, Maryland: Nitinol studies/broken keys/cracked rings.
9.30 - 10.15 p.m.	Dr Friedbert Karger, Max Planck Institute for Plasma Physics, Munich: A discussion of some recent results on high-temperature phenomena.

23 February

9.00 - 9.30 a.m.	Dr Andrija Puharich: A little about the past, a lot about the future.
9.30 - 10.15 a.m.	Dr Wilbur Franklin: Scanning electron microscope observation of fracture surfaces.
10.15 - 11.00 a.m.	Dr E. Alan Price, Institute of Parapsychology, Johannesburg: The Uri Geller effect.
11.00 - 11.20 a.m.	Dr Friedbert Karger: Psychokinesis.

11.20 - 11.40 a.m.   Dr Evan Harris Walker, Ballistic Re-
                      search Laboratories, US Army R and
                      D Center, Maryland: Changes in our
                      physical view of the world.
11.40 - 12.00 noon   Closing discussion

In addition, the names Edgar Mitchell, George Owen, Lyall Watson,
Fred Wolf, Joel Whitten and Brian Josephson appeared on the list
of participants.

THE VIGILANTES

The unusual amount of energy that critics of parapsychology have
expended has already been mentioned. The vigour of some of the
criticism of the research on Geller and PMB, especially in sections
of the media such as 'Time' magazine and 'New Scientist', has also
been described. In more recent years, some of the critical energy
available has been directed through new institutions.
    Between about 1972 and 1976 the sociologist Marcello Truzzi
circulated a pamphlet called 'The Zetetic', which was subtitled
'A Newsletter of Academic Research into Occultisms'. In the issue
of June 1975 Truzzi first mentioned plans for the setting up of
an association which was intended to be called 'Resources for the
Scientific Evaluation of the Paranormal'. As well as Truzzi, the
initiators were Martin Gardner (regular writer for 'Scientific
American' and author of 'Fads and Fallacies in the Name of Science'
(1957)), Ray Hyman (sceptical psychologist) and 'the "Amazing"
(James) Randi (known to many of you for his replications of the
tricks of pseudo-psychics on national television)' (Truzzi, 1975).
All three of these last-named were to write many articles critical
of Geller and other parapsychological research. Gardner later
wrote a small book satirising Geller's performance from a supposedly autobiographical viewpoint. This book was called 'Confessions
of a Psychic' and was published under the pseudonym 'Uriah
Fuller' (1976). Randi wrote 'The Magic of Uri Geller: As Revealed
by the Amazing Randi' (1975). Between mid-1975 and mid-1976
the American Humanist Association became involved in Truzzi's
plans. The 'Humanist' magazine had well-established credentials
in the attack on the so-called pseudo-sciences. Its most notorious
attack was published in the issue of September/October 1975 and
was entitled, 'Objections to Astrology: A Statement by 186 Leading Scientists'.[6] Paul Kurtz, editor of the 'Humanist', was a member
of the editorial board when the first issue of the official journal
of what was now called 'The Committee for the Scientific Investigation of the Claims of the Paranormal' appeared. Kurtz and Truzzi
were the co-chairmen of the committee. The journal, under the
editorship of Truzzi, kept the title of 'The Zetetic' and first
appeared in Fall/Winter 1976.
    With this membership, the committee only lasted long enough
to produce two issues of its journal. By the end of 1977, Marcello

Truzzi had resigned because of what he saw as the growing
danger of the committee's excessive negative zeal at the expense
of responsible scholarship; because of the decision to change the
journal from an academic to a popular organ; and because of what
he perceived as the undemocratic nature of the committee which
would prevent any rectification of the problem (1977b). Kurtz
took over the chairmanship of the committee and Kendrick Frazier,
formerly editor of 'Science News', became editor of the journal,
which changed its name to the 'Sceptical Inquirer'. Subsequently
Truzzi has started another newsletter called 'The Zetetic Scholar'.

The committee and its journal do not figure largely in the
account which follows, but the foregoing description will perhaps
highlight both the zealousness and the degree of social and
institutional organisation of some of the sceptical opinion which
faced PMB research. As well as a broadly hostile scientific environment, PMB researchers faced a small informal network of active
critics and formal critical organisations. It must be said that
among the informal group were scientists who were approached
but refused to join the committee, believing that it was inappropriate to institutionalise opposition in this way. There was a full
spectrum of styles of sceptical opinion. In Truzzi's words: 'Just
as there is a spectrum of responsible-irresponsible proponents
[of the paranormal], the same is true on the critical side' (Truzzi,
1977a).

The motivation of critics seems to have been various. Respondents included among their answers to questions on this point:
worries about the growth of pseudo-sciences and about scientists,
especially undergraduates, being 'conned' by things they do not
understand; worries about a general occult revival; worries about
children and the public being fooled by Geller; and simple fasci-
nation with the whole subject. It may be germane that at least one
member of the committee admitted to making lots of money from
debunking Geller, and one other mentioned smaller rewards of the
same kind. (Doubtless some proponents have done rather well out
of the whole thing also.) Some of the motivation for the zealous
opposition, which gave rise to what one might refer to as the
growth of a group of 'scientific vigilantes', is perhaps nicely
expressed in the following quotations. The first is from an editorial in 'Nature', the second from Christopher Evans, a member
of the committee, and the third from Paul Kurtz:

> It would have amazed the Victorian steadfasts of science how
> confused some of our attitudes towards science still are. Instead
> of the logical world they hoped for and tried to work in, there
> is a discernible tendency for the public and even some prac-
> titioners of science to turn their backs on science and become
> preoccupied with the bizarre and the magical. Mr Uri Geller is
> only the most recent to cast doubt in the public mind of the
> efficacy of rational explanation ('Nature', 1974, p. 541).

How can man ever hope to solve the problems of his existence

on this planet if, in crisis, he seeks comfort and guidance from
the mystical and occult rather than stare reality in the face?
For this, I believe, is what is happening to Western Society
in its present state of turbulence. Where science and technology
fail, superstition steps in as a welcome house guest. When we
look at our world and see only a cruel present and soulless
future, then ghosts must walk and metal bend to comfort us.
When politicians and philosophers fail to guide and console the
time of the psychic Messiah is nigh (Evans, 1976, p. 53).

Often . . . the least shred of evidence for these claims [for
the existence of paranormal phenomena] is blown out of proportion and presented as 'scientific' proof. Many individuals now
believe that there is considerable need to organize some strategy
of refutation. Perhaps we ought not to assume that the scientific
enlightenment will continue indefinitely; for all we know, like
the Hellenic civilization, it may be overwhelmed by irrationalism,
subjectivism and obscurantism (quoted in Frazier, 1976, p. 346).

MYTHS AND RUMOURS

The positive and negative passions within which PMB research
was carried out and the subsequent air of paranoia, plots and
rumour can be further judged by the following two accounts of
the area that the authors were offered at one time or another
during the course of the project. The first of these accounts came
from sceptics, the second set of accounts from believers in the
phenomenon.

PMB AS A SCIENTOLOGISTS' PLOT

According to some critics, the results of the work done at Stanford
Research Institute have emerged out of deliberate conspiracy or
unconscious bias by members of the Church of Scientology.[7] The
existence of paranormal phenomena would be consistent, it seems,
with the scientologists' creed. Certain of the 'vigilantes' have
drawn attention to Puthoff's beliefs and connections in criticising
SRI work. For instance, Ray Hyman, writing in a critical context,
has drawn attention to the fact that Puthoff 'has made it to the
level of a Class III operational Thetan in the Church of Scientology'
(Hyman, 1977, p. 16). Martin Gardner described Puthoff as 'a
physicist and scientologist' (Gardner, 1975b, p. 114), and Joe
Hanlon (1974a, p. 182) made the connection more specific:

Puthoff has gone through encounter groups and other West
Coast fads, and is now a Scientologist (as is Ingo Swann) [a
psychic subject used at SRI]. In an area where observation is
difficult anyway, have the SRI investigators taken enough precautions to ensure that their natural desire to see Geller succeed

does not cause them to unconsciously make errors or misinterpret the data to Geller's benefit?

The scientology plot explanation was also put by a respondent in an interview. Referring to a claimed 'exposé' of the SRI work, he said:

this has all been published in a recent book . . . it was greeted by howls of protest from the scientologists at SRI . . . it reveals lots of experimental details of what went on when Geller was at SRI . . . the whole thing was being videotaped by X, who is a scientologist. Puthoff is a scientologist. Two other psychics they tested, R and S, are both scientologists as well. R said there were fourteen scientology 'clears' working at SRI. The original research done by Puthoff and Targ was in part funded by T, who is also a scientologist. . . . This is all very relevant because scientologists believe in psi and in effect Puthoff is confirming church doctrines . . .

Another respondent suggested:

I do not think that Targ and Puthoff are very competent personally and I think the scientology thing is a very important condition to be aware of. . . . There is definitely some sort of scientology conspiracy. It is slightly paranoid but from the things I have picked up that seems to me to be the most likely explanation. There is a very strong ideological religious bias in their work. Scientology and that sort of stuff is something that appeals to second-rate scientists quite a lot.

PMB, THE CIA AND THE MILITARY

A view cultivated by believers was that PMB and related Geller phenomena were important to government and the military.

The SRI researchers refuse to disclose their sources of funding but there were rumours that large amounts of money originating from military sources have found their way into the project. One respondent who claimed to be knowledgeable about the SRI set-up reported that the project had been kept running for much longer than overt funding would allow, suggesting either an unusual subsidy by the commercially minded SRI management or some kind of secret source of money. One researcher (not at SRI) was able to reveal to us 'off the record' that his work on the PMB phenomena was supported either directly or indirectly by the US Navy.

A rumour in the same vein concerned Pat Price, one of the most successful of the SRI 'remote-viewing' subjects. Price, it was said, had been frighteningly successful in his remote viewing of secret military targets. It was suggested that he may have been so successful that he became a danger to the state. Perhaps his death, officially reported as being caused by a heart attack, had a more sinister cause! Again it was said that one scientist (a respondent in the project) who had previously been sympathetic to psychic phenomena was now openly hostile to the work because he had been 'got at' by the CIA, who would prefer the value of the work to remain a military secret.

Finally, one respondent said that the SRI work was a 'front' for the real research which was going on in secret behind locked doors in another part of the same establishment. It was suggested that an acquaintance of this respondent had been taken to SRI purportedly to take part in some remote-viewing experiments. However, when this person was introduced to 'Dr Puthoff' and 'Mr Targ', it transpired they were not Targ and Puthoff at all – the acquaintance apparently knew them by sight. The experiment was conducted under the pretext that it was a part of Targ and Puthoff's normal and overt programme, but in reality it was part of a separate programme entirely. It was suggested by this respondent that the overt SRI programme served to draw attention and criticism from the real, secret military programme. That was why it was subsidised, and, what is more, if the overt programme did not appear to be too successful, then so much the better!

BELIEVERS AND SCEPTICS

With the two accounts presented above we conclude our thumb-nail sketch of PMB research and its milieu. Some of the charac-teristics of the background of those whose research will be described on the pages to follow should now be clear. In particular, the cognitive location of most experimenters and of the 'vigilantes' should be apparent. However, throughout the text we will also be referring to believers and sceptics. A word of explanation is in order.

'Believer' and 'sceptic' will be used here to apply to very loose social categories. They are not psychological traits. Thus, their use is not meant to rule out the possibility that members of one category or another might now and again have moments, or even days, of doubt about their beliefs. No testing of this possibility was done or even considered. In any case, most persons with scientific backgrounds will not admit to absolute certainty about anything. Indeed, most will readily state that they are willing to be convinced of things contrary to their beliefs, provided they are shown appropriate evidence.

However, a modal quality of the 'believer' category (most, but not all, share it) is that its members have taken the paranormal spoon-bending phenomenon sufficiently seriously to run experi-ments in which they have tried hard to observe the phenomenon; or they have been present in situations where they were led to feel that a very strong prima-facie case for the phenomenon had been made. Of the 'sceptic' category, a modal quality would be that its members are so certain that the phenomenon is explicable as some form of fraud or trickery that they do not feel the need to do experiments of their own or theorise about other possible explanations. If they do carry out experiments, these are designed as 'demonstrations' that cheating was the mechanism involved.

3 IS PARAPSYCHOLOGY COMPATIBLE WITH SCIENCE?
Science, physics, psychology

*The notion of compatibility – forms of argument that have been
used – comparison with cognitive dissonance – incompatibility
with science – incompatibility with physics – incompatibility with
specific physical principles – the inverse-square law – precognition – incompatibility with psychology – with learning
ability – some tangential views*

INTRODUCTION

Our intention in these next chapters is to analyse the relationship
between parapsychology – metal bending in particular – and the
rest of science. A conventional way to proceed – if 'conventional'
is an appropriate adjective to describe any procedure within such
an unusual project – might be first to determine the 'cognitive
relationship' between the two endeavours by some sort of philosophical inquiry, and then determine the social relationship between
the respective communities of scientists. Such a division of inquiry
is implicit in certain traditions in social psychology. For instance,
cognitive dissonance theory examines the accommodations of individuals to conflicting beliefs. An inquiry establishes that the individual holds two conflicting beliefs, and then the resolution of
this dilemma is examined. However, as Brown's superb analysis
shows, in particular case studies of cognitive dissonance, the
first part of this process is not only implicit, but incomplete, and
this leads to confusion in the second part of the operation (see
Festinger et al., 1956; Brown, 1965, pp. 584–603).

This chapter and the next constitute an exploration of the process of carrying through an inquiry of the 'philosophical' type to
determine whether or not the subject matter of parapsychology
contradicts the rest of science in some absolute, a-temporal,
logical fashion. It will be concluded that such an inquiry would
have no determinate answer – a conclusion that fits well with the
underlying hypothesis of this work: that to divorce the social
and the cognitive is to misunderstand the process of knowledge
construction in science and a fortiori to misunderstand the process
of knowledge construction in general.

ARGUMENTS ABOUT COMPATIBILITY

To begin to think about what might be meant by saying that the content of two sorts of endeavour are in contradiction is to realise how unclear such a notion is. The only things that philosophers can be sure do contradict (with reservations, of course) are 'p' and 'not p', but any attempt to show that elements within scientific endeavours are related in the same way as 'p' and 'not p' must be attended by difficulties concerning disagreements between parties over the correct translation of 'p' and 'not p' into other symbolic universes. Do all parties mean the same thing by, for example, telepathy and precognition and science and causality? Again, would philosophers agree about the fundamental elements within scientific systems that need to be compared in order to establish a broad relationship of contradiction? One would imagine that they would not. For instance, would not a Kantian attempt to demonstrate contradictions at the level of the a priori perceptual categories that make available the world of phenomena? In such a scheme a Kantian might rule out precognition by virtue of its conflict with categories related to Newtonian time and causality. On the other hand, a logical empiricist would, presumably, be much more concerned with a conflict of potential experimental evidence, refusing to accept that the manipulation of logical symbols other than those of an observation language could yield any new knowledge about the existence or otherwise of phenomena. Students of the history of philosophy could, no doubt, extend this discussion further, but here it will be adjourned in favour of an examination of arguments that have actually been put forward in order to make one sort of claim or another about the relationship between parapsychology and other scientific work.

Arguers, on the whole, do not seem unduly exercised by philosophical principles. They do not seem to worry, for example, about the analytic nature of the notion of contradiction, or logical reasoning in general. Thus some critics of parapsychology argue that psi phenomena cannnot exist because of their incompatibility with science. For instance, G.R. Price, a well-known sceptic, sets out to show the improbability of the existence of the paranormal 'by showing that ESP is incompatible with current scientific theory' (Price 1955, p. 360). Similarly, C.E.M. Hansel, another leading sceptic, suggests: 'In my view *a priori* arguments determine our attitude towards an experiment, and may save time and effort in scrutinising every experiment' (Hansel, 1960, p. 176). Proponents of the paranormal find such arguments of sufficient merit to require replies in kind.

Views like these, and counter-arguments, have been presented in the following formats:

1   A belief in the unity of science (implicit) and the incompatibility of psi phenomena with science or certain of its characteristics leads to the conclusion that psi phenomena are spurious.

2   A belief in the existence of psi phenomena and the incompatibility of psi phenomena with some part of science leads to
the conclusion that science must be changed or undergo a
revolution (led by parapsychology and therefore psi phenomena are important).

These two arguments have at their core the same claims regarding the incompatibility of psi phenomena and science though they
are deployed respectively by sceptics and believers - hence some
of the strange bedfellows that will be found in the later sections.

3   Psi phenomena are compatible with science so they are not
impossible.
(This is one type of answer to argument 1.)
4   Science is open-ended, or pluralistic, so that even if psi
phenomena are incompatible with science or parts of science
this does not mean they are impossible.
(This is another type of answer to argument 1.)
5   Science is full of incompatible pieces called anomalies. Psi
phenomena are like these and not very important.
6   Psi phenomena are incompatible with current science, as it is
perceived, by definition. (This says nothing about their
existence.)
7   Everything that exists must be brought under the aegis of
science and therefore psi phenomena are part of science irrespective of any contradiction they seem to entail.

The majority of what follows consists of incompatibility claims
generated by proponents of formats 1 and 2 and answered by proponents of format 3. All the other formats are represented too.
The authors have taken a number of liberties with the arguments
of writers. In particular, most of them have been lifted out of
context with scant regard for the justification which their authors
would have given them. In the main body, little attention has
been given even to the interests that authors thought their arguments were serving, although this is discussed now and then.
What is intended is to show the essentially open-ended nature of
the whole incompatibility debate, and so all that is claimed about
the argument 'fragments' assembled is that the beliefs they embody
would have been held by 'rational' men and put into print in
'responsible' forums. There is no attempt here to write a history
of the debate, or a history of ideas. The authors are not concerned to do each argument justice but to try to suggest that
there are enough tenable viewpoints available to rational men to
make an a priori decision on the compatibility question unlikely,
as either side can be defended by an appropriate shift of ground
or by deployment of one kind of subsidiary argument or another.
The attempt to subsume human actions under logical categories
fails.
A model for this kind of failure is presented by Brown in his
discussion of cognitive dissonance theory (Brown, 1965). He gives

as an example of a pair of beliefs that are prima facie in contradiction 'man will reach the moon' and 'man will never leave the earth's atmosphere'. As Brown points out, these beliefs are not in contradiction, and therefore no dissonance is involved, if it is also believed that the moon may enter the earth's atmosphere, or perhaps if atmosphere is defined in such a way that the moon is already within the earth's atmosphere. Elsewhere, it has been argued that the analysis of Festinger et al. (1956) is ethnocentric for similar reasons (Collins and Cox, 1976). In this work, which deals with changes in meaning frame, it is of vital importance to exorcise ethnocentric a-priorism.

The arguments are arranged in subsections, with claims of incompatibility coming first and arguments which avert this conclusion following on. One might imagine the arguments which propose incompatibility as translating something scientific and something parapsychological into p's and q's in such a way that p = not q or q = not p, so that to hold p and q would be to hold p and not p. (For a diagrammatic representation of the argument see Figure 4.1 at the end of chapter 4.) The next arguments show how a different translation avoids the contradiction. Nothing as hard or well-defined as logical entailments are ever broached or suggested. What are being looked at are practical arguments in the spirit, it is hoped, of Toulmin (1958).[1]

THE CASE OF PARAPSYCHOLOGY

1   *Parapsychology incompatible with science?*
At the highest level of abstraction, arguments or argument fragments can be found which claim simply that some or all parapsychological phenomena contradict the whole of scientific knowledge. This view is represented by Hansel (as quoted in Burt, 1967a, p. 3),[2] 'The whole body of scientific knowledge compels us to assume that such things as telepathy and clairvoyance are impossible.'

Other arguers have claimed that parapsychological phenomena contradict certain basic principles pertaining to science as a whole. For example, G.R. Price (1955, p. 360) writes 'But the conflict is at so fundamental a level as to be not so much with named "laws" but rather with basic principles.'

That the conflict is with immutable scientific knowledge is claimed by Willis (quoted in Burt, 1967b, p. 62):

> The conclusions of modern science are reached by strict logical proof, based on the cumulative results of numerous *ad hoc* observations and experiments reported in reputable scientific journals and confirmed by other scientific investigators: then, and only then, can they be regarded as certain and decisively demonstrated. Once they have been finally established, any conjecture that conflicts with them, as all forms of so-called 'extra-sensory perception' plainly must, can be confidently dismissed without more ado.

These authors have been interested in establishing the non-existence of psi phenomena via an argument of type 1. Broad, Mundle, H.H. Price and Shewmaker and Berenda have argued a broadly similar thesis to a different end. Rather than using the contradiction to cast doubt on the reality of psi, they instead use it to question the status and general validity of the principles with which psi is held to conflict.

Broad defines several 'Basic limiting principles' of four main types: causation, the relation of mind to matter, the dependence of mind on brain and limitations on ways of acquiring knowledge. The scope of these principles is outlined by Broad (1949, p. 296), 'I think that they will suffice as examples of important restrictive principles of very wide range, which are commonly accepted today by educated plain men and by scientists in Europe and America.' Broad then goes on to show that certain paranormal phenomena are prima facie in contradiction with one or more of his principles.

Mundle adopts certain principles outlined by the philosopher Bertrand Russell for the analysis of science. In particular Mundle claims psi phenomena contradict a principle of causal connection, and he justifies the use of this principle by an appeal, similar to Broad's, that 'most scientists seem confident that the principle is universal and necessary' (Mundle, 1950, p. 221).

If the contradiction between these principles and psi phenomena is to be used to question the general validity of the principles, then clearly this serves to emphasise the importance of psi phenomena. For instance, H.H. Price (1948-9, p. 113) writes:

Psychical Research has succeeded in establishing various queer facts about the human mind, but [some people] think that these facts are mere curiosities and oddities of no particular import-ance. . . . On the contrary these queer facts are not at all trivial, and it is right to make the greatest possible fuss about them. Their very queerness is what makes them so significant. We call them 'queer' just because they will not fit in with ortho-dox scientific ideas about the universe and man's place in it.

It is clear that Price is here concerned to draw attention through his arguments to the significance of psi rather than its non-existence. Similarly, both Broad and Mundle are concerned with exploring the relationship of accepted (or at least hypothetically possible) psi phenomena with science as it is currently under-stood, and therefore with exploring any (hypothetically) necessary changes in such knowledge.

Shewmaker and Berenda (1976, p. 413) make a similar point: 'These phenomena appear to violate principles which are basic to our entire scientific mode of explaining all other physical and psychological phenomena. Yet they, no less than any other events, demand explanation.'

These attempts to establish the contradiction between parapsy-chology and science at the level of general principles are examples of what we described earlier as argument formats 1 and 2 (see

pp. 48-9). However, these types of argument can be answered by
an arguer who claims that psi and science do not entail any contradiction (format 3). One philosopher who has consistently argued
for the compatibility of the two fields is Michael Scriven. For instance, he finds such claimed contradictions between general
principles of science and psi phenomena to be insubstantial and
a matter of philosophy rather than physics. He writes (Scriven,
1962, p. 101):

> It is true that certain vague general principles which charac-
> terize many of our laws are rejected by ESP supporters, but I
> would class these general principles as being at the level of
> philosophical rather than physical insights, and consequently
> even more readily subject to reformulation.

One particular principle with which it has frequently been
claimed psi phenomena conflict is the doctrine of 'epiphenomenalism'
and its close relative 'the materialistic conception of personality'.
Hansel (a sceptic) and H.H. Price (a believer) again make strange
bedfellows when it comes to their opinions on this principle.
Hansel (1959, p. 457), in suggesting principles of knowledge
which conflict with ESP, includes the epiphenomenalist notion that
mental processes are dependent on physical processes in the
nervous system of the person who experiences them. Hansel uses
this as an a priori argument against psi phenomena. Price finds
the same contradiction, though he is using it to argue against
the universal applicability of the materialist principle: '. . . if
we consider the implications of telepathy, the most elementary and
the best established phenomenon in the whole field of Psychical
Research, we shall see that they are incompatible with the Materialistic conception of human personality' (Price, 1948-9, p. 107).
Although Hansel is arguing against the existence of psi phenomena
by this principle (format 1) and Price is arguing against the
validity of the principle (format 2), both again accept that there
is a contradiction.
    This contradiction between psi and science, established through
the intervening variable of materialism, is defeasible too, however.
Both Mundle and Ducasse think that it is possible that a way will
be found to reconcile psi phenomena with the materialist viewpoint.
For instance, Mundle points out that current theories of physics
may not be complete or correct and that materialism, even in current physics, allows for the explanation of certain inter-phenomena
such as the 'force' of gravity. He sees no reason why explanations
of ESP should not be found which do not challenge materialism.
As he writes (Mundle, 1967a, p. 57):

> It may be argued that 'X cannot be explained by physics' does
> not entail 'X disproves materialism', unless 'materialism' means,
> among other things, that the current theories of physics are
> correct and complete, which no one would claim. . . . 'Material-
> ism' need not be defined so as to entail that physical things can

interact only by contact or by means of physical radiations or fields. A materialist is free to maintain that the 'interphenomena' of physics (radiations, the 'force' of gravity, etc.) are logical constructs, and that the failure, so far, to construct inter-phenomena to explain ESP need not cause ontological discomfort.

Ducasse (1954, p. 816) makes the similar point that there may be an, as yet, undiscovered part of physics, such as a sub-subatomic level, which might lead to the explanation of psi phenomena but would not overthrow the materialist conception of science:

> That matter may have sub-sub-atomic constituents, and that these might have properties capable of accounting for ESP and PK is, of course, at present pure speculation. I introduce it only to make clear that the reality of these and of other kinds of paranormal phenomena would not in principle require abandonment of a materialistic conception of the universe . . .

These moves defeat the materialism/psi incompatibility (format 3) and open the way for psi to be compatible with a materialistic science.
Thus, in our survey of the literature we have found nothing that would demonstrate definitively that the content of parapsychological ideas is in conflict with general scientific principles.

2 Parapsychology incompatible with physics?
For some authors, there is no sense in making a distinction between the relationship of psi to science and the relationship of psi to physics. For instance, Michael Scriven (1960a, p. 214) suggests that 'physics is, in an important sense, *co-extensive* with science' (italics in original). But to others (see below, p. 61), the distinction is important. Thus the following extracts of arguments which suggest that psi is incompatible in particular with physics (as we know it) might be significant:

> it is true that the evidence and conclusions of parapsychology . . . do not seem to fit into the panorama of physics today (Chauvin, 1970, p. 216).

> Psi and physics are irreconcilable in terms of what we know today, and present knowledge is the only knowledge we have at our disposal in trying to relate them (Pratt, 1960, p. 24).

Mundle makes the same point for physical mechanisms in general and with specific reference to clairvoyance and PK:

> The relevance of psi phenomena is, of course, that it seems impossible in principle to explain these powers in terms of physical mechanisms . . . (Mundle, 1952, p. 267).

Would any physicist agree that P.K. is compatible with what is thought to be established in physics? Most physicists would, I think, be inclined to take it as certain that a person's volition cannot be a *proximate* differential condition of physical events occurring at a distance from that person's body . . . (Mundle, 1950, p. 215).

These suggestions, that there is a contradiction with physics, are also defeasible. The definition of physics must be related to the definition of physical, and certain collections of arguments have shown that this definition is by no means unproblematical. For instance, in the collection of papers 'Science and E.S.P.' (Smythies, 1967), concerning the relation between parapsychology and science, several meanings of the word 'physical' emerge. For example, Mundle (p. 204) defines physical to be 'visible and tangible'; Price (p. 36) claims that in the ordinary meaning of the word nothing is a physical event unless 'it is perceptible by means of the sense-organs either directly, or indirectly'; and finally Dobbs (p. 225) claims that physical agencies are the kind 'acceptable in principle to physics as currently practised'. Again, no clear meaning of the term 'physical' emerged from a debate in the 'Journal of Parapsychology' on the issue of 'Physicality and Psi', with C.D. Broad (1960, p. 16) and Michael Scriven (1960b, p. 14) both pointing out that it was not possible to give an agreed meaning to the term, and with Pratt (1960, p. 24) asserting that physics dealt with changes within the material universe that are capable of being described in terms of 'time-space-mass-energy-relations'. This definition was in turn questioned by Scriven (1960a, p. 214), who pointed out that concepts based on information theory, such as entropy, were an integral part of physics. As ESP phenomena, such as telepathy, could also be treated in terms of information theory there was no necessary incompatibility. It seems that whether or not there is a contradiction between psi and physics depends on the definition of physicality adopted and no agreed definition can be seen to have emerged from this debate.

Another way of removing incompatibilities between psi and physics is suggested by McConnell (1947). He exploits the logical possibility entailed in the dual interpretation of any psi experiment (see below p. 60) to avoid the conclusion that PK (mind over matter) is incompatible with physics. By interpreting PK experiments in terms of clairvoyance (mind sensing the state of matter) it is possible to avoid breaking the cause-and-effect chain; a break which it is claimed means that PK is in contradiction to the notion of cause and effect in physics (i.e. it is non-physical):

However, the demonstration of the lack of these relationships must be exhaustive to be conclusive - a logically impossible task . . . there would appear to be a logical difficulty . . . in any attempt to show violation of causal sequence. If our wish follows the dice throw, is it PK or clairvoyance? This difficulty would seem to rule out for PK any positive test for non-physicality as we have defined that term (McConnell, 1947, p. 116).

It has also been argued that many of those wishing to press the case that psi and physics are incompatible have a restrictive view of physics. As Scriven (1960b, p. 14) puts it:

Now the interesting claim would be that there is some *impossibility* about the idea of physics encompassing psi. But I see no possible way of justifying that claim . . . the opposition to it [psi] is largely based on an absurdly parochial idea of the limitations of physics (italics in original).

Murphy and Honorton make a similar point:

It is the physics of the 19th century, persisting in terms of current space-time patterns, that makes the phenomena 'impossible' (Murphy, 1968, p. 65).

The debate over the incompatibility of physics and ESP has been conducted almost exclusively within the framework of nineteenth-century deterministic physics, wherein the ultimate constituent of physical reality was still believed to be solid matter (Honorton, 1975, p. 112).

Burt (1960, p. 29), too, stresses the amenability of contemporary physics to parapsychological notions:

. . . it would seem that there is nothing whatever in *contemporary* physics which would preclude the apparent anomalies presented by psi phenomena (italics in original).

Many of the unexpected phenomena encountered in the study of quantum physics would seem to be 'characterized by not conforming to physical laws' as ordinarily understood.

Murphy and McConnell stress the 'open-ended' nature of physics (a format 4-type move):

Of course what the *physics of the future* may reveal none of us should be foolish enough to predict; this is perhaps one of the reasons for being a little hesitant about insisting so strongly today that we know we are dealing with psychic or spiritual factors rather than physical ones (Murphy, 1953, p. 42; italics in original).

Perhaps at the sub-atomic level physics borders on parapsychology in some not-yet-understood sense, so that the distinction between them cannot be clear-cut (McConnell, 1947, p. 115).

In these arguments it is as though the question of the compati-

bility of psi with physics depends upon which 'historically
frozen' moment of physics is selected for comparison with parapsychology. The final point is that, as the history of physics
will continue to unfold for ever, a final decision for incompatibility can never be reached.

Thus it seems that the nature of physics in general does not
mean that parapsychology is necessarily in conflict with it.

3 *Specific physical principles*
It might be thought that the incompatibility of psi and science
can be argued away more easily at the general levels of science
and physics we have been looking at, but when specific physical
principles are considered, the room for argument is much less. It
transpires that this is not the case.

The argument regarding incompatibility has been carried into
discussion of such specific physical principles as, for instance,
energy. Murphy (1953, p. 42) makes the following comment regarding energy problems and psi phenomena 'We know, as we do,
with some degree of certainty that we are not dealing with any of
the types of physical energy with which contemporary physics is
concerned', and Mundle (1967a, p. 56) and Burt (1966, p. 373)
suggest that energy resources in the brain are too small. The
problems of space and time are mentioned by H.H. Price and
McConnell:

> In telepathy one mind affects another without any discoverable
> physical intermediary, and regardless of the spatial distance
> between their respective bodies (Price, 1948-9, p. 107).

> Specifically, physics is the expression of matter relationships
> in space-time co-ordinates. Thus the absence of any regular
> relationship between experimental phenomena and space or time
> should, by definition, be proof of non-physicality (McConnell,
> 1947, p. 112).

A similar point is made by G.R. Price (1955, p. 360).

Another problem put forward is the informational one. For
example, Mundle (1950, p. 222; 1967a, p. 56) and G.R. Price
(loc. cit.) - again, strange bedfellows - point out that a subject
can obtain information paranormally from a specific target (e.g. a
card in the middle of a pack) without interference from other
physical objects in the surrounding area (e.g. the other cards in
the pack). Beloff (1970, p. 138) makes a similar point:

> . . . the crux of the problem, as I see it, lies, not so much in
> specifying what kind of energy might surmount spatial and
> temporal distances or material barriers, but rather in explaining
> how it comes about that the subject is able to discriminate the
> target from the infinite number of other objects in his environ-
> ment.

A related point is made by Mundle (1967a, p. 56) and G.R. Price
(loc.cit.) in remarking that physical barriers seem to be pervious
to ESP. Finally, Burt (1967b, p. 91) suggests that there is no
structure in the human body capable of transmitting or receiving
ESP signals.
Thus it is argued that all these physical principles are in conflict with psi phenomena.
The way that some of these specific points have been answered
will be looked at: before taking up, at slightly greater length,
another specific incompatibility claim, namely, that psi phenomena
do not obey the inverse-square law – thought to be typical of all
physical forces.
With regard to the energy incompatibility, Margenau has
suggested that in some cases parts of physics itself do not obey
normal energy relationships. Thus he writes (Margenau, 1966,
p. 221):

At the forefront of current physical research, in the fields of
quantum theory and elementary particle physics, the principle
of conservation of energy is frequently breached because we
find it necessary to invoke the existence of 'virtual processes'.

This has the effect of undermining the rhetorical power of any
contradiction between psi phenomena and such energy considerations.
Regarding the informational problem, Meehl and Scriven (1956,
p. 14) write:

. . . no simple radiation theory can explain the Pauli Principle
and one can no more refute it by saying 'How could one electron
possibly know what the others are doing?' than one can refute
the ESP experiments by saying 'How could one possibly read a
card from the middle of the pack without interference from those
next to it?'

Again this has the effect of undermining the incompatibility.
And, of course, regarding any of the other objections, the
open-ended nature of science may be cited just as before in the
case of seemingly more abstract physical incompatibilities. Thus,
Burt (1966, p. 374) writes:

The foregoing objections [Burt mentions many of those
listed above] . . . would seem to completely rule out the ever
popular notion of 'brain radio'. They do not of themselves,
however, exclude all other physical modes of transmission. The
new theories of quantum physics may conceivably contain possibilities which have not yet been adequately explored.

Thus it has not been demonstrated decisively that there are
any specific physical principles that conflict with parapsychology.
We will now go on to consider a specific physical law with which,

many arguers claim, parapsychology is in conflict.

4 *Inverse-square law*

The inverse-square-law objection ties in with the apparent lack of attenuation of telepathic signals over distance. Most physical forces seem to be reduced in strength as the square of the distance from the source and it is expected that all physical forces should be reduced in the same way (e.g. see Mundle, 1967a, p. 55).

One answer to this suggestion is to produce a counter-example from physics itself, as do Margenau, Dobbs and Rush:

it should also be recalled that not all interactions obey an inverse square law - in fact almost none do. . . . An electric field in front of a charged plane of infinite extent shows no attenuation at all (Margenau, 1966, p. 222).

the inverse square law does not necessarily apply, even to ordinary electro-magnetic radiations. For in the case of radio waves the strength of a signal as received may even increase with increase of distance between transmitter and receiver, due to ionospheric effects and various forms of 'ducting'(Dobbs, 1967, p. 229).

it must be borne in mind that the inverse-square propagation of energy is seldom realized in practice. Such effects as diffraction, reflection, refraction and absorption, as well as deliberate 'beaming' in the case of radio signals, modify the simple spatial distribution (Rush, 1943, p. 48).

Essentially Rush is claiming here that, if the radiation analogy is pushed far enough, we have to accept that psi radiation can be modified away from the ideal inverse-square law in the same way as he claims for other physical radiations.

The advantages, in terms of avoiding the incompatibility, of pushing the radio analogy even further, are shown by Mundle, (1967b, p. 200) who writes, 'ESP is being assimilated to radio transmission; radio sets have amplifiers and volume controls; we may suppose then that the brain possesses an automatic volume control which amplifies weak ESP signals.' This means that the lack of attenuation can be explained by large amplification in the brain for distant signals and small amplification or even reduction for near signals. So, in extending the analogy, Mundle is also removing the incompatibility by pointing out that psi can still obey an inverse-square law.

A similar approach is adopted by Meehl and Scriven (1956, p. 14): '. . . since we have no knowledge of the minimum effective signal strength for extrasensory perception, the original signal may well be enormously attenuated by distance and still function at long range.' So ESP may again obey an inverse-square law over some of its range.

Another alternative is suggested by Burt (1966, p. 373), who writes:

> . . . the transmitter's brain might include a mechanism which, like the laser, could produce amplification by stimulated emission of the relevant radiation. The radiation could then perhaps be concentrated and directed in almost linear fashion towards recipients . . .

A different sort of objection to the inverse-square-law incompatibility is raised by Rush (1943, p. 47), when he considers the information content of the assumed radiation:

> ESP is the perception of a *signal* i.e. of a systematic pattern impressed on the assumed radiation, much as audible speech frequencies are impressed on a radio wave. The mind interprets the *relative* intensities which compose this pattern; it does not respond to intensity as such (italics in original).

In other words, ESP radiation may be following an inverse-square law but the subject's response, which depends on interpreting the different parts of the signal, may not necessarily fall off with distance, as interpretation involves assessing relative intensities within the overall radiation.

Finally, the evidence that psi is not attenuated by distance can be questioned. As Dobbs (1967, p. 230) puts it:

> First, accepting that telepathy has occurred over great distances, as well as over small distances, it does not follow that distance is wholly irrelevant to its occurrence, or *to the probability of its happening*. We have, for instance, no systematically compiled data to test whether it has happened as frequently over long distances as over short distances, taking into account the number of occasions when it has been tried experimentally.

The relative ease with which these arguers overcome the inverse-square-law objection illustrates that, even when forced to argue within the confines of specific parts of physics, arguments may still be found to overcome such objections. Indeed it seems that the closer arguers get to contradictions with hard-and-fast physical principles, the more easily they can be avoided, by simply making use of the rich variety of ideas already available within physics.

5 *Precognition as a special case*
If particular physical principles cannot be used to establish an immutable and necessary contradiction with psi phenomena in general, perhaps it can at least be said that particular psi phenomena do entail such a contradiction. One particular phenomenon of parapsychology - precognition - has been claimed by many arguers to be in necessary contradiction with science. For instance,

even if arguers were to feel themselves able to accept the physical possibility of telepathy and psychokinesis, many would still baulk at the possibility of precognition. For example, Knight (1950, p. 13) writes, '"Straight" telepathy poses vast theoretical problems but precognition – with its apparent implication that causation can work backwards in time – seems to violate one of the essential presuppositions of science.'
Similarly, H.H. Price, Ducasse and Rhine himself feel that precognition is 'outstandingly incompatible' with physical science:

> Precognition seems to require a mode of causation in which the effect occurs *earlier* than the cause, and there is clearly no room for such a process in a Materialistic universe (Price, 1948-9, p. 112).

> Of the several modes of extra sensory perception, precognition is the one *prima facie* most paradoxical; for how can a non-existent event – an event that has not yet occurred – cause anything? That an effect, for instance a precognitive dream, should occur earlier than what causes it is a contradiction *ex vi terminorum* and is, therefore, impossible (Ducasse, 1959, p. 95).

> Nothing in all the history of human thought – heliocentrism, evolution, relativity – has been more truly revolutionary or radically contradictory to contemporary thought than the results of the investigation of precognitive psi (Rhine, quoted in Price, 1955, p. 361).

One way out of this impasse is to reinterpret precognition in terms of some other psi modality; typically this is PK – the subject causes his predictions to come about rather than foresees them – a tactic which McConnell was seen to employ above (p. 54). This maintains the arrow of causality without any problem. Indeed objections to any particular type of psi functioning could be escaped by reinterpreting in terms of another. As Mundle (1950, p. 219) points out, 'There has been, and still is, much controversy between psychical researchers as to how many different primary hypotheses must be invoked in order to account for the facts.' Though, as Mundle himself notes (1952, p. 266), he would not find such a reinterpretation process plausible in all cases, particularly cases where large-scale disasters have been precognised, implying that the visionary *caused* the disaster:

> It does not seem very plausible to me in view of: (1) spontaneous cases in which the events precognised are major catastrophes. I find it very hard to believe that someone's dream could cause a train crash or an earthquake.

Even if the reinterpretation ploy is not acceptable, so that apparent time-reversal is inescapable, there is still no need to

conclude that precognition is incompatible with physics. For instance, some authors have claimed that physics already incor-
porates time-reversal (e.g. Feinberg, 1975), theories advocating
more than one dimension for time have been postulated (e.g.
Broad, 1937), and it has also been suggested that precognition
involves 'subjective time' and hence is irrelevant to the objective
time with which physics is concerned (Margenau, 1966).
   An alternative response to the objection that it is logically impossible for an effect to precede its cause is provided by Bob
Brier (1974) in his book 'Precognition and the Philosophy of
Science'. Brier's arguments have been neatly summarised by Beloff
(1975, p. 154). First, the logical objection to backward causation:

   Let A and B be two hypothetical events which we are taking to
   be causally related, where A precedes B. Now, once A has
   occurred, B cannot possibly make it not occur; similarly, if
   A fails to occur, B cannot then make it occur. Hence since B
   can have no effect on A, B cannot be the cause of A.

Brier combats this type of objection by arguing that just the
same type of objection can be raised against forward causation,
where we assume A to be a cause of B. Again in Beloff's words
(loc. cit.):

   . . . either B will occur or it will not occur. If we assume that
   B will occur, we cannot also suppose that A can prevent it from
   occurring; similarly if we assume that B will not occur, we cannot suppose that A can make it occur. Hence A cannot be the
   cause of B, which is absurd.

Brier (1974, p. 101) concludes, after his examination of the
logical difficulties of a cause succeeding its effect, that 'even if
precognition did necessarily involve backward causation, it cannot
be ruled out on the grounds that backward causation is a logical
impossibility'.
   Thus, logic alone does not seem to provide an unambiguous
answer to the possibility of precognition, and does not therefore
make even precognition 'anti-rational' or unscientific.
   To conclude the discussion of physics and parapsychology, it
must be remembered that, even if it were decided that they are
incompatible, it does not follow that parapsychology and science
are incompatible (compare Scriven, above p. 53). Pratt, Ehrenberg and Chauvin in these argument fragments, which are of the
format-4 type, show that some arguers are happy to accept a
'pluralistic' notion of science which can accommodate psi into
science even if not necessarily into physics:

   Physics is not synonymous with science . . . such an assumption
   begs the question. If there ultimately should prove to be some
   range of natural (parapsychical) phenomena that are irreducibly
   beyond the scope of physics, this state of affairs would not of

itself be a contradiction of the concepts of that area of knowledge. It is simply a question of whether parapsychology represents an extension of physics or an extension of science beyond
the borders of physics, as that branch can properly be defined
(Pratt, 1960, p. 24; italics in original).

Coming from modern physics to parapsychology, I, unlike most
of my fellow-parapsychologists, do not consider the two fields
of experience incompatible. From my point of view, physics
embraces the range of occurrences below the biological level,
while psi phenomena transcend mere biology (Ehrenberg, 1960,
p. 216).

In regard to parapsychology, then, we may affirm only that at
the present time we do not know how to reconcile modern physics
and psi. But we are not entitled to use the word 'contradict'.
The existence of psi does not annul the laws of electrical cur-
rents, for on a proper scale and for the facts they regulate,
they are true (Chauvin, 1970, p. 217).

Similarly, Tart (1972, p. 1204), in arguing for a special science
to study altered states of consciousness (ASC's, i.e. states in
which psi phenomena may become manifest) and for pluralistic
(state-specific) science in general, does not see the clash with
conventional psychology as negating the scientific nature of his
enterprise:

The vast majority of phenomena of ASC's have no known physical
manifestations, thus to physicalistic philosophy they are epi-
phenomena, not worthy of study. But in so far as science deals
with knowledge . . . the essence of scientific method . . . is
perfectly compatible with an enlarged study of the important
phenomena of ASC's.

6 *Parapsychology incompatible with psychology?*
Certain objectors to psi phenomena have argued that the incompatibilities lie not (or not only) with physics or science in
general, but with psychology. For example:

The subject matter of psychical research, as has already been
noted, is poorly defined. It deals with phenomena which apppear
to be contrary to *physical* laws. The same idea finds expression
in the term ESP. . . . In this instance, the subject is defined
as dealing with matters which appear to be contrary to, not
physical, but psychological, laws (Szasz, 1957, p. 97).

the conclusions advanced by parapsychologists would be utterly
incompatible with the cardinal assumptions on which present-
day psychology rests (Willis, quoted in Burt, 1967a, p. 3).

Though no arguments can be quoted which directly counteract

the incompatibilities proposed by Szasz and Willis, their defeasibility can be seen from Mundle's (1952, p. 260) claim that two of Broad's principles are rejected by most biologists and psychologists and thus that the principles cannot be described as part 'of the framework within which all our practical activities and our scientific theories are confined'.
The polar opposite position to that of Szasz and Willis is perhaps that of Burt. It appears that he is putting forward a case for the unification of psi and psychology in pluralistic isolation from the rest of science: 'Psychical processes and psychical phenomena [form] . . . the very crux of psychology as a separate branch of science' (Burt, 1967a, p. 16). This can be regarded as another version of the format 4-type argument.

7 *A specific psychological principle*
In the same way that specific physical principles have been claimed to be incompatible with parapsychological phenomena, it is found that specific psychological principles can also be held to be in contradiction. Such a claim is made by G.R. Price (1955, p. 360), 'There is no learning but, instead, a tendency towards complete loss of ability', but answered by (among others) Meehl and Scriven (1956, p. 14):

Now it would be reasonable to expect, in a series of experiments intended to show that learning does not occur, some *trial-by-trial* differential reinforcement procedure. Mere continuation, with encouragement or condemnation after *runs of many trials*, can hardly provide a conclusive proof of the absence of learning in a complex situation. We ourselves know of *no* experiments in which this condition has been met and which show *absence* of learning; certainly one could not claim that this absence was established (italics in original).

There is, then, nothing in psychology that definitely makes parapsychology unscientific.

8 *Some tangential views*
Some idea of the degree of complexity of the compatibility question may, by now, have been given. It is made still more complex by writers' suggestions that, even if it were not possible to absorb psi phenomena into science as it is known, this would not make the phenomena important, but rather it would involve a small or non-existent problem. Thus Scriven (1962, p. 100) suggests:

the relationship between current physical laws and extra-sensory phenomena is that if accepted, the latter would require that the former be viewed as having a slightly more restricted range. . . . It is only when the laws are extrapolated from the regions in which they have been directly supported by experimental evidence that they could come into conflict with ESP.

and Thouless and Flew believe:

> The demonstration of the reality of ESP, of precognition, and
> of psychokinesis is a demonstration of the presence of a series
> of anomalies (Thouless, quoted in Pratt, 1974, p. 133).

> apart from the anomalous set of very weak effects, everything
> else is just as it was before. Once the correlations are admitted
> as exceptions to the various general principles against which
> they offend, there seems no reason why most sciences (scien-
> tists) should be upset further (Flew, 1953, p. 124).

In a similar way, critic Boring (1955, p. 113) has said that
ESP data represent an 'empty correlation' and Stevens (1967, p.
1) that 'the signal to noise ratio for ESP is simply too low to be
interesting'. Hoagland (1969) has suggested that 'Unexplained
cases are simply unexplained. They can never constitute evidence
for any hypothesis', and A.J. Ayer (1965, p. 51) has written:

> The only thing that is remarkable about the subject who is
> credited with extra-sensory perception is that he is consistently
> rather better at guessing cards than the ordinary run of people
> have shown themselves to be. The fact that he also does 'better
> than chance' proves nothing in itself.

These kinds of comment, which mainly fall within format 5 of
the general arguments we have identified, must be set alongside
definitions of psi phenomena which constitute the field by reference to perceived incompatibilities with current physical knowledge
(format 6). Thus Pratt and Beloff suggest:

> Psi phenomena are precisely those psychological events which
> defy description in terms of any physical theory now available
> (Pratt, 1960, p. 25).

> Parapsychology means the scientific study of the 'paranormal',
> that is, of phenomena which in one or more respects conflict
> with accepted scientific opinion as to what is physically possible
> (Beloff, 1974, p. 1).

To add a final baroque twist, Scriven (who believes physics is
coextensive with science; see above, p. 53) cannot countenance
a definition of the physical which is incompatible with the proven
facts of parapsychology (format 7): 'The principles of physics do
not include those of . . . psi, but they must not be incompatible
with the behaviour of . . . successful psi subjects' (Scriven,
1960a, p. 214).

SUMMARY

Arguers have attempted to find principles and laws either belonging to science as a whole or to specific parts of science with which
all of parapsychology or parts of parapsychology can be shown
to conflict. Counter-arguments have been posed which seem to
deny these incompatibilities. The different formats of argument
available suggest that arguers are not compelled to reach any one
conclusion over the compatibility issue and its consequences for
the scientific status of parapsychology. In the next chapter, the
special case of quantum theory will be examined. This is an area
of physics which, of late, has frequently been cited as promising
an explanation for parapsychological phenomena.

4 IS PARAPSYCHOLOGY COMPATIBLE WITH SCIENCE?

The quantum theory

Outline of quantum theory – the measurement problem – Schrö-dinger's cat paradox – Einstein-Podolsky-Rosen paradox – (non-locality) – resolutions of the paradoxes – avoidance – statistical interpretation – macroscopic instruments collapse wave function – consciousness collapses wave function – hidden variables – many-worlds interpretation – time-reversal – superluminal information transfer – other views – arguments within quantum theory – 'philosophical' nature of quantum theory interpret-ations – this 'low-status' area permeable to parapsychological ideas – parapsychology not necessarily incompatible with science – arguments inconclusive

The revolution in physics associated with the development of the quantum theory was described by the eminent physicist, Henry Margenau (1966, p. 223), as follows:

Toward the end of the last century the view arose that all inter-actions involved material objects. This is no longer held to be true. We know now there are fields which are wholly non-material. The quantum mechanical interactions of physical . . . fields [described by the symbol 'psi'] . . . have a certain abstractness and vagueness of interpretation in common with the parapsychologists' psi – these interactions are wholly non-material, yet they are described by the most important and the most basic equations of present-day quantum mechanics.

The possibility of a connection between quantum theory and parapsychology, hinted at in this comment, forms the subject matter for this chapter.[1] By examining the relationship between parapsychology and quantum theory we continue the work of exploration of the cognitive links between psi and science started in the previous chapter. The analysis in this chapter, then, makes little concession to the history of the relationship between the ideas, but treats the relationship like a relationship in logic; such relationships are generally understood not to change through time.
  To begin with, a simple exposition of the relevant aspects of quantum theory and two of its apparent paradoxes will be at-tempted. Then the various interpretations of the theory will be discussed in terms of the way these can provide resolutions of the paradoxes. It will be shown that some of these resolutions are naturally compatible with parapsychological phenomena, but

also that the disagreements between proponents of the various resolutions are such that no determinate, atemporal answer to the question of the compatibility of the two fields is possible.

AN OUTLINE OF QUANTUM THEORY

The quantum theory was developed in the period 1900–1930, in order to deal with certain phenomena observed at the atomic level which could no longer be explained satisfactorily within classical mechanics (Kuhn, 1978; Jammer, 1966). Of particular importance were Einstein's discovery that light was quantised (existed in discrete packages or bundles of energy), and thus behaved like particles, and de Broglie's discovery that particles, such as electrons, exhibited wavelike effects. The wave–particle duality of matter was a central theme in the emergence of the theory. In some experiments matter exhibited wavelike properties and in other experiments particlelike properties. The notion of complementarity developed from this duality. Bohr showed that in some experiments it was appropriate to describe what was going on in terms of waves and in other experiments in terms of particles. The two types of description were not to be mixed and they were considered to complement each other. This type of description contrasts with the unambiguous descriptions of classical mechanics.

The complementarity aspect of quantum theory is just one of several startling changes brought about by the new theory. Perhaps the most well-known element of the new theory is Heisenberg's Uncertainty Principle. This principle states that when certain pairs of experimental parameters are being measured, such as, for example, the position and the momentum of an electron, the value of only one of these parameters can be determined with certainty. While one paramenter is measured, the other parameter cannot be exactly determined. If we know the exact position of an electron, for example, its momentum will be uncertain; on the other hand, if we know its momentum, its position will be uncertain. It appears that when we look at an electron the act of looking disturbs the system. This type of 'observer effect' is rather like that encountered when we measure tyre pressure. The act of making a pressure-gauge measurement 'disturbs' the system because a small amount of air is released from the tyre, thus reducing the pressure by a small amount. This analogy is, however, defective in an important way. In classical measurements, such as the measurement of air pressure, we can in principle determine the exact effect of our disturbance of the system. In quantum mechanics the disturbance is itself inherently unanalysable. Thus, in quantum theory there is a radical new type of observer effect not present in classical mechanics. It is no longer possible to account for the effects of making a measurement on the measured system.

The other main difference between classical mechanics and quantum mechanics is the statistical nature of quantum theory.[2]

In quantum theory it is possible to say that events, such as decays of atoms, are only probable rather than certain. For instance, quantum theory cannot predict the exact moment when a radium atom will decay. All that can be derived are probabilities which will tell us that in a certain time period there is a certain probability that the atom will decay. The statistical nature of the theory allows for the possibility of very unlikely events, though these are almost certain not to happen.

This statistical nature has given rise to a great deal of controversy. Some physicists have been unhappy with the fundamental randomness in nature which quantum theory seems to imply. As Einstein put it in his famous aphorism, 'I do not believe that God plays dice'. The problem has been particularly perplexing because one of the basic equations of quantum mechanics, the Schrödinger Equation, describes quantum systems in a deterministic manner. It seems that the statistical nature of the theory results only from the measuring process.

Although the statistical predictions of quantum theory have been borne out by experiment and the theory has been highly successful in a formal sense, certain difficulties have remained. Physicists and many philosophers interested in the foundations of the theory believe that such fundamental notions as complementarity, the uncertainty relations and measurement are unsatisfactory or even incomprehensible (Bastin, 1971; Colodny, 1972; Jammer, 1974; d'Espagnat, 1976). The remarks of respondents often reflected this. Thus one respondent, famous for his experimental work in the quantum area, related the following anecdote:

> I could not understand the quantum theory and I went back to the old literature. . . . It slowly became clear that there was no orthodox view, that there were various orthodox views and each one claimed to be orthodox. . . . I would say to this point that I still don't understand it. My thesis supervisor was very upset about this. He was trying to groom me as his pet astrophysicist and I was not exactly playing along with his game plan. He thought I was spending too much time on things that obviously were of no importance.

Similarly one quantum physicist, who had spent much of his career researching the foundations of quantum theory and who had published one of the leading texts on quantum theory, told how he came to write this text:

> Now you see, when I taught the course in quantum theory at P, I did it really to understand the quantum theory. I had always been very interested in the fundamental theory, what it meant. I thought that perhaps I could understand it by teaching the course and writing. . . . Then I finished the book and began to reconsider whether I understood it, and gradually I began to feel that I didn't.

Physicists, then, have found many aspects of quantum theory less than satisfactory. Two important paradoxes will now be looked at. The ambiguities in the notion of complementarity, the uncertainty relations and the statistical nature of the theory have become entwined within the first of these – 'the measurement problem'.

THE MEASUREMENT PROBLEM IN QUANTUM MECHANICS

The measurement problem in quantum theory can be seen as stemming from the difficulties encountered in squaring the common-sense view of reality with the description of reality provided by quantum mechanics. The common-sense view is that objects such as, for instance, tables and chairs have a definite, fixed reality or concreteness. Such objects are not thought to disappear when they are not observed and they are assumed to possess a degree of stability such that independent observers can agree on their reality. However, it seems that in quantum mechanics this reality becomes much more hazy.

The haziness results from the description given to objects and systems in quantum theory. This description is carried out in terms of the state of the system under consideration. The notion of 'the state of a system' is in itself controversial but it is usual to take it as a measure of our knowledge of the system. Such knowledge is represented by mathematical functions known as state vectors, or wave functions or psi functions. In order to describe a particular quantum system a 'state vector' is written for that system. Now, whereas in classical mechanics systems are generally in only one state at a time, in quantum mechanics a multiplicity of states is possible. For instance, in a typical quantum system a radioactive atom can, in many cases, decay in more than one way. After an interval of time an atom, say of type A, may have decayed into an atom of type B, or one of type C, or it may not have decayed. All these possible developments form part of our knowledge of the state of the atom. Thus, when we come to write a state vector for the atom before we measure it (observe it), we must include in the state vector all the possible states A, B and C. This is done by writing a state vector which is the sum of the separate state descriptions for A, B and C. The proper state vector for this particular atom is therefore the sum of A and B and C, and the state of the atom before it is measured can be said to be a combination of the three states or a superposition of the three states.

Of course, when a measurement is carried out on the atom it is found to be in only one of the states A, B or C but, until the measurement is made, we do not know which of the three states we will find. There are no causal laws for determining the final state of the atom for individual measurements. All quantum theory provides are statistical rules which give the likelihood of finding one of the states A, B or C in many measurements. For any indi-

vidual measurement it can only be said that there is a certain
probability that a particular state will be found.

Thus, in quantum theory, before a measurement is made a
quantum system seems to exist in an irreducible multiplicity of
states but the effect of measurement is to reduce this multiplicity
to one definite state. It is as if, on measurement, the atom 'de-
cides' which state to be in. The change of state on measurement
is known as the 'reduction of the state vector' or 'collapse of the
wave function' because it appears that the state vector or wave
function has been 'reduced' or 'collapsed' so that it now describes
only one of the many possible states. The measurement problem
is to account for this collapse.

The picture of the world painted by quantum mechanics is one
in which objects have no fixed reality until they are measured. It
has been described frequently as a world of potentiality, which
only achieves actuality on measurement. It is as if objects exist
in a blur between all possible states and only become fixed into
definite states when they are observed or measured. Inevitably,
it is difficult to produce an explanatory metaphor from conventional experience. Perhaps the analogy of a shaken kaleidoscope
is not inappropriate. The mirrors and coloured shapes of a kaleidoscope could be said to contain all the patterns that the kaleidoscope
can produce. What is more, the production of some patterns is
more likely than the production of others. Although all these
patterns, with their associated probabilities, are in some sense
already in the kaleidoscope system, only one pattern at a time can
be observed, and only one pattern is actualised upon observation.
It must be realised, however, that this analogy breaks down in
two ways. Firstly, it is possible to think of a way of explaining
how a particular kaleidoscope pattern is produced in terms of the
classical-mechanical interaction of the coloured shapes, the
inside of the kaleidoscope case, and the shaking to which the
device is subjected. In principle, given perfect knowledge of all
of these parameters and the starting point, we could predict the
resulting pattern. In a quantum system we could not predict the
observed state of a system either in fact or in principle. Secondly,
in the case of a kaleidoscope it is sensible to think of a particular
pattern existing within the device after it has come to rest, even
if it has not been observed. In quantum systems, the superposition
of states is usually taken not to collapse into one until it has been
observed.

Now it might be thought that quantum mechanics only deals with
tiny, invisible objects, such as atoms, which make up the nebulous
micro-world and that these are of little concern to the world in
which everyday life is conducted. This view, it seems, is mistaken,
because quantum theory is a fundamental theory and attempts to
provide a description of the whole of physical reality, not just the
smallest parts. The disjunction between quantum-mechanical description and the common-sense view of the world is indeed most
severe when macro-objects are considered. This was demonstrated
by Schrödinger when he formulated his famous paradox, known as

'Schrödinger's Cat'. In this case the consequences of quantum-mechanical measurement are considered for an everyday object, namely a cat.

THE SCHRÖDINGER CAT PARADOX

Schrödinger imagined the following situation. A cat is placed in a closed steel container along with a small amount of radioactive element and a device which ensures the death of the cat if the element decays. Quantum physicists have suggested several such devices. Schrödinger's idea involved a hammer which is triggered by the decay and breaks a flask of cyanide. The radioactive element is chosen so that there is a 'fifty-fifty' chance that it will suffer decay during one hour. This means that, if the cat is left in the contraption for an hour, there will be a fifty-fifty chance that it will be found alive at the end of the experiment. It is possible to describe this system in terms of quantum-mechanical state vectors or wave functions. There are two possible states in which the cat may be found: 'cat alive' and 'cat dead'. The state of the entire system after one hour can be described by a state vector which is simply the sum of these two states (cat alive and cat dead). In other words, before the box is opened, according to quantum mechanics, the cat is in a combination, or super-position, of dead and alive states. Of course, when we look in the box we always find the cat to be either alive or dead. This is explained by the combination of wave functions collapsing into one of the definite states, cat alive or cat dead, when the system is measured (observed). However, it seems paradoxical that, until we look in the box, we must say that the cat is neither alive nor dead but is in this peculiar state of half-life. It would seem that cats ought to be either fully alive or fully dead. Certainly the cat itself should know whether it is alive. A resolution of this paradox seems to require an answer to the question - how, when and where does the wave function collapse?

Another paradox generated by quantum theory seems to require that two separated systems can interact instantaneously.

THE NON-LOCALITY PROBLEM OR EPR PARADOX

The Einstein-Podolsky-Rosen (EPR) paradox was put forward by Einstein and his colleagues in 1935 (see d'Espagnat, 1976; Jammer, 1974). It consisted of a thought experiment ('gedanken experiment') involving measurements on two separated quantum systems which had previously been in interaction. The original argument was designed to show that the quantum theory was incomplete, but since the expansion of the argument by Bohm (1951) and Bell (1964), the paradox has largely revolved around the issue of 'non-locality'. This is the notion that, in quantum theory, it is possible that causes may not be spatially and temporally local to systems (i.e. a sort of action at a distance). In the EPR case measurements are made on one system, which has previously been in interaction with another system but which is now spatially separated from it. This measurement seems to produce an instant correlation in the other system.

The correlations between these spatially separated systems (known as EPR correlations), although theoretically predicted, were not decisively demonstrable by experiment until the work of John Bell (Bell, 1964; Clauser et al., 1969; d'Espagnat, 1976). He derived a mathematical inequality concerning non-locality in the context of formulating constraints to test various classes of 'hidden variables' theory (these types of theory are outlined below). Bell's inequality (known as Bell's theorem) was testable by actual experimentation as opposed to thought experiments. In the last ten years a series of experimental tests of Bell's theorem have been carried out, the principal experiment being performed by John Clauser at Berkeley (Freedman and Clauser, 1972; Clauser and Horne, 1974). These experiments (despite one or two notable exceptions (Harvey, 1981; Holt and Freedman, 1975)) have tended to confirm quantum theory and indicate that the EPR correlations are part of experimental actuality.

In these experiments an atom produces two photons (light 'particles'), which fly off in opposite directions. The polarisation of either photon can be measured and it is found that, when the polarisations of both photons are measured simultaneously, they are correlated. For instance, in the simplest cases, if one photon is polarised in one direction, the other is found with the opposite polarisation. However, each photon may be polarised in either direction and, according to quantum theory, each must be thought of as having an equal probability of being found to be polarised in either direction before the direction is measured. Again a macroscopic metaphor may help, provided that it is not taken too literally.

Each photon can be thought of as a coin spinning through the air after being tossed. When the direction of polarisation of the photon is measured, this is equivalent to looking at the coin to see if it is 'heads' or 'tails'. The coin has an equal probability of being found in either 'state'. The paradox of non-locality resides in the fact that, if a pair of coins are tossed at the same time so that they fly apart in opposite directions, when we look at one and it comes down 'heads' we know that the other will be 'tails', if someone looks at it simultaneously, wherever he or she is! Seemingly, the coins can communicate with one another, faster than the speed of light, in some acausal way.

Though experiments have now seemingly corroborated the correlation for distances of a few metres, there is as yet no theoretical agreement on the implications of these experiments for quantum theory and relativity theory, and several physicists consider the non-local correlations to be mysterious and in need of explanation.

PROPOSED RESOLUTIONS TO THE PARADOXES

Thus far, the emergence of quantum theory has been described and its problems outlined through looking at two major apparent paradoxes. It must be pointed out that these paradoxes present no problems for those who work routinely with the quantum theory.

It is conventional to think of quantum theory as being made up of two parts. The *formalism* is an esoteric mathematical theory, which does seem to explain the behaviour of the subatomic physical world in purely abstract terms in so far as it is mathematically self-consistent and enables statistical predictions to be made of the behaviour of micro-systems. The second element in quantum theory, an element that would be considered strictly unnecessary by many physicists, is the attempt to generate an *interpretation* that would give some physical meaning to the formalism and its power of prediction. This conventional separation of the two elements should not be taken to mean that they were completely separate in the development of the theory (Jammer, 1974). However, for most physicists, a 'solution' to the paradoxes is to ignore them and work with the formalism. If this solution is adopted, the present state of quantum theory will be thought to be adequate and it will have nothing special to say to parapsychology. Rather, the usual claim will be that physics deals with theories testable by experiments and that anything that does not raise an experimental question is an issue of 'taste', 'comfort' or 'philosophy', but *not* physics. A typical expression of this attitude is the following statement from one of our respondents:

> Most physicists see no need for any interpretation of quantum theory. Most physicists are very happy with the present status of quantum theory. This is because it gives results. The more thinking ones will bend a bit, but they are rare. We have got so satisfied with quantum theory that we have become quantum engineers.

Another respondent, who was a 'straight' quantum physicist, commented:

> These paradoxes are not a problem for the theory; the theory predicts what will happen. They are only a problem for the interpretation. Philosophers generally take those issues. Generally physics is objective and mostly experimental. One can argue forever about the interpretations; they make no difference. . . . If the collapse of the wave function is needed in physics to actually calculate something, then that's the way physics should proceed, but if it's an unobservable then it doesn't really matter what you do to calculate it.

When asked about Schrödinger's Cat paradox, this respondent replied, 'That again is a philosophical issue; the results are always

clear. It's no problem for the cat; it's no problem for the observer.' In the same way, referring to the EPR paradox, Gerald
Feinberg (Oteri, 1975, p. 107) made the following remarks at a
conference on quantum theory and parapsychology:

> . . . it seems to me that one is not talking here about an experi-
> mental problem, but rather about how comfortable one is with a
> particular theoretical description. That was certainly the prob-
> lem of Einstein, Podolsky, and Rosen. They simply did not like
> the logical consequences that this description led them to. Other
> physicists have had no particular objections to it. But in no
> case, to my knowledge, is there a disagreement between an
> experiment that has been done, and the prediction of this par-
> ticular state.

Yet another respondent said, 'I think non-locality is proved, but
I don't really understand it. I don't think it's a serious question.
Philosophers have written several books on it!'
The resolution to the paradoxes obtained through avoiding
questions of interpretation is the one that is most common among
physicists and implies no promise for psi phenomena. Nevertheless, certain other resolutions formulated to solve problems in
quantum theory do seem also to precipitate the possibility of
explanation of psi phenomena and this has been recognised among
parapsychologists and some of those physicists who are interested
in the interpretive problems. Thus, the parapsychological community recently sponsored an international conference of physicists
in Geneva entitled 'Quantum Physics and Parapsychology' (Oteri,
1975). Six of our respondents attended this conference.[3] Other
indications of the 'coming together' of the two fields include the
results of a recent survey of quantum physicists (Harvey, private
correspondence), which showed that several considered their
work to be relevant to parapsychology, and the formation (around
a group of physicists at the Lawrence Berkeley Laboratory,
University of California, in 1975) of the 'Fundamental "Fysiks"
Group' for the purposes of research and discussion into matters
of physics relevant to consciousness. This group has initiated
several discussions amongst interested scientists in the San Francisco Bay area on the relevance of quantum theory to parapsychology. Their 1975-6 seminar programme included talks by several
eminent theoretical physicists, including quantum physicists.[4]
Also, at least ten of our respondents subscribed to some version
of the quantum mechanics-psi link and a further six (including
three specialists in quantum theory) had considered the link in
sufficient detail to be able to make in-depth comments.
The solutions for the paradoxes that have been offered will be
examined overleaf. All of these are presented in Table 4.1, including
the non-solution or 'avoidance solution' discussed already.
As will be seen, those that are listed to the left of Table 4.1
do not seem to make quantum theory specially compatible
with psi phenomena, whereas those to the right have been taken

Table 4.1 Solutions to the paradoxes

Proposed Solutions to Measurement Problem

	NO SPACE FOR PSI	COMPATIBLE WITH PSI			
	Statistical-interpretation resolution	Macroscopic instrument resolution	Entry-of-consciousness resolution	Hidden-variables resolution	Many-worlds resolution
Avoidance resolution					
Not a problem for physics	Treat ensembles only and problem of collapse will not emerge	Macroscopic measuring instruments collapse wave function	Consciousness collapses wave function	Additional variables collapse wave function	No collapse but world splits

Proposed Solutions to EPR Paradox

	Statistical-interpretation resolution	Hidden-variables resolution	Time-reversal resolution	Super-luminal resolution
Avoidance resolution				
Not a problem for physics	EPR correlation is only statistical	Additional variables explain inter-action of separate systems	Timelike vectors explain inter-action of separate systems	Faster-than-light signals explain inter-action of separate systems

to hold explanatory promise either by themselves or in combination with others. The solutions will be discussed in sequence, working left to right across the Table.

THE STATISTICAL-INTERPRETATION RESOLUTION

This is a general approach to interpretation in which the quantum theory is considered to be about ensembles of similar quantum systems rather than individual systems.[5] The superposition state, which in the orthodox interpretation is assumed to collapse on measurement, represents in this interpretation an ensemble of similar systems which will yield particular values in a given statistical frequency, on measurement. Similarly, in the EPR paradox, the apparent correlations between individual quantum systems is taken to be merely a statistical correlation between ensembles of systems. This solution has not been put forward as having implications for parapsychology.

The statistical interpretation or ensemble interpretation was put to us as a solution to the measurement problem in the following way:

> The ensemble interpretation is complete, it doesn't allow you to talk about such questions as Schrödinger's Cat and there is no collapse of the wave function whatsoever. If you have a philosophical predilection which requires you to describe single systems, then that's up to you, but if you do, you get into some hairy philosophical problems; but quantum mechanics doesn't. . . . There is no chance of determining the collapse of the wave function.

The same respondent told how the EPR paradox was dealt with in his approach:

> If you want to have non-local theories, people tried to introduce these in the 1950s and they gave up. It's not mainstream physics. . . . The EPR paradox is a failing of the understanding of what the ensemble interpretation will let you talk about. No I'm sorry, I'm a hard-nosed scientist when it comes to this. I think they are wasting their time completely.

The references to 'philosophical predilections', 'hairy philosophical problems' and 'not mainstream physics' hark back to the avoidance resolution. Indeed, it seems that the statistical interpretation nicely complements the 'hard-nosed' scientist approach, and this respondent was able to oscillate happily between the two. The statistical interpretation solved the problems by not allowing the questions to be asked; to ask the questions was to go beyond quantum theory into philosophy. As this respondent put it, 'The formalism of quantum mechanics today doesn't allow you to say anything more than about probabilities and ensembles; anything that goes to explain the individual system is going beyond quantum theory.'

Macroscopic–instrument resolution
This solution is specific to the measurement problem.[6] Some characteristic of a piece of macroscopic measuring apparatus, such as 'irreversibility', is put forward as explaining wave-packet reduction. The irreversibility may be postulated as a general thermodynamic property of macroscopic systems or as a property of a particular piece of measuring apparatus such as a non-linear amplifier. It is the irreversible element of the measuring process which leads to the reduction of the state vector or collapse of the wave packet.

This solution to the measurement problem does not seem to lead its proponents towards parapsychology because consciousness is given no special role in the measuring process. As Feinberg (Oteri, 1975, pp. 48-9) has put it:

Analysis of the reduction of the wave packet indicates that what's involved is a change from a pure state to a statistical mixture and is characterized by a thermodynamically irreversible transition.

It also suggests that such a reduction occurs when a microscopic system interacts with a class of macroscopic systems which can undergo such irreversible transitions, not especially when it interacts with a human observer.

Similarly, one respondent remarked, 'Once you have put the signal on a non-linear amplifying device, you have made the experiment. You have made the measurement already and you do not need a human.' This solution is not germane to the non-locality issue. Both Feinberg and the respondent above favoured the 'avoidance solution' approach as an answer to the non-locality problem.

Consciousness–Collapse Resolution
This is a specific solution to the measurement problem (but see Zweifel, 1974), first proposed by von Neumann in 1932 (see von Neumann, 1955) and recently taken up by Wigner (1963). In this view it is the intervention of the human mind and, in particular, consciousness that characterises every measurement in quantum mechanics.[7] Thus, in contrast to the previous position, here it is assumed that, in some way, consciousness leads to the collapse of the wave function. This view is adopted by many physicists who argue that current quantum theory and parapsychology are compatible. It is not difficult to see that if human consciousness is thought to be essential in the process whereby a physical system comes to take on a definite state, the possibility that mind can influence matter becomes less bizarre.

Quantum theory, being a probabilistic theory, can allow for a

measuring (observation) process to have a very unusual outcome.
These are outcomes that would be thought of as impossible in
classical physics, and, of course, so-called paranormal events
are like this. Within the Wigner-von Neumann interpretation, consciousness is involved in making every measurement (observation)
definite. In these circumstances, it is suggested, consciousness
has succeeded in bringing about an unlikely measurement. As
Brian Josephson (1975, p. 225) remarks:

> Quantum mechanics only tells us the probability distribution of
> observed values of physical quantities. If the observer was
> emotionally involved in the outcome of the experiment and
> particularly wanted one result to come out rather than another,
> perhaps that would shift this probability distribution.

Two of the theoreticians who have adopted this element of
quantum theory as the linchpin for explaining how the mind is
coupled with matter are O. Costa de Beauregard and Evan Harris
Walker. Costa de Beauregard writes (1976, pp. 549-52):

> As stated by von Neumann, London and Bauer, Wigner and
> others, *the quantum event occurs if, and only if, there is an
> active intervention of the psyche.*
> . . . if we believe in symmetry between cognizance and will,
> we are logically led to the working hypothesis that *collapse of
> the state vector can be caused not only by knowing awareness
> but also by willing awareness.*
>
> . . . what we are speaking of has a name in the realm of para-
> psychology, and that name is *psychokinesis* (all italics in
> original).

Walker (1975, pp. 7-8) puts it as follows:

> It is the consciousness of the quantum mechanical process that
> is responsible for the collapse of the *state vector.* . . . In the
> light of the above considerations and the Copenhagen Interpret-
> ation [the 'orthodox' view] of quantum mechanics, the action of
> consciousness to secure the collapse of the state vector has the
> physical consequence of determining the subsequent states of
> that system in a manner that corresponds to the concept of the
> 'will' (italics in original).

Both of these writers go on to develop their ideas in technical
detail.[8]

Hidden-variables interpretation resolution
This is a general approach to the interpretation of quantum theory
which attempts to explain the statistical nature of the theory by
assuming that there are well-defined variables acting at a 'subquantum' level which produce the apparent randomness at the

quantum level. It is analogous to the explanation of Brownian motion in classical mechanics. Brownian motion is the apparently random motion observed when smoke particles are suspended in a gas. The random 'joggling' of the smoke particles can be explained in terms of the invisible gas molecules, which have well-defined variables associated with them (such as position and momentum), colliding with the smoke particles. The only difference is that in quantum mechanics the sublevel, where the well-defined variables are assumed to act, is not (at least yet) accessible to measurement, and so the variables remain hidden. These 'hidden variables' can be used to explain both the collapse of the wave function and the EPR correlation. The main developments in the hidden-variables approach have been associated with David Bohm (see Bohm, 1952, 1957). This approach has been used in two ways by physicists arguing that present quantum mechanics and parapsychology are compatible. Sarfatti has suggested that the hidden variables can be controlled by consciousness in some way. Walker has tried to combine the Wigner-von Neumann approach with hidden variables, suggesting that the hidden variable is consciousness.

Sarfatti (1974a, p. 7) writes, 'The subquantum Brownian movement of the hidden variable theory of Bohm and Vigier in the nonlocal version is 'mental' in origin, proceeding from the uncoordinated and incoherent mental activity of the participators everywhere and everywhen.'

As noted above, Walker's theory is worked out in some detail. However, the 'flavour' of his views may be seen in his remark at the Geneva conference (Oteri, 1975, p. 49):

What I'm saying is that in quantum mechanics one can introduce hidden variables. This is not done exactly as Bohm would do; but these variables are quantities such that if their values are identified, however you determine what they are, a reduction of the state vector will be obtained.

The role of the hidden variables in the EPR paradox is also stressed by Walker (ibid., p. 5), who stipulates that 'the hidden variables . . . must be nonlocal in character' and cites Bell's work in this context.

The many-worlds interpretation – or Everett-Wheeler interpretation - resolution

This is a general approach to quantum theory first outlined by Hugh Everett III in 1957,[9] that resulted from an attempt to rid quantum theory of wave-function collapse. In this interpretation all the elements of the superposition state are assumed to exist but not all in the same world. It is postulated that, every time a quantum transition occurs, the world splits, and that in one world one part of the superposition has reality whilst in another world another part has reality. This avoids the need to say that, on measurement, the wave function collapses; the wave function never collapses but continues through the existence of many worlds.

These worlds are not worlds in the sense that one could visit them in a spaceship. The idea is somewhat more vertiginous. According to this interpretation there are a near-infinite number of near-replica universes, of which we inhabit one. The others – continually splitting into new near-copies of themselves – contain the other possible quantum states that have not been actualised here. They are not part of our space-time system. The most well-known physicist associated with this interpretation is John Wheeler. This approach has also been seen as leading its exponents toward parapsychology. Two of our respondents advocated this interpretation. One of them, John Hasted, presented us with an unpublished manuscript (since revised and published, 1981) in which his views were set out (see also Hasted, 1979). In this, discussing the measurement problem and the many-worlds interpretation as a possible solution, Hasted (1976a, p. 125) writes:

The many-worlds interpretation of quantum mechanics has not received the attention from physicists that it deserves . . . the existence of this interpretation gives us an opportunity to propose a speculative hypothesis on the basis of which these paranormal phenomena might be explained.

The essential step in applying the theory to parapsychology is to assume that people with psychic ability manage to achieve some sort of interaction between the different worlds, which would not happen in the normal way.

In the other worlds various possible states of affairs are actualised. If the appropriate sort of interaction between worlds can be achieved by a psychic, such states of affairs can be made visible, or can be made to affect events in this world.

Time-Reversal Resolution
This has been proposed by the French physicist, O. Costa de Beauregard, as a solution to the EPR paradox. Essentially, the two separated systems are seen as interacting via timelike vectors which link them together in their common past. That is, the EPR correlation is explained by allowing time-reversal, so that the previous interaction of the two systems becomes the source of the present non-local correlations. The previous interaction is appropriate because the current situation retroactively determines the prior situation.
Although when Costa de Beauregard first formulated his solution to the EPR paradox he did not draw any implications for parapsychology from it, in his more recent work it has been a key element in his argument that present quantum mechanics is compatible with parapsychology. For instance, he writes (1975, p. 100):

When leaving classical statistical-mechanics and entering quantum mechanics the sting of the EPR paradox becomes painful . . . between observers E and P [spatially separated] we do not have

only *telediction* . . . but also *teleaction*. The latter conclusion
is the one that Einstein, Podolsky and Rosen were ruling out
as obviously absurd. But it is the one I must accept as the
only one consistent with my overall philosophy. Moreover, *it is
a conclusion that can be experimentally tested in the form of
parapsychological experiments* (italics in original).

Superluminal-Information-Transfer Resolution
This solution to the EPR paradox will not be found in most texts
on the foundations of quantum theory as it is a possibility only
recently suggested following work on Bell's theorem. The physicist
most closely associated with these ideas is Henry Stapp (1975a,
1975b, 1976). His suggestion is that Bell's theorem implies that
our view of relativity may need modification. That is, it is possible
that some sort of signal (although the meaning of 'signal' is crucial
here) travels faster than the speed of light and is the means
whereby the two spatially separated systems are instantaneously
correlated.[10]
Sarfatti (1975, 1976a, 1977) has advocated this solution:

> Recent theoretical discoveries in the quantum effect known as
> EPR. . . . allow for the transmission of information *instantly*
> between any two places in the physical universe. There is no
> violation of Einstein's theory of relativity because the information
> transfer does *not* require the propagation of energetic signals.
> The quantum information utilizes energy already present at a
> particular place. If this hypothesis is confirmed, then psycho-
> kinesis, telepathy and precognition are likely to have a unified
> explanation within the presently known framework of modern
> theoretical physics (Sarfatti, 1975, pp. 279-80).

While the idea of non-locality seems to imply the possibility of
instantaneous signalling between separate systems, and therefore
seems to allow for paranormal phenomena, the reality is more complex. In non-locality experiments the correlation is between separate random events. It is only possible to see that there has been
a correlation by looking at the two series of random events side-
by-side. Each separate sequence of events will not appear to have
any order, so that it is not easy to see how an observer of only
one sequence could obtain information from it. It is as though
one has communication without transfer of information (Herbert,
1975). Thus, theories of psi which make use of this notion must
make use of it in a subtle way.

Other views
The analysis offered here, as might be expected, does violence
to the full complexity of the debate. For instance, under the
'consciousness resolution' the researchers encountered views such
as that consciousness should be seen as residing, not only in
humans, but also, for example, in Schrödinger's cat (which could
collapse its own wave function) or even in inanimate objects. Also

encountered was the view that none of the resolutions were adequate. For example, one physicist renowned for experimental work
in the area of quantum theory referred to the problem of collapse
as follows:

> I haven't the foggiest. I find it very hard to understand the
> collapse of the wave function. I find it very hard to understand
> the quantum-mechanical superpositions, and I do not yet, at
> least personally, understand, nor have any resolution to the
> various paradoxes. I do not know where it occurs, and I do
> not know if it occurs. But somehow something is wrong and I
> do not know what it is.

Another respondent made the same point with specific reference
to the suitability of current quantum theory as a basis for the
explanation of psi:

> I think the collapse of the wave function is such a theoretical
> monstrosity. I think it's the weak point of a theory which is
> inadequate in this respect anyway and I certainly wouldn't want
> to start there.

THE ARGUMENT OVER PSI AND QUANTUM THEORY

In providing in this way an exposition of quantum theory, and its
possible link with parapsychology, the scope for argument over
this relationship has already been revealed. In discussing the
matter in terms of the different possible solutions to the paradoxes
thrown up by quantum theory, it has been shown that the choice
between different solutions may provide the means of arguing over
quantum theory's explanatory power for psi phenomena. In Table
4.1, those who choose solutions to the paradoxes that lie in the
category 'No Space for PSI' (left-hand) will find that quantum
theory solves none of the problems of parapsychological happenings.
Those who adopt solutions in the category 'Compatible with PSI'
(right-hand), according to the exact variant of the interpretation
they adopt, may find parapsychological phenomena still unexplained
(e.g. Bohm and Hiley – see below), potentially explained (e.g.
Hasted), actually explained (e.g. Walker) or even *necessary* if
their version is true (e.g. Costa de Beauregard). It should be noted
that the 'right-hand' resolutions are not necessarily more heterodox
with regard to physics than the ones on the left. For example, the
'statistical interpretation' was once considered to be very heterodox. All the interpretations have at least one Nobel Laureate or
otherwise distinguished physicist associated with them.
    All of these positions have emerged in the debate, along with
others, such as that the argument is futile in the current underdeveloped state of either quantum theory or parapsychology (or
both), or that a radical new conception of quantum theory which
might be relevant to parapsychology is needed. Of course, few

arguers would agree with the authors that all these different positions are equally reasonable. And some would argue that none of them were reasonable. Three respondents who argued the incompatibility case said, respectively:

> The ideas to do with quantum mechanics being involved with ESP are, as far as I am concerned, not on at all. In fact, it's a remarkable misunderstanding by a large number of people who should know better about what the correct interpretation of quantum mechanics is.

> It is absolute bunk. It is just tremendously far-fetched and there is no evidence whatsoever. The whole thing is very doubtful and it seems unlikely that this feeling that people have had for thousands of years should suddenly turn out to be quantum mechanics. I think, on the contrary, in ten thousand years time parapsychology will not be any further advanced.

> They are all going in the wrong direction as far as quantum mechanics is concerned and I would be very surprised if quantum mechanics *per se* had anything to do with parapsychology. . . . I think that Q [one of the quantum men] is doing nonsense.

Compare this with the comments of Costa de Beauregard (Oteri, 1975), who favours what we have called the 'time-reversal solution' to the EPR paradox:

> My feeling is that the problem is merely one in the interpretation of quantum mechanics. . . . I am convinced we do not need any more equations to understand the specificity of parapsychological facts (p. 271).

> . . . relativistic quantum mechanics is a conceptual scheme where phenomena such as psychokinesis or telepathy, far from being irrational, should on the contrary, be expected as *very* rational (p. 101; italics in original).

Positions between these extremes were also put by respondents, or have been published. A negative comment by one respondent contained the suggestion that the only link between parapsychology and physics was their shared problematic nature:

> The connections between my work on quantum mechanics and parapsychology are two-fold. In one case you have non-local correlations which you do not understand, and in the other case you have non-local correlations which we do not understand.

Another respondent said:

> I don't think it's fair for people to be explaining one unknown in

terms of another unknown. To explain the unknown of psi in terms of the unknown as explained by a paradox isn't really an explanation at all.

A less pessimistic but nevertheless cautious stand has been advocated by David Bohm and his colleague Basil Hiley (1976, p. 178), talking of the EPR experiments:

> We believe that non-locality will only reveal itself in very subtle ways and investigations should proceed by exploring the precise conditions under which such effects appear. At present these conditions are too ill-defined to justify their use as possible explanations in psychophysics without a more careful investigation into the phenomena themselves.

On the other hand, an eventual reconciliation need not be ruled out by those who agree that the current situation is too nebulous to provide any positive explanation. For instance, such a position would be held by C.T.K. Chari who, though he said (1975, p. 74) at the Geneva conference, 'Parapsychology and quantum mechanics are still in too unfinished and controversial a stage to admit of generally agreed or acceptable connecting bridges', would go on to argue that a particular novel conception of quantum theory might be a fruitful heuristic for the explanation of psi.[11] Similarly, one of our more radical respondents told us:

> I have a big axe to grind with Z [a physicist who thinks psi can be explained by current quantum theory] because Z on his own admission accepts the whole of the formalism of the quantum theory as a complete description of what happens in the physical world. He has never questioned that. . . . Z thinks that within conventional quantum theory he can produce something to handle PK. I think this is a very unpromising line to start with.

Thus to follow through the twists and turns of the argument about the compatibility of psi and quantum theory, one must follow through the twists and turns of the arguments between upholders of the various different interpretations of quantum theory. The nature of parapsychological phenomena is almost irrelevant. Even parapsychologists find the leeway for debate is in quantum theory, not parapsychology. This is surprising because one would expect that where one area of scientific endeavour faces up to another it would be the least prestigious that would suffer most cognitive manipulation. In this case, however, though physics is undoubtedly prestigious, the particular sub-sub area of physics being dealt with - the interpretation (as opposed to the formalism) of quantum theory - is not a particularly prestigious area (see Pinch, 1976). What is more, it is characterised by a long history of debate of a sort which orthodox scientists would call 'philosophical', with the worst connotations. In the current state of the interpretation of quantum theory, there is no need for scientists to extend themselves in complicated refutations of the psi-quantum theory link; there is sufficient leeway in the physics to allow any position to be maintained. Should one interpretation come to dominate, however, arguments may become more definitive.

This is not the place to enter into a long exposition of the purely physical argument, but certain of the tactics that were encountered are of sufficient interest in themselves to merit a brief review. Among other things it is hoped that this will demonstrate the unsettled state of the debate about interpretations of quantum theory (Dewitt and Graham, 1973a). For example, respondents thought it quite reasonable to argue against the 'many-worlds interpretation' because it is literally *incredible*.

Comments from respondents about the many-worlds interpretation included the following:

I am not in sympathy with the many-worlds interpretation because it is even more fantastic than my own interpretation.

The branching-universe theory I think is quite crazy. [Branching-universe is an alternative name for the many-worlds interpretation.]

I just can't conceive that in some world I am getting the girl and in some world I'm losing her!

It seems rather incredible that the whole universe including the stars and the galaxies have been changed when we look in another universe.

The many-world model is an appalling model psychologically and I hope that it isn't true.

I think the Everett quantum mechanics, which comes out of Princeton and is very respectable, is in fact quite bizarre, and I very much doubt if it should have been published in a scientific journal.

These comments, though they all refer to the most extraordinary many-worlds interpretation, are not untypical of the debate as a whole.

The openness of the physics can again be seen by respondents' references to the 'Copenhagen interpretation' of quantum theory. From a distance, it appears to most physicists that Bohr and Heisenberg did produce a definitive interpretation, which is given this name. Probably all would agree that this is the most 'prestigious' interpretation of quantum theory, but close examination reveals that there are different opinions as to what the Copenhagen interpretation is. The following comments are revealing:

I ascribe to the interpretation that is the most conservative. That is the Copenhagen interpretation in an amplified form.

This is superluminal information transfer.

I am just playing with the orthodox interpretation and putting in one more thing; this is advanced potentials [time-reveral solution]. My interpretation is the Copenhagen interpretation plus not rejection of advanced waves.

The basis of my theory is simply the Copenhagen interpretation of quantum mechanics with the postulate that the observer is true [i.e. the observer's consciousness collapses the wave function].

A rather interesting tactic is to claim that the favoured interpretation is the universally accepted one:

The ensemble approach is quantum mechanics; it is taught in all schools because it works.

And at least the interpretation which most physicists presently accept for the reduction of the wave packet involves simply such a thermodynamically irreversible transition. [This refers to what we have called the 'Macroscopic Instrument Resolution'. The comment was made by Feinberg, in Oteri, 1975, p. 50.]

Again, arguers may suggest that an interpretation that they do not like goes beyond quantum theory. Thus Walker, arguing against the macroscopic instrument resolution, said (Oteri, 1975, p. 49):

The idea that a macroscopic thermodynamic state is responsible for wave packet reduction is not derivable from the equations of quantum mechanics. . . . It is precisely *as beyond conventional quantum theory* as is the prediction of the state in which the system will be found on observation (italics added).

In the same way, a respondent arguing against interpretations such as Walker's said:

By and large they are on the wrong track. They are trying to re-do quantum theory in a way that changes it significantly. . . X [a physicist] is doing nonsense. . . . X is trying to introduce consciousness into quantum mechanics and I can see no need for this.

A similar criticism seemed to be implied by Mattuck (in Oteri, 1975, p. 127) at the Geneva conference: '. . . if you have a hidden variable theory in which consciousness acts in some way as a hidden variable in its effect on quantum systems, then it seems that you go outside of the realm of quantum mechanics.' Finally, the openendedness of the debate can be seen in the argument that there is no real distinction between the various interpretations. For instance, one respondent remarked: 'The thing about interpretations is that they are totally equivalent. The many-worlds-interpretation is just as valid as the Copenhagen one. There is no basic reason to choose one over the other.' Another said:

> . . . that is indistinguishable from my theory. It is simply another language. You can take any of the interpretations of quantum mechanics and modify them in the same way as I have taken the Copenhagen interpretation. They are all interpretations of the same equation and they are all open-ended and they are all valid philosophical systems.

But compare this with Bohm and Hiley's (1976, p. 174) criticism of Sarfatti:

> Perhaps our most serious criticism of Sarfatti's paper is that he has taken parts of two such basically incompatible interpretations in an effort to justify his speculations without attempting to discuss how these disparate ideas can be brought together.

In the immediately preceding section no distinction has been made between the comments of 'believers' and the comments of 'sceptics' because no particular significance can be drawn from the distinction within the physical debate. Believers may be found who think that quantum theory does have explanatory power for parapsychology and other believers may be found who think that it is not relevant. Sceptics, of course, are not likely to be exercised by the problem, but clearly would not be inclined to think that any interpretation makes psi phenomena necessary.

The impact of quantum theory on parapsychology is not one that can be definitely specified in terms of compatibility or incompatibility. Again, the relationship between the fields does not appear to yield to a priori analysis. However, quantum theory has, without doubt, had a considerable impact upon parapsychology.

Perhaps the most useful way of looking at this is in terms of an area of science being sufficiently underdeveloped, or 'philosophical', or culturally unconstrained (Collins, 1975, 1976) as to be permeable to parapsychological ideas. What appears to have happened is that the interpretation of quantum theory has become divorced from the social practice of physics. Physicists in their everyday practice do not, by and large, engage with the issues raised by the debate over the interpretation of quantum mechanics. That debate has occurred more in the area of philosophy - but it must be said that many eminent physicists have made contributions. Thus, although the interpretation of quantum mechanics has some of the rhetorical power and prestige of a hard science (an attribute which no doubt makes it all the more attractive to parapsychologists in search of scientific legitimacy), it is at the same time a curiously unconstrained, open-ended area of science. The recent attempts from within physics to make the interpretation of quantum theory more relevant to actual scientific practice (the attempts to test consequences of Bell's theorem - see Harvey, 1981) can be seen as mirroring the attempts by parapsychologists to make the interpretation of quantum theory more relevant to scientific practice by the tie-up with ESP effects. It is these dual developments which have undoubtedly encouraged some parapsychologists to become more interested in quantum theory, and has led some physicists to be more receptive than they otherwise might have been. It has also provoked at least one eminent physicist (John Wheeler) explicitly to dissociate quantum mechanics from parapsychology as part of a more general attack on the status of parapsychology (Gardner, 1979).

CONCLUSION TO CHAPTERS 3 AND 4

In these two chapters attempts to determine the relationship between the ideas of science and the ideas of parapsychology have been examined. The style of incompatibility argument that has been discussed is set out schematically in Figure 4.1.

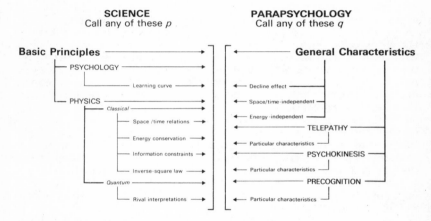

To argue that science and parapsychology are incompatible choose any pair *p* and *q* and show that

science ⇒ *p*
parapsychology ⇒ *q*
p ⇒ not ⇒ *q*

Figure 4.1 How to show that psi is incompatible with science

This examination of the issue has been conducted as though it were an issue which could be settled without reference to its social context. It has been treated as a matter of 'logic'. In fact, however, it has been found that all the arguments that have been put forward are answerable in one way or another, so that no definitive a-cultural and a-temporal answer to the question of the relationship between psi and science has been located. This might have been argued from the general relativistic presuppositions of the whole work, but it was thought to be important to review these arguments, for clearly the arguers do not share the authors' presuppositions. Of course, the evidence may not be convincing. Whole books have been written about some of the issues to which only a few lines are devoted here, so arguers may still feel that some treasured a priori argument for incompatibility is valid.[12] What is more, at best the above analysis is a species of induction. The claim is that, as all the arguments that could be found were defeasible, all such arguments will be. The determined a-priorist may look for better arguments to arise in the future. Against these objections the manifest richness of human ingenuity is urged. Whatever you say, someone will get round it. Quine (1953) has even shown that, in a sense, it is not possible to be completely certain that all bachelors are unmarried!

Assuming that the conclusion of these chapters is correct, the authors are released from certain obligations and left free to pursue certain sorts of analysis. There is no obligation to see scientists who investigate parapsychology as involved with two sets of ideas that are in logical contradiction. Talk of accommodation to problems thrown up by working in the two fields simultaneously will follow, but these difficulties should now be seen as one consequence of a conflict between cultures or paradigms. This will often be manifested in conflicting requirements as regards particular actions, e.g. reading meters (see chapter 7), not as problems of resolution of logical paradoxes. It is possible to think now in terms of paradigms or meaning frames where the social and the cognitive are inextricably mixed, without imagining that a formal solution to problems is available. It is possible then to feel free to look at the way that PMB and physics are 'incommensurable'. Actors do not have to be treated as though they have missed some vital point of logic.

5 PARANORMAL METAL BENDING AT BATH
Investigating and publishing

The experiments done at Bath – the published description and other sorts of description – first observations – subsequent observations and growth of scepticism as cheating observed – some scientists easily duped – construction of drafts of published account of experiments – first re-examination of evidence of cheating – use of modalities in descriptions

THE BATH EXPERIMENTS

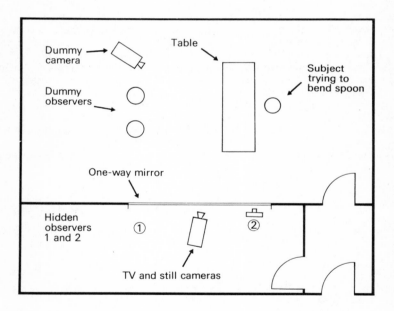

Figure 5.1 Plan of observation room

Between May and September 1975 Dr Brian Pamplin and Dr Harry Collins, both of the University of Bath, conducted a series of observations on children who claimed to have Geller-like powers. In all, they observed six youngsters. The conditions of the experiment were such that the experimental subjects were not aware

90

that they were being observed by one group of experimenters, who were concealed behind a one-way mirror (see Figure 5.1). Five out of the six children were seen to 'cheat', that is, they appeared to bend metal test objects by physical force, such as wrenching between two clenched hands, when they should have been using their paranormal powers to accomplish the deformation. None of the children showed any convincing demonstration of the operation of paranormal powers except that the 'dummy observers', who were not concealed (Figure 5.1), were not always aware that they had been duped. One 'dummy observer' on one occasion felt very strongly that he had witnessed paranormal metal bending.

The results of these experiments were published in the scientific journal 'Nature'. They attracted considerable attention and seem to have had some effect on the credibility of paranormal claims. The 'Nature' publication is reproduced below.

CORRESPONDENCE

Spoon-bending: an experimental approach
SIR, - We have investigated six young people who claimed the power of bending objects by stroking in the manner demonstrated on television recently by Uri Geller and others. In this report we will call these people A, B, C, D, E and F. A, B, and F are young girls all aged eleven years. C is a girl of thirteen, while D and E are boys aged ten and eight respectively. All were contacted with the aid of local press and television. A, B and C had received publicity in the local evening papers. Subsequently Dr Pamplin appeared on BBC 'Points West' local television news programme when B demonstrated her ability quite convincingly. The parents of D, E and F subsequently contacted Dr Pamplin claiming that their children could also bend cutlery by stroking.

Most of the subjects were first visited in their own homes where they showed their ability in the casual atmosphere of their sitting rooms. A succeeded in bending a weighed and measured rod of mild steel of $^3/_{10}$ths inch diameter supplied by the experimenters as well as her own cutlery.

All six subjects were subsequently tested in Bath University's psychology laboratory. This laboratory has three large one-way mirrors behind which the experimenters can observe, photograph and take television videotape unseen by the subject. In all cases, except A, one or more observers sat in the laboratory with the subject. In the first four experiments there was a second television camera in the laboratory with the observers. The subject was handed the spoon or rod after its outline had been drawn on a sheet of paper and was allowed to stroke it in the approved manner between forefinger and thumb of one hand and to report what they felt was happening. B reported that the spoon 'felt soft' before bending. C stated that it 'felt like plaster,

then running water'. The running water feeling occurred, it
was said, just before bending occurred. However, at no time
did C bend anything for us while experimenters were watching.
The others all succeeded in bending spoons and B bent a rod
of mild steel as well.

The aim of the experiment was to obtain a photographic or
videotaped record of the actual moment of bending. The observer
in the room measured the spoon against its outline at intervals
during the session, noting the time.

The observers in the room were instructed to deliberately
relax their vigilance at intervals after the first twenty minutes.
The experimenters were specially alert during these periods
and in all cases except C they observed and photographed
cheating by the subjects. A put the rod under her foot to bend
it; B, E and F used two hands to bend the spoon using considerable muscular power, while D tried to hide his hands under a
table to bend a spoon in both hands out of sight of the observer.

We can assert that in no case did we observe a rod or spoon
bent other than by palpably normal means. We cannot, of course,
conclude that all instances of the so-called Geller Effect are due
to cheating. However, we offer details of our experimental procedure in the hope of helping other experimenters design experiments that can be used when cheating is suspected.

DR BRIAN R. PAMPLIN
MR HARRY COLLINS

Bath University, UK

In the next two chapters these experiments will be redescribed
in detail. In this chapter a chronological account of the gathering
of the data and the construction of the 'Nature' publication will
be given. In chapter 6, the assumptions and predispositions of
the experimenters that made their account possible will be more
systematically explored.

INTRODUCTION

The results of the Bath experiments were written about in the
media and discussed by some sections of the scientific community.
News of the experiments passed rapidly among members of the
sceptical 'network' of scientists and others, described in chapter
2 as 'vigilantes'. The negative results of the experiments found
a sympathetic audience in that group. It is only the fact that the
experiments had this impact that lends what follows any intrinsic
interest. What will be recounted is not on a par with the discovery
of the 'double helix' or the first optical pulser, so the unsympa-
thetic readers may feel that the authors are 'gilding the lily' in
expending so much descriptive effort on such a trivial experiment.
However, we are making a general point through the study of a
particular case, the intrinsic interest of which is not germane, except in so far as it makes the chapter more or less pleasant to read.

All descriptions are abstractions. If Cleopatra's nose can be described in an indefinite number of ways, then certainly the experimental series discussed below could be described in an indefinite number of ways. Here, however, attention is drawn to certain peculiarities of the scientific accounts of the experimental series. They are contrasted with another description in which an attempt is made to reconstruct some of the observations and feelings of one of the experimenters (Collins) at the time the experiments were being done. Implicitly, certain claims about the relevance of this description are made: it is not just any description - it is better in some ways than other descriptions for the purposes in hand.[1] However, no claim is made that it is 'the definitive description'. This point will be made clear in the next chapter, but a more superficial point needs to be made first. A description of the same general kind as that given here, but from the point of view of another experimenter, might differ and be equally relevant for the purpose in hand.

In what follows, one author, Collins, is going to make comments which will reveal that at points during the series he felt in less than complete agreement with actions of the initiator of the experimental series, Dr Brian Pamplin. It is necessary to include such comments if the appropriate description is to emerge. It should come as no surprise that two researchers from such different backgrounds - Pamplin is senior lecturer specialising in solid-state physics, especially semi-conductors - should see things in different ways. It must also be remembered that Collins had less to lose through being associated with paranormal phenomena. (See chapter 7 for this point expanded from a methodological point of view and chapter 8 for more discussion of the pressures on physical scientists working in the field of the paranormal.) A small example of what would usually be the unspoken opinion of Pamplin's colleagues appeared in the Bath University academics' magazine, 'Assembly News and Views'. The author was Professor C.R. Tottle, who at the time was Head of the School of Materials Science and Pro-Vice-Chancellor. In the course of a letter (1975, p. 36) he wrote:

> Dr Pamplin recently appeared on television in connection with a BBC Bristol watered-down version of Uri Geller's tricks with spoon and fork bending. Dr Pamplin remarked that he would want to see a scientifically designed experiment before comment. Had he been a materials scientist, he would have to know that our knowledge of the mechanical properties of metals is such that these conjuring tricks rely on sleight-of-hand and subterfuge. It is not possible to bend a silver or stainless steel spoon or fork by stroking it. The creep of metals can be roughly estimated in terms of the melting point and to perform this trick requires a melting point below 100°C, as shown by Wood's alloy - frequently sold in jokes and tricks shops in the form of spoons and forks. The spoons melt when used to stir hot tea, for instance. All Dr Pamplin had to do, was to ask the composition of the material used - but then Dr Pamplin is a physicist and not

a materials scientist, who, incidentally, also studies chemistry. There is one other material which can be used for this trick - an alloy of nickel and titanium, which can demonstrate 'memory' effects when heated, but I am not aware of any similar alloy that can be affected by blood temperature. Some of our colleagues have seen me demonstrate the properties of this alloy with a match or cigarette lighter.

By this time Pamplin was able to reply (1975, p. 37):

With regard to my experiments on Uri Geller phenomena, I would refer the reader to my recent letter to 'Nature' (see below) which exposes the cheating of local young people by means excluding the use of unusual special materials.

Where possible, then, comments referring to Collins's unease with regard to certain matters are tempered by including a reconstruction of what might have been Pamplin's quite legitimate point of view. If Pamplin were writing this chapter, it would, no doubt, look different and would perhaps contain comments on his irritation with Collins's pedantry and 'hidden sociological motives'. If this were the case, then Collins could make no claim as to the validity of his feelings over Pamplin's; both descriptions would stand equal from an epistemological point of view. The difference in the experimenters' viewpoints would be the most significant thing as far as this chapter is concerned.

A second point: the description that will be presented will make the experiment look very 'sloppy'. Whether it really was sloppy or not by the standards of routine work in physics or psychology it is impossible to tell without an impracticable series of comparative studies where some attempt would be made to reconstruct the experiments to be compared in the same way as is attempted here. Such work as has been done would suggest that the relationship between the experiment and its eventual description, as presented here, is not untypical (Collins and Harrison, 1975; Latour and Woolgar, 1979; Knorr, 1979). However, we suspect that critics will say that it is untypical as compared with (distorted?) memories of their own work or with the canonical versions of proper research procedure. The authors readily acknowledge that by these standards the work described is sloppy. Irrespective of the 'truth of the situation' the important point is that there are many descriptions of the work available that would make it look the opposite of sloppy, and that Pamplin and Collins eventually availed themselves of such an interpretation, as did critics of PMB when they made use of the results. Still more significantly, the suggestion is that there are descriptions of all scientific work which would make it look sloppy. One might go about constructing such an account by detailed scrutiny of minute-by-minute procedure in any experiment, pointing out discrepancies between claimed protocol and actual procedure. As all accounts depend upon some kind of glossing procedures, and *ceteris paribus* clauses, for they

can never capture the infinite richness of the moment, a 'sloppy'-
looking account must always be available.

The requirement of generating the description which captures
some of the observations and feelings belonging to the period
when the experiments were actually being conducted has necessi-
tated a certain amount of what might appear to be self-indulgent
introspection on the part of Collins. This is rather embarrassing
in a scientific text, but the very fact that it is embarrassing is
itself revealing of the nature of scientific texts. The neutral
third-person-passive style of writing is not an accident of scientific fashion but is intended to give an impression of objectivity.
The personality and individuality of the writer is of no account.
The work described reveals universal characteristics of nature.
Anyone could do it at any time. (See the end of this chapter for
a longer exposition of this point.) However, as the scientific
paper which emerged from the Bath experiments is to be contrasted with the narrative account, this latter account will be
rendered in the first person. It is hoped that the points thus
made will compensate for the consequent lack of stylistic uniform-
ity throughout the book. Thus, henceforward in this chapter
only, the personal pronouns 'I' and 'me' refer to Collins, and the
collective 'we' means Pamplin and Collins.

AN EXPERIMENTAL APPROACH

On 5 May 1975, I was present while an eleven-year-old girl attempted to demonstrate that she could bend metal by 'paranormal'
means. First contacts with children who claimed this ability were
made, through a local newspaper advertisement, by Dr Brian
Pamplin of the physics department of the University of Bath, who
had independently become interested in observing the phenomenon.
Dr Pamplin had asked another member of the Humanities School
(W) if she would be interested and, knowing of my previous research into the paranormal, W had asked whether I would like to
collaborate.

At this first session, held in a private house, the child 'Sally',
her parents, a psychologist, Pamplin and myself were present.[2]
At the time I recorded in my notes that after a couple of hours
Sally had succeeded in bending several objects, including spoons
and two mild steel rods provided by the experimenters, which
were too strong to bend by hand. The actual moment of bending
was not observed. Indeed, on two such occasions Sally was out
of the room, and on the others she sat with her back to the observers but with one hand behind her back. Sally's father showed
other objects that she had bent at home, including some more
which were too strong to bend by hand. My notes include the
comment that it was 'all pretty convincing' but 'a bit boring until
one can think of something to do with it'. I felt entitled to be
blasé because (I suppose) I had become used to thinking about
the marvellous phenomena of the paranormal over a period of

years and had developed some of the thickness of skin of researchers in the field – they do, after all, deal with such matters
every day of their lives from 'nine to five'. However, I was quite
excited at the prospect of getting a record of paranormal bending
on videotape. Such a tape, it seemed to me, would be a remarkable scientific document as well as a superb instrument for probing
scientists' attitudes to the paranormal. Referring to my notes I
see that the psychologist was deeply impressed by the demonstration and asked questions such as whether Sally ever experienced 'trancelike states' and whether she had reached the men-
arche. The physicist wanted to take electroencephalograph records
while Sally performed her bending operations. Even at this early
stage differences in our view of the situation were evident. We
agreed that she would come to the university to be videotaped
the following week.

   After Sally and her parents had left we discussed the forthcoming experiment and particularly the problems presented by
Sally's apparent inability to bend the objects while being watched
directly. Eventually we decided to film her from the far side of
one-way mirrors so that she would be unaware that she was being
watched by cameras and observers, which might 'put her off'.
At this stage we had not seriously considered the possibility of
fraud, except that I was concerned lest our film be devalued by
being open to accusations of fraud. Eventually I wrote out an
experimental protocol to be followed during the filming, and tried
to press this on my co-experimenters. This caution was prompted
by my research on the sociology of the paranormal, which revealed that accusations of fraud were frequently directed by
sceptics at supposed demonstrations of paranormal phenomena.
   My protocol was headed:

   *I would suggest that the following protocol be observed to
   minimise the credibility of accusations of fraud.*

The details concerned such issues as continuity of the film, starting and stopping the run, and so forth.
   According to my notes, the day before the experiment the
psychologist telephoned me with the news that a friend of hers
'trained in science' who 'knows about these things' had told her
that the metal-bending effect was well known and that a book had
recently been written showing how it happened and, what is more,
that it was common knowledge among materials scientists. The
psychologist seemed no longer particularly interested in the experiments. She was now somewhat dismissive of what we had witnessed
and of what we might witness. It was, after all, 'a phenomenon
well understood in informed circles'. It transpired eventually that
the book referred to was 'The New Science of Strong Materials'
(Gordon, 1968) and that it could not explain the phenomenon, nor
was the phenomenon well understood in materials-science circles.
Indeed, the consensus of opinion in materials-science circles
would now be that the effect does not exist. Other 'debunking'

explanations were to be produced by materials scientists before
this felicitous stage was to be reached, however. The incident is
typical of the way that experts in other fields make confident ex-
cathedra pronouncements while maintaining their distance from
relevant experimental work. 'Expertise at a distance' is easy to
come by.
  Our first experiment started at 7 p.m. on 13 March. Sally was
taken into the experimental area while Pamplin, W, myself, W's
husband, 'Mike' the cameraman, and sometimes Sally's parents
watched from the other side of the one-way screens. As far as
we knew, Sally was not aware that we were there. There was an
air of expectancy. The protocol broke down quite soon, as observers entered the experimental area, or Sally turned her back
to the camera, thus hiding the object being rubbed, or Mike went
for a 'reaction shot' taking the object out of frame. All of us had
different interests and priorities, which involuntarily dominated
our actions as soon as we began to concentrate on our individual
projects. Sally sat in a chair in the experimental area rubbing
at one object or another, showing great concentration and in-
creasing signs of distress as the minutes ticked by. I would guess
that some of the observers became sceptical quite quickly as time
went by. I was certainly disappointed, but also worried that the
observers' scepticism would be transmitted - paranormally - to
the subject and make things still worse. Many parapsychologists
believe that the presence of sceptics may prevent the manifestation of paranormal phenomena. Eventually, after many disturb-
ances of the protocol and breaks for orange squash, we observed
that a spoon had become bent. The time was 8.12 p.m., so more
than an hour had passed. Sally had had her back turned to the
camera at various times immediately preceding this, and Mike
claimed that he had seen her cheat. At 8.18 p.m. the run was
terminated. We were all rather deflated, but I at least felt that
it was not surprising that nothing positive had happened under
the stressful circumstances of Sally's first visit to a university
laboratory. I attempted to make cheerful arrangements for her
next visit. Perhaps she had cheated toward the end of the session,
but by that stage she was under tremendous, if subtle, pressure
to produce something. Our next session was fixed for the following week.
  The next session started at 7.15 p.m. on 20 May. The arrangements were roughly as before, but there were several other
observers who had heard of our efforts and asked to be present.
By 7.40 p.m. nothing had bent although Sally had been concen-
trating and rubbing the mild steel rod we had provided. At 7.40
p.m. we changed the lighting on request, 'so that it wouldn't
shine in her eyes'. At this stage in the experiments we were using
two or three floodlights in addition to the fluorescent lighting in
the room to provide enough light for good picture quality through
the one-way mirrors. The experimental room was white-painted
and, as the sessions went on, the temperature increased and the
glare must have been disturbing. Until now Sally had remained

alone in this room, but her mother now entered to encourage her and stayed there for a while, though out of frame. According to my notes, by this time the observers were chattering among themselves, having largely lost interest in the experiment, and showed signs of unveiled scepticism. I recorded:

8.00 p.m.   Now no confidence at all – strange how even I feel totally pessimistic after what are, after all, only two hours of attempts under what are the most adverse of circumstances.

8.05 p.m.   It's actually getting very boring – fancy giving up so easy!

8.18 p.m.   Mr S takes in some squash for S. Tells her to try with the other hand. Mr S takes the place of Mrs S . . . encourages her. 'Forget the lights are on', 'Bend it quickly', etc.

8.22 p.m.   Nothing . . . Mr S still encouraging her.

8.25 p.m.   S looks as though she's summoning up courage to bend it manually – keeps turning it from hand to hand – putting it in position to bend it by force.

8.26 p.m.   Tries to bend it by force – doesn't succeed. Mr S putting pressure on her – 'You must bend it before you go.' S is trying to bend it by force – whole thing very sad!

At this point we stopped the experiment proper, and most of the party went to the Senior Common Room for a break, telling Sally that they would be back in a while and she should stay there and try again on her own. Actually Mike and I stayed behind the mirrors and continued to film. I think the idea was that by this stage it looked as though Sally had some notion that she was being watched from somewhere and that this might be putting her off. Perhaps we would at last be able to capture the real, but elusive, event when the pressure was finally removed. What happened, however, was that Sally immediately 'cheated' in a crude way. She searched agitatedly for a crack in a chair or other laboratory furniture to serve as a lever with which to bend the rod. She eventually bent it underneath her foot. At the same time she was exhibiting signs of enormous distress and agitation, which it is fortunate only Mike and I were privy to.[3] I found the whole episode, firstly surprising – I had not expected it – and also embarrassing. Nevertheless, we arranged for a further run in another four weeks. After all, it was evident from Sally's actions when she thought she was not being observed that she was under tremendous pressure. This negative observation, then, said nothing about her capabilities under more propitious circumstances.

A new problem in the way of our maintaining a positive attitude to the experiments was that one of our major reasons for believing strongly in Sally was that she had bent a rod that was too strong

for any of us to bend by hand. We now discovered that it could
be done by putting it under a foot, a method that simply had not
occurred to us before. We also realised that on the occasions she
had bent these very strong objects, she had been out of our sight
completely, so could have used the foot method.

I noted, after returning home, that I was now a complete sceptic. I honestly felt that the whole so-called 'Geller effect' was a
fraud. But I also noted that this feeling was due to the outcome
of only one observation of one little girl cheating on one occasion,
which by all the rules should have been as adverse an occasion
as possible for the production of the genuine phenomenon and a
favourable occasion for fraud. From an epistemological viewpoint
this feeling that it was all fraud was the most naive of inductive
generalisations - indeed, still worse, it was a generalisation from
one instance. What we had discovered was the rhetorical power
of demonstration. The drama of the incident completely swamped
any kind of cool analysis. This is precisely what well-designed
individual experiments are about, of course. Dramatic happenings
force one to believe in what it is claimed is being demonstrated.

On 22 May we visited the house of another small girl who had
been brought to our attention via the media. The party from Bath
consisted of physicists, Pamplin, 'Dobbs', and myself. The little
girl, 'Tina' was very precocious and replied to our questions in
a forthright and charming manner. Not all her answers seemed
quite consistent to me, but at this stage I was very sceptical
and was looking for anything suspicious at all. These suspicions
were reinforced when some gentlemen from local TV arrived (un-
expectedly as far as I was concerned) and it transpired that
Tina's father was a TV cameraman. I then began to wonder if it
was we 'scientists' who were being 'set up'. Tina began to go
through a routine. She tried to bend an object in front of us, but
could not succeed. Slowly, conditions and vigilance became more
relaxed. Eventually she ran to the kitchen to fetch a teaspoon
to bend, and brought back one that looked already slightly bent.
Pamplin looked at it immediately she brought it in but Tina said
that it had 'already started' - 'it all happened very quickly in
the kitchen'. She continued to try to bend it, while sitting in
an armchair. She raised her leg very high into a rather uncomfort-
able position in order to hide the spoon from us as she tried,
apparently, to cheat.

After this Tina was interviewed for local radio and TV. Pamplin
was interviewed also, but I demanded that my name be kept out of
it. (I was still not sure whether we were being 'set up' and also -
a less-admirable motive - I felt that I must 'keep my nose clean' as
far as possible for future fieldwork with scientist respondents.) As
far as I understand, the broadcast TV commentary on Tina's performance suggested that she produced quite an impressive feat of
paranormal spoon-bending, whereas to me, watching the TV filming, it was clear that there were considerable periods when she
had the spoon beneath the table top and out of sight of everybody.
I guess this observation would not make for exciting television.

Other tests on Tina were performed by Dobbs. He drew some
simple shapes on paper, and Tina was able to reproduce these on
her own sheets of paper. During one or two of these tests she
was out of the room while Dobbs drew the test drawings. I saw
her peep through the french windows to see what he was drawing.
Tina could not reproduce any of the shapes that I drew on paper,
but I made certain that she couldn't see my pen top while I drew.
According to my notes, by the end of the session I was a thorough
sceptic and did not believe that we would ever see paranormal
metal bending.

I had assumed that Tina's cheating had been as transparent to
the others as it had been to me but on the journey back to Bath
I discovered that I was completely mistaken. While Pamplin was
non-committal or sceptical, it transpired that Dobbs had been
bowled over by the afternoon's events. He remarked 'It has been
a red-letter day in my life.' He believed completely in the paranormal abilities of the little girl. As we journeyed back I tried to
point out his errors - how the spoon she brought in from the
kitchen was already bent; how she hid the spoon behind her
bizarrely raised leg; how I had watched her peeping through the
french windows; how she could easily see the end of his pen when
she was in the same room. Dobbs would accept none of this at first.
He argued from the sweetness and innocence of the little girl that
she could not have cheated. (I had an 'advantage' here, for I
had taken an instant dislike to the child. Also, of course, I had
already suffered the shock of discovering a preparedness to cheat
in the case of another little girl.) Dobbs said that as far as he was
concerned the phenomena existed. There was no need to do any
controlled experiments in the laboratory unless you wished to
convince others. As for convincing ourselves, we had already done
it, we now knew the phenomena existed. I argued that it was not
possible to make a distinction between convincing oneself and
convincing others.

As I have said, by this stage I was completely sceptical, but I
was not sure that I would be able to maintain this stance in the
face of Dobbs's protestations. After all, we were arguing about it,
and I expected to be able to change his mind, so why shouldn't
he change mine? On the other hand, we had begun to build up a
library of physical artifacts to support our beliefs. Our sessions
with Sally had been videotaped, and I had taken still photographs
on occasions when she could be seen to cheat. Actually, the videotapes were not too much use as 'reinforcing artifacts' because of
the time it would take to set them up and find the place on the
tape where the cheating took place. At the time of writing this,
we have never looked at the early videotapes of cheating but we
know they are there! We have the still photographs, which fortunately turned out rather well. I recall seeing them when they were
returned from the university photographer, and thinking how
well they had turned out and how they reinforced my fading memory of the scene. These photographs, pasted into my laboratory
notebook, now constitute that memory, along with my notes of the time.

Interestingly, the photographs are not very convincing to other people. When they have been shown to believers in the phenomenon, the latter have often pointed out that the photographs merely show little girls with their hands in strange positions. They do not show the little girls bending spoons by physical force. In such circumstances one falls back on the other artifacts. One agrees that it is not possible to capture a scene with a still photograph, but the videotapes and the notebooks make it clear that there could be no doubt about what was taking place if one was there! For example, one might point out comments in the notebooks that coincide with taking photographs such as: '"X" takes spoon in both hands and bends it by force, photograph taken'; then a few minutes later, '"X" shows the observers that it has been bent'. Thus used, these artifacts may or may not convince others that cheating has been witnessed but they carry only a little of the dramatic power of seeing it live. However, the dramatic power of live demonstration soon fades if it is not reinforced. But the artifacts help to convince the experimenters of what they had seen live! Active and circular reinforcement is required if certainty is not to fade. The extent to which certainty can be maintained in this matter will depend on what it is one is trying to stay certain about, and how it is viewed in the wider society.

I argued some of this out in my head as I argued with Dobbs that there is no distinction between convincing oneself and convincing others. Thus, if one can't produce the evidence to convince others, I suggested, then one can't be sure that one will remain convinced oneself. My notes made at the time include the comment, 'The paper is an artifact for accomplishing objectivity – for the author too!'

On Thursday 29 May we ran a test on Tina in the psychology laboratory. In addition to Pamplin, Dobbs and myself, 'Briggs', a member of a committee of the Society for Psychical Research (SPR), came to help out and observe. Briggs had heard of our work through the local media and was interested in our suitability for receiving funds from the SPR for further research. On this run, the protocol was rather different. Both Dobbs and Briggs sat in the experimental room with Tina, while watching her. At the same time the hidden observers stayed on the other side of the one-way screen, as in previous runs. Our TV camera observed from behind the screen as before, but in addition a second TV camera was kept inside the experimental area in full view of Tina. She knew of the existence of the second one only (see Figure 5.1).

We started at 2.45 p.m. I wrote in my notes:

The whole emphasis of the experiment has changed now. We seem no longer to be interested in proving the existence of the phenomenon, for now there is no stress on continuity. Now, rather, protocol has been arranged to catch her cheating.

By 3.02 p.m. nothing much had happened though I believe Tina had been trying to bend, by the physical force of one hand, a

small, weak spoon she had brought with her. At 3.02 p.m. she
asked for the camera to be turned off as it was 'putting her off'.
The camera in the experimental area was ostentatiously pointed
away from her. We kept the hidden camera switched on, of course.
At 3.04 p.m. she claimed she 'felt it go'. Dobbs compared the
spoon with a drawn profile and agreed that it had 'gone a bit'.
We, behind the mirror, were not sure whether this was true or if
Dobbs was just encouraging her. At 3.05 p.m., the same thing
happened. At 3.06 p.m. Tina asked for the floodlights to be turned
off. Dobbs turned one of them off. When we looked back, the
spoon had quite obviously bent further. I had my attention misdirected, but Pamplin said he saw her bend it with both hands.
Mike said the camera was on her the whole time. Little more happened and we took a break at 3.15 p.m. During the break Tina's
parents showed me a letter they'd received from a well-known
'fringe scientist' asking if he could conduct experiments with her,
and promising her a trip to America among other things.

At 3.50 p.m. we recommenced. At 4.10 p.m. nothing had happened and we again turned away the camera in the experimental
area. At 4.13 p.m. Tina bent the spoon by force. At 4.14 p.m.
she showed it to Dobbs, who confirmed that it was bent. At 4.17
p.m. she bent it by force again, and I caught the moment with
my still camera. At 4.17½ she showed it to Dobbs again, who confirmed that it had gone further. My notes state: 'All at back of
screen are now convulsed with laughter.' This charade continued
until 4.29 p.m., when 'we are all rolling about'. There seemed
little point in continuing. According to my notes, she had distracted the attention of Dobbs and Briggs every time she bent
the spoon by force.

I noticed that Dobbs and Briggs seemed to allow their attention
to be distracted rather easily, but I have no record or memory
that this was part of the experimental protocol.

At 4.30 p.m. we got her to try a few drawing experiments with
Dobbs drawing the objects and Tina trying to copy them without
watching. As far as we could see she did everything she could
in the way of peeping, either directly or via the mirrors.

Afterwards, Dobbs professed that he had not seen her cheat,
and we had to show him my notes and stress to him that the only
times she bent objects were when he was distracted. This time he
did not take too much persuasion, but I was surprised at the
extent to which he seemed unaware that the fraud was so simple
and crude. This may be a property of the one-way mirrors, of
course. It may relate to the feeling of disappointment one has
when told how some magicians' tricks work. As long as you do not
see the subterfuge you can not imagine that it could be anything
so tawdry.

Some of the foregoing may seem callous, or irresponsible, or
not ethical. Ordinarily such details as that the experimenters
found themselves laughing at the antics of a little girl who was not
aware that she was being observed would be rigidly censored in
any public account, and would be irrelevant in a 'scientific' account.

These details have been reported here because they represent a part of the way that the experimenters' view of the experimental results were generated. It is part of what made the existence of the phenomenon seem ridiculous at times. But it also shows how easily the experimenters were prepared to adopt such a view.

Though the account of our mirthful reactions must not be censored, it is still wrong for scientists to laugh at their victims, so perhaps some excuses would be appropriate. What must be imagined are the emotions of boredom and indignity that result from sitting cooped up in a small dark room for several hours while watching nothing of interest. All the while one has to maintain the notion that one is doing important work. This is difficult, but not impossible, for the experimenters themselves, who at least have some notion of where the work will lead. However, one cannot expect any helpers or observers, who are not so committed, to be anything but bored after an hour or so of forced attention at so mundane a scene. In such a situation, the 'Candid Camera' aspect will finally force its way through the pretence of pompous objectivity, and laughter will relieve the pent-up frustrations. It is not only the little subject who is being laughed at, but the whole incongruous situation of the little subject doing trivial things and one's respectable adult colleagues, the 'dummy observers', taking it all so seriously. Excuses aside, to reiterate, the laughter shows how the situation was being 'seen' - the experimenters would not have been laughing if they had thought there was even a remote possibility that anything paranormal was happening - and the laughter itself in turn committed the experimenters to a 'normal' view of the situation.

On 2 June Pamplin told me that he wanted to write a letter to 'Nature' saying 'more or less' that spoon-bending was fraud. He suggested that we be co-authors of the letter. This came as somewhat of a surprise to me, and at first I refused. As far as I can recollect, I did not think that we had seen anything worth reporting. That is, I did not think that the fact that a few kids had cheated when invited to bend spoons under laboratory conditions would be of interest to anybody. It seemed to me that what we should do was to continue the experiments for a reasonable length of time and if (which now seemed unlikely) we found someone who could bend spoons paranormally then we should report this. Otherwise, we had no findings to report. I felt that reporting the trivial observations we had made would make us look silly. Another, 'unscientific', subsidiary point was that I did not want to be seen as a sceptic at the outset of my sociological research project on psychokinesis, as this might damage my relationships with potential respondents. It was to transpire that my fears were unjustified on both counts. Our experiment, as has been mentioned, proved to be of interest in both public and scientific circles, trivial though it may have been. Also, as far as I can tell, having an 'experimental pedigree' did me nothing but good where fieldwork response was concerned and led into a useful further programme of participant observation. However, for the time being I said I would prefer that my name not appear on any paper Pamplin was contemplating writing.

On that date, 2 June, we visited subject 'Annie' at her home and spent two and one quarter hours while she tried unsuccessfully to bend objects. At least she did not try to cheat, even though we deliberately provided her with the opportunity to do so. On the journey back Pamplin agreed that we were now looking for cheating, rather than looking for the paranormal.

On 13 June Pamplin gave me a copy of an initial draft of a letter to 'Nature' that he had written. At first, it seemed to me that its account bore little resemblance to what we had actually done, except in principle. It was, as one might say, the 'chronological big lie'. Essentially, it described an ideal experiment to detect fraud, as though that were the experiment that we had actually done. At the time, I was somewhat shocked, and in my notes I recorded that I considered some of what Pamplin had written to be simply lies! But in retrospect, if one were conducting an experiment in physics, as Pamplin said at the time, that was precisely how it would be written up. From the point of view of the physicist, small differences in the behaviour of the humans serving the apparatus are insignificant. In the social sciences and in parapsychology, they are of the essence. This is perhaps why what came naturally to Pamplin seemed like a significant bending of the truth to me.

Much later in the project Pamplin was interviewed and asked to comment on these aspects of the published letter. He remarked:

It's not strictly accurate. . . . In the first one or two experiments no instructions of this kind were given. There's a bit of journalistic licence in the reporting of the experiment.

It is scientific licence when you are writing up something . . . you put the best light on it as a scientific and well-thought-out thing . . . and if something came to you half-way through the experiment and you didn't do it from the beginning you don't always let on, if you don't think it's material evidence to the conclusion you are drawing.

Some of the discrepancies were as follows: details of protocol that had been followed only once were described as the usual protocol (remember, only three runs in the laboratory had been conducted by this stage, and on only two subjects); it was claimed that the subjects had been *instructed* to rub the spoons between the finger and thumb of *one* hand, and *report* what they felt was happening; it was claimed that the experimenters in the room were *instructed* to measure the spoon by drawing its shape in outline on a piece of plain paper (sic) and to compare the spoon with the drawing at *roughly five-minute* intervals. If no change was observed after *twenty minutes* they were *instructed* to avert their eyes from the subject. Included in the description was the case of Sally bending the rod under her foot, which took place under none of these conditions. Indeed, the description only very approximately fitted one of the runs. The details of the careful planning and timing were imaginary. My recollection is that the drawing of the outline was Dobbs's idea on the spur of the moment and that, far from using a 'piece of plain paper', he used the back of an envelope. I noted at the time that Pamplin's account had far more rhetorical power than would the sort of account that I would give. My account would seem far less 'technocratic' and efficient and certain. But, of course, this is simply one 'principle of selection' against another, for no account can be completely accurate. Probably, to a physicist my account would seem pedantic and even misleading, to the extent that it hid the point of the exercise in petty and pointless details.

On 16 June we ran three more experiments on children recruited by Pamplin. The first run started at 1.50 p.m. and lasted until 2.30 p.m. At one point, the subject Annie claimed that the spoon had 'started to go', but examination proved that this was not the case. No bending at all took place during this session.

At 2.45 p.m., another subject, 'Alec', attempted to bend. According to my notes, at 3.20 p.m. I took a series of pictures of Alec apparently trying to bend the spoon by force in one hand. I seem to remember Alec's hand giving the appearance of strain and his looking a bit desperate, but my photographs show nothing very much. There is no record anywhere of whether or not the spoon was actually bent.

At 6.20 p.m. we tested our third subject, 'Nick', and at 6.50 p.m. I noted that I took a series of photographs of Nick with his hands under the table, apparently trying to cheat. Again, the spoon didn't actually seem to have become bent.

I wrote an 'alternative letter' for 'Nature' and passed it to Pamplin on 18 June, remarking that I would be much happier with it than with the one he had written. I tried to construct some sort of compromise in my letter. It contained a paragraph explaining that our experiments did not show that all cases of the Geller effect were cheating, and, what is more, we considered that in our later experiments, where we were expecting cheating, we had probably created an unfavourable 'psychological ambience' for the production of paranormal effects. My motivations for wanting this in were, first, my feelings about the naive inductivists we were being and, second, my desire not to be branded as a sceptic, a label which must do harm to my prospects of doing successful fieldwork. I now felt that I should co-author the letter in order to keep some control over what went into it.

My description of the experiments to date in this counter-letter started as follows:

The five subjects were examined for periods between 1 hr and 3 hrs. Two did not succeed in bending the test objects, while three succeeded by palpably normal means.

Looking at my notes, I can find no record of more than two sub-

jects who succeeded in bending the test objects, though it looks
as though there were 'good grounds' for suspecting at least four
subjects of cheating or trying to cheat. It is not now immediately
obvious where the figures in my description come from.

On 1 July Pamplin handed me a rewritten version of the intended
'Nature' piece. In this he talks of experiments with six subjects,
anticipating the results of the next experiment arranged for 24
July. This version included many of the technocratic details of
the first version, but claimed that of the six subjects (he called
them A, B, C, D, E and F) only:

> A put the rod under her foot and bent it, B used both hands
> quickly while the experimenter turned away, and D put both
> hands under a table to bend his spoon out of sight of the exper-
> imenters. The only examples of bending observed in the labora-
> tory were achieved by such palpably normal methods.

Thus Pamplin's account here agrees with mine as far as our claims
of who cheated is concerned, but there is no record in my notes
that the child whom Pamplin called D (Nick) actually succeeded
in bending anything.

Pamplin's laboratory notebook, which he was kind enough to
allow me to make use of, makes the issue clearer. He suggests
that at one time I commented aloud during the experiment on subject Annie, the subject of whom I have just written as the one
who did not even attempt to cheat. His report of this comment
reads, 'Harry reported [Annie] attempting to bend it with one
hand on her leg.' Going back to my notes I now find the following:

> 2.20 [Annie] says it's starting to go [bend] after picture [taken]
> of bending against leg. BUT HAS NOT [bent] IN FACT.

It looks very much as though I eventually interpreted our first
case of a child not succeeding at bending the object at all as a
case of her not attempting to cheat even though I had prima-facie
evidence, and a rather good photograph, of what looked like an
unsuccessful attempt at cheating. This evidence now looks at least
as good as the evidence in the other two cases that afternoon, but
for the other two I did not read back their lack of success as
showing they did not try to cheat. I am not sure why this is, but
it certainly is the case that Annie had become a 'subject who did
not try to cheat'. To stress the point, on the evidence of the experiments as far as can be reconstructed from experimental notebooks, Annie was only one among three who did not succeed in
bending spoons. However, the notebooks record what looked to
us, at the time, like attempts to cheat by all three. Clearly, our
assessment of what was taking place was based on social cues
that were not recorded in our notebooks.

Further, Pamplin's notebook contains outline drawings of the
spoons at the beginning of the experiments, against which he
checked the spoons from time to time to see whether they had

actually bent. Neither Annie's nor Alec's spoons show any change, but the drawing for Nick (his D) is as shown in Figure 5.2. As can be seen, the bend is very slight, scarcely detectable, and quite unlike the obvious bends we have seen in other cases. But it looks as though Pamplin is counting this as a 'normal' bend produced by fraud, along with the other two cases of 'obvious' fraud in his account of the experiments.

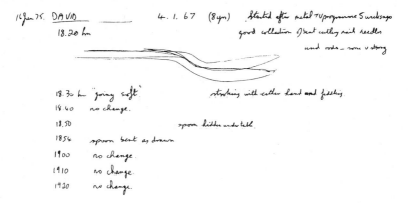

Figure 5.2

I agreed to Pamplin's account, but asked for it to be shortened and for something about 'psychological ambience' (which had been cut out) to be left in.

On 24 July we ran an experiment on another subject, 'Gay'. I recorded that I was somewhat bored and not at all excited by the prospect of the forthcoming run. We started at 3.45 p.m. At 3.58 p.m. I noted 'what looks like an attempt at forcing with both hands using thumb pressure'. At 4.06 p.m. subject claims that spoon has 'gone'. But Dobbs, in the room, checks it against his outline drawing and says it hasn't.

4.07 p.m.   Spoon bent in both hands.
4.08 p.m.   SAME AGAIN. Caught it [with camera].
4.09 p.m.   Shows it to Dobbs amid great exclamation from all.
At 4.14 p.m. and again at 4.17 p.m. these events were repeated.

We decided to enter the experimental area and tell Gay that we had been watching, and what we had seen. After denying that she had been cheating, Gay continued trying to bend one of our test rods. I recorded that she had an 'amazing amount of face' and that 'OBVIOUSLY WE ALL KNOW NOTHING WILL HAPPEN'.

On 3 August Pamplin showed me another draft of the account of the experiment. The psychological ambience point was still left out of the account, but I decided to let well alone. Later when we interviewed Pamplin, we asked him why he had dropped the section about psychological ambience. He remarked:

> I can only really say that I didn't like it. I didn't analyse more
> deeply than that. Now if you ask me to, I can, I think. I would
> say that you're writing this for a scientific journal called
> 'Nature', not a psychological journal, plus my ignorance of
> psychological terminology. . . . I thought I'd leave that out and
> send the version back to you. . . . I tried to be as accurate as
> I could without being pedantic . . . and this one here didn't
> strike me as a point I wanted to make so I didn't put it in.

What worried me still more was that Pamplin had started to talk
about the experiments to the local press. Apparently he had told
the local paper about our one-way mirror set-up.

On Thursday 4 September I was surprised to discover my name
along with a description of our experiments on the front page of
the 'Guardian'. It seemed that 'Nature' had published our letter
that day, and it had been picked up by the press at large. When
I arrived at the university I found the building full of reporters
and cameramen with Pamplin being interviewed, apparently, by
several people at once. I was in demand for copies of the still
photographs I had taken, and later that day was telephoned by
the BBC and invited to confront Professor John Taylor in the
'Nationwide' programme that evening. I agreed, for I wished to
meet Taylor, potentially our most important respondent, and I
wanted to try to 'cool him out', that is, to make it clear that I
was not a complete sceptic by any means.

The printed letter to 'Nature' was reproduced on page 91. It
is going to be discussed as an artifact in itself. In order to make
the point properly, of course, it would be necessary to reproduce
the whole issue of 'Nature', with its crisp but conservative cover,
its rich black print on shiny pages, its understated, ceremonial
presentation of learned articles whose very titles are incomprehensible except to those in the appropriate specialised field. All
of these are the outward signs of a tradition of authority in
matters pertaining to knowledge. However, what is important for
the moment is to note that Pamplin and Collins were claiming that
they had witnessed cheating in all cases except that of Annie.
But in going through my notebooks and Pamplin's notebook in
order to write this chapter I found, as I have pointed out, that
at least one more of the subjects did not actually bend objects in
the laboratory (according to the notebooks) and one other produced only the slightest of bends. In fact, only half the subjects
cheated in any 'gross' fashion, that is, in a fashion which required a minimum of interpretative discretion.

The publication of the 'Nature' paper will be used as a punctu-
ation mark in the description of the experiments. More experiments
were done after this, but the circumstances were different. For
instance, Pamplin more or less dropped out of the series, and
some of the later experiments were done in collaboration with
other scientists such as Professor Taylor and Professor Hasted.

Also, the experiments were different in so far as the secret of the one-way mirror was no longer a secret. In the next chapter points will be drawn from the later experiments (in most of which Pinch took part) as illustrative material in the reanalysis of the experiments described above.

END NOTE

At the beginning of this chapter it was suggested that many different accounts of the same experimental series were possible. In the chapter an account which reveals glossing procedures, and thereby gives rise to an impression of sloppiness, has been contrasted with the scientific account. It was suggested at the beginning that it should always be possible to produce a 'sloppy-looking' account of any piece of scientific work.

One thing that corroborates this suggestion is the treatment of experiments by critics and proponents of paranormal phenomena. A major technique for revealing 'inadequacies' in the work reported by parapsychologists' laboratories has been painstaking reconstruction of the day-to-day events which took place during the carrying out of experiments later to be reported in published form (see, for example, Hyman, 1977; Randi, 1975; and Wilhelm, 1976). However, as will be seen in this chapter and the next, it is no surprise to find that very close attention to laboratory procedure can precipitate accounts which make claimed findings seem far less well-founded. The reason that this is not obvious is that most experiments are not subject to this kind of detailed examination. For example, journalists do not watch experiments in physics or psychology being done, nor do they try to reconstruct them critically. It is suggested here that if they were to do so they could discover the same sorts of uncertainties as they find in parapsychological experiments. This has to do with the way that accounts are constructed. It may be of significance that no such painstaking examination was made of the Bath experiments by the critics (see end of next chapter for examples). They were happy to accept the account at face value, although it was, as has been shown, at least as open to rewriting as most parapsychological experiments.

One other research project has been recently carried out, the results of which seem to engage with the above argument. Latour and Woolgar (1979) have studied the way that claims about the existence of phenomena in a biology laboratory change in style as the phenomena become accepted or 'objectified'. In a valuable and original section of their work they use a case study to show that types of statement about the existence of some phenomenon or relationship can be divided into several categories. Some of these categories contained 'statements about other statements', which they refer to as 'modalities'. They write (Latour and Woolgar, 1979, p. 78):

A statement clearly takes on a different form when modalities drop. Thus, to state, 'The structure of GH.RH was reported to be X' is not the same as saying, 'The structure of GR.RH *is* X'.

Latour and Woolgar distinguish a range of modalities which can broadly be associated with the 'facticity' of the phenomenon or the relationship being discussed. At the least-factlike end of the spectrum they found modalities such as are included in the following statements (ibid., p. 79):

1   Peter (ref.) has suggested that in goldfish the hypothalamus has an inhibitory effect on the secretion of TSH.
2   There is also this guy in Colorado. They claim that they have got a precursor for H. . . . I just got the preprint of their paper.

Latour and Woolgar's work seems to strike a chord with what is being suggested here. Minute re-examination of laboratory practice is bound to lead to a reintroduction of modalities into scientific discourse about the paranormal phenomena under discussion. The modalities may then be of an extremely 'soft' kind which tend to reduce the facticity of the phenomenon. Minute examination of laboratory practice will change statements from the form

The mechanism of remote viewing is related to that of clairvoyance

to the form

Jones, who is a short-sighted scientologist, has foolishly claimed that Geller, the stage magician, was able to see the Hoover Tower on 20 September without looking at it. He has since related this ability to what equally gullible parapsychologists call clairvoyance. Actually, on 20 September Jones had a serious head cold that impaired his sight even further, and was not even aware that seven of Geller's associates were in the room during the whole time that the experiment was being carried out. (See Collins and Pinch, 1979, for real examples.)

Thus, re-examination of laboratory procedures, through the reintroduction of 'soft' modalities into scientific discourse, reduces the facticity of the phenomena under discussion. This is a more systematic way of talking about the appearance of 'sloppiness' than can be given to any experiment by reconstructing the appropriate account. On the other hand, the treatment given to psi phenomena by critics is of such a radical nature that the term 'sloppiness' more accurately describes the transformation obtained than does the 'reintroduction of modalities'.

6 PARANORMAL METAL BENDING AT BATH
Using the past in making the present

Chronological and methodological lies in constructing the scientific account of experiment – inductive jumps – ignoring environmental factors – deciding what had 'really' been seen – ambiguity of individual pieces of evidence – taken-for-granted background knowledge as determinant of interpretation of evidence – other peoples' interpretations and descriptions of the Bath experiments

LEVELS OF CONSTRUCTION OF A SCIENTIFIC ARTIFACT

1 *Chronological and methodological lies*

As has been suggested, at the time of publication Collins felt that the paper published in 'Nature' did not quite reflect his reservations about the generality of the conclusions that could be drawn from the experiments; nevertheless, it reflected pretty well Pamplin's and Collins's feelings about what had been observed. Collins's reservations about the conclusions were of two types. These were firstly some essentially 'studied, intellectual' reservations – perhaps pedantic – over whether the experimenters were not being naive inductivists in giving a general interpretation to what had been seen in only five instances, and whether they had really given the 'phenomena' a chance to appear in their unfavourable experimental set-up. But the terms in which these reservations were cast were not really 'scientific', but rather 'philosophical'. If Collins's wider interests had not included unscientific things such as the problem of induction, he would probably not have thought about them in this context. After all, it is important for a scientist to be a naive inductivist that is, to believe what he sees.

Collins's other type of reservation concerned the impact that the paper would have on potential respondents, and here the interest was definitely illegitimate. Thus, when all was said and done, intellectual reservations aside, the paper reflected what Pamplin and Collins felt, namely, that the phenomenon of 'spoonbending' was a fraud and that they had gone some way toward showing it.

To say this clearly and concisely required a 'chronological lie'. That is, it required the description of the experiment as an ideal fraud-detection experiment, and it required the claim that Pamplin and Collins had caught nearly everyone cheating. Also, it required them not to spell out in detail exactly what was meant by cheating, or exactly how the term had been operationalised. It therefore required the experimenters not to be concerned that Collins had remarked that he had observed what he thought was Annie trying to bend a spoon against her leg and that he had observed Alec in a broadly similar piece of behaviour, but that the two pieces of behaviour had eventually been interpreted as different actions, one not cheating, and the other cheating. And it required that Pamplin and Collins not mention that one of the pieces of spoon-bending was so slight as to be ambiguous.

Now, putting this in terms of a failure to operationalise what was meant by cheating is itself a retrospective reconstruction of a piece of 'sloppiness' which was not evident at the time. Remember that the experimenters did not set out to discover cheating. Consequently, an exact definition of cheating did not seem to matter. Now these actions can be explained in more 'objective' terms. It can be said, for example, that the experiments crossed certain boundaries between physical and human science. Paranormal metal bending seems to be a physical phenomenon, and so does normal metal bending. But the idea of cheating refers to an internal state, to a human intention without externally observable correlates. Thus, as physical scientists, the experimenters might feel confident in most cases to make statements about whether or not a spoon had bent, but they could not read the intention behind such events in an unambiguous way. Hence, attributions of cheating were made not purely on the basis of observation. They were made on the basis of observation and understanding of subjects' actions. (This will be still more clear in the discussion under section 4 of this chapter.) In terms of this retrospective model of our experiments, it is not entirely surprising that it is not possible to reconstruct, from recorded observations in notebooks, the way that the description 'cheat' was attributed to subjects.

The description must have emerged from more than simple laboratory observations. It certainly emerged from observations that included those made outside the laboratory. None of this makes the 'Nature' account 'incorrect' but it is more complicated than it seems at first sight. The paper exemplifies scientific rhetoric appropriately applied.

2 *Adventures in induction*

At a more profound level than methodological fictionalising is the deception of self and others regarding the generality of the findings. That is the deception involved in the rule-of-thumb solution to the problem of induction. This deception is normal scientific practice.

Three to five cases of cheating had been witnessed, that is, three to five cases of young people bending cutlery or other objects by physical force when they were supposed to be doing it by paranormal means. Now, only six children of the hundreds who claim to be able to produce the feat had been observed, yet, on this basis, the experimenters felt in themselves that they had seen all that was necessary to draw a conclusion. More claimants could have been tested but since the experimenters had 'known what they were going to see' in the last two or three cases before they even did the experiment, it seemed pointless to go further. In any case, where does one stop? At some point prior to examining all possible cases one must stop and say what has been found (see Collins (1976; p. 17), for the same point in a different context). As remarked above, Collins thought that the experiments had stopped too early, and were rather trivial. But Collins, it seems, was proved wrong by the public reaction. (Of course, Collins did go on to do more experiments, but - see below - the driving force here was firstly, the remote hope of finding something positive and, secondly, the sociological project behind the series.)

The experimenters, then, had been adventurous. They had glossed three to five cases as all the cases there were. But, of course, there was another layer of gloss beneath this, for the experimenters only saw the subjects attempting to bend the spoons on a small number of the total set of occasions when they had bent spoons. All (or nearly all) the subjects had a collection of twisted and battered cutlery and other objects which they had bent 'paranormally' on other occasions when they had not been under laboratory observation. This paranormal bending was quite a normal feature of their everyday lives, so they claimed. Thus one might say that our inductive adventures were adventurous to the power 2.

3 *Environmental escapades*
Following the second stage of 'inductive adventure' is the serious matter of the peculiar conditions under which this inductively insignificant set of observations were made. Not only were the observations few, they were also 'untypical'. Most bendings, it was claimed, took place in the familiar surroundings of the subjects' own homes, and most were not observed by anybody other than the subject. To find out whether paranormal bending takes place, a set of instances of 'attempts at paranormal bending under laboratory conditions in the presence of observers some of whom were concealed' had been examined. The experimenters' feeling, that spoon-bending was fraudulent, rested on the assumption that the obvious change in conditions between the subjects' homes and the laboratory was not relevant to the outcome of the experiment. It was implied that these variables could not be counted as relevant experimental parameters.

However, one of the subjects, who was confronted with the evidence of her cheating, claimed that this variable was relevant. She admitted that she had cheated in the laboratory. She said that she found herself unable to bend the spoons under laboratory conditions and so, not wishing to displease the experimenters and make them feel that she had completely wasted their time, she cheated. This subject did not cheat until her third visit to the laboratory, and around her sixth hour under observation, so one

can sympathise with her feeling of being under pressure to produce something. Perhaps the experimenters should have tried to
imagine what they would have felt like if asked to produce, say,
a 'specimen' in a limited time in front of bright lights and television cameras and a panel of doctors who did not believe that
they could do it.

This, then, was one obvious set of changed parameters that
were not taken into account in drawing conclusions from findings.
The parapsychology literature could have given guidance on a
number of others. These include 'the decline effect', the hypothesised negative influence of observers on the manifestations of
psi phenomena, the negative influence of sceptics in the environment – Pamplin and Collins had certainly become sceptics after a
short while – and the hypothesised general inaccessibility of psi
phenomena to scientific investigation.

Of course, there are an infinite number of non-obvious variables
which were not counted as relevant parameters. Who knows what
are the relevant variables in experiments connected with psi
phenomena (Collins, 1976), or in any experiment (Collins, 1974,
1975)? Perhaps Pamplin and Collins should have looked carefully
at the ambient temperature, the number of women over sixty-five
within twenty miles of the laboratory, or the depth of snow on
the nth plant of some star in another galaxy. None of these
matters was allowed to disturb the conclusions drawn.

4   *Seeing is believing*
Given that observations were made of a statistically insignificant
number of occasions on an insignificant number of subjects (not
that seeing more would have solved this problem), under extremely
untypical, and possible unfavourable, circumstances, and reported
in of necessity an 'objective' fashion, is it possible to be sure
of what was seen on even those occasions? The answer, at a
superficial level, is 'no'. It is 'no' at a more profound level, too.

At a superficial level the experimenters could report difficulties in making up their own minds about what they were seeing.
Though at the time of the experiments they could often feel certain of what had been seen, it was found that this certainty would
soon fade, especially in the face of the arguments of a believer.
In these circumstances, the experimenters would need to refer
back to 'artifacts' – still photographs – to reassure themselves
that cheating had really been observed. Recall now the argument
in the car between Collins and Dobbs over what had occurred on
one of the visits to a subject's house. Collins reasoned then that,
if it was not possible to persuade others about the evidence, the
experimenters could not be sure of staying persuaded themselves
over a long period. Sometimes, when the experiments were discussed with others, the photographs would be shown to 'prove'
that the experimenters' own observations were valid. But often
the experimenters were surprised to find (they became less surprised as the experience repeated itself) that others would not
be particularly impressed with the pictures, seeming to be fully

satisfied only with the ones showing one of the subjects actually
bending down to place the specimen under her foot. Thus, the
following conversation took place between Collins (C) and one
scientist respondent (H). Collins and Pinch were in H's office,
discussing the question of cheating, while leafing through
Collins's laboratory notebook in order to show copies of the still
photographs to H. At this time, H's response came as a surprise.

1 C: [Indicating one of the pictures] That's being bent by
       manual force.
2 H: Where is the object?
3 C: In between the two hands. It's a spoon held like that
       [indicates].
4 H: What is that doing? I mean . . .
5 C: That is bending it. I mean, the experimenter in the
       room is looking away – this is at a moment when she's
       got hold of the thing, got both hands, and is going like
       that. The end of the spoon would be just about under
       that finger there.
6 H: You know, I find it a little bit difficult to accept that
       one because the muscles are all relaxed round there.
7 C: Well, possibly it's not . . .
8 H: I'll tell you one thing, that if it is a force bend, it is
       of unbelievable subtlety because she's looking the other
       way, so to speak.
9 C: Oh yeah! [knowingly] That's no problem [sniggers].
       Um! . . . I wonder if . . . Do you know this girl by
       any chance?
10 H: No.
       [C names girl, H repeats that he doesn't know her.]
11 C: For her I'd bet any money you like that everything that
       she has ever done is a cheat.
[Pause]
12 H: [Looking at another photograph] What's that? That's a
       thumb on top, is it?
13 C: Yeah, that's her thumb from her right hand.
14 H: Yes, yes, that does look a bit messy.
15 C: There's [names subject] again having another bash.
16 H: No, I don't accept these.
17 C: Well, O.K.
18 H: That one, that one might be one, actually. But that one
       doesn't . . .
19 C: I mean, I think you're quite justified in the sense of
       saying that the photographs themselves. . . . No [look-
       ing at other photographs] . . . I don't think either of
       these. These just show what – in fact, we decided in
       the end that this girl had not cheated and had not bent
       a spoon.

Here, in statement 1, C claims that the photograph he is pointing out shows a clear case of cheating. By statement 5 he is

forced into spelling this out by H's unexpected reaction. By 7 he
is prepared to concede that the photograph is not as unambiguous
as he had thought. By 11, he is having to resort to arguments
quite separate from the evidence of the photograph to make his
point. By 17, C has conceded for another photograph. By the
first half of 19, C has conceded that the use of still photographs
as evidence on their own is not unambiguous. He is about to go
on to say that 'nevertheless, if the photographs are read in conjunction with the notebook, their evidence becomes overwhelming'.
He is interrupted in making this final point because H is looking
at the photograph of subject Annie, the 'one who didn't cheat'.
This photograph shows what Collins thought at the time was
Annie's attempt to cheat by pressing the spoon against her leg
(as mentioned on page 106). To H, the evidence in that photograph
is comparable with that in the others, so Collins hastens to point
out to him that this was not to be counted as evidence. That was
what 'we had decided in the end'.[1]

The same points could be made through examining the use of
videotapes as evidence. The 'natural conversational' evidence in
this example comes from an experimental run performed in the
series that followed the publication of the 'Nature' paper. Here,
Collins, Pinch and others had performed observations during the
course of an afternoon on a subject brought to our laboratory by
Professor Taylor.

On this occasion the notes were made by Pinch. At one point,
Pinch, P (Dr Pamplin), John Taylor, Eduardo Balanovski and
Collins were behind the one-way screen. Pinch's notes record:

P says: 'Bent by force.' (Taylor and Balanovski were playing
with video camera.) Taylor says we can go back.

Thus, one of the party had seen and commented on a bend by
force and the rest of the party had not been watching, since it
was decided to check back on the videotape.

Later, Pinch again notes:

She bent it with both hands . . . 17 [this records the time on
the filmed clock]. P noticed it . . . she used both hands.

Pinch's notes show that by the end of the session all the experimenters were sceptical.

After the subjects had left, the observers spent some time
looking back through the videotape. The tape-recorder which had
been used during the experimental session was left on by accident
and it recorded the discussion. None of the experimenters were
aware of this at the time. The transcript shows the difficulty
experienced in picking out from the videotape the section which
shows unambiguous cheating. Thus, one section of the transcript
reads as follows (the videotape is running the whole time and the
experimenters are commenting on it):

Taylor:	It's pretty hard to see.
Pinch:	There's a bend there.
Taylor:	No.
Collins:	No.
Taylor:	No bending there.
[Pause]	
Collins:	I wouldn't like to swear on that one.
Taylor:	No.
[Pause]	
Taylor:	Here we go.
Taylor:	No.
Pinch:	No.
[Pause]	
Collins + Pinch:	. . . and there.
Taylor:	It's not bent yet.
[Pause]	
Taylor:	What about there?
Balanovski:	Yes. Yes.
Taylor:	Has it gone yet? It's not bent.
Balanovski	Yes. Yes.
Taylor:	No, it's not bent, it's not bent.

After some considerable discussion of this sort it was eventually agreed that at least one bend by force had been seen but there was general confusion over whether more than one had been seen. Also, it was not clear that the one that had been seen corresponded to the records in the notebooks. Certainly the motivation for looking again and again through the tape is to be found in the experimenters' recorded certainty that they had seen cheating with their own eyes. They knew that they had seen it because they had recorded the fact in written form!

Some ten months later Pinch and Collins looked at the same videotape again. On that occasion they agreed that they were able to spot one 'force-bend' early in the recording, and they felt fairly certain about another. However, they could not find one that should have been there, according to the earlier transcript, at time 13. And, between what appeared to be the last possible force-bend and the end of the tape, the spoon seemed to have become bent still more. Collins and Pinch decided, finally, that in order to make absolutely certain whether or not the spoon was more or less bent by the end of the tape it would be necessary to take still photographs of various points of the video display and compare those!

These episodes show the way that what counts as evidence of cheating becomes 'negotiated' during discussions, and that a quest for absolute certainty develops into an unending regressive search for new artifacts to reinforce earlier ones. This, then, is the process of glossing 'what-we-really-saw', which goes on at a superficial level. This process is involved when observers come to agree that they had seen movements consonant with cheating - movements that looked like cheating.

At a less superficial level are the glossing processes involved
in deciding that movements consonant with cheating really are
cheating. The episodes described above show that the mere movements could not be unambiguous, for part of the decision-making
process involved checking to see whether the spoons had actually
bent during the apparent cheating period. Precisely the same
'cheating' movements could not be counted as 'force-bending' if
no bending had taken place. But, of course, where bending did
take place, all agreed that movements that were agreed to look
like cheating were in fact cheating. One of the subjects, who was
confronted with evidence of her cheating, disagreed with this interpretation. The following extract records the discussion as Pamplin
and Collins entered the experimental area toward the end of that
day's session:

4.18 p.m.
P: We've been watching you, 'J'.
J: Have you?
P: Yes, and we saw you do this with both hands when they
    [the dummy observers] weren't watching. [Indicates crude
    bending action.]
J: Oh. Didn't know that.
P: [Laughter of the 'caught-you-out' variety.]
J: Well, I wasn't only bending it by force.
P: You weren't?
J: No.
P: It really did go because you were holding it, you think?
J: Yes, yes - I do that sometimes when I change hands but it
    doesn't mean I bend it by force.
P: I see.
    [Non-relevant discussion]
P: [Indicating another of the test objects already bent] You've
    certainly bent that one, 'J', haven't you?
J: Yes, yes. You sometimes have to go like that [indicating
    cheating motion] to get bits of dirt off it.
P: Hm [understandingly].[2]

Naturally, Pamplin and Collins took the subject's comments for
dissembling, but they show that these same movements may be
interpreted in different ways. But what if the subject had agreed
immediately that she had been cheating and that she had been
'caught out'? Would this enable the experimenters to say that she
was unequivocally cheating and that no glossing on their part had
been required? The answer is 'no', for if it can be accepted that
one sort of answer is dissembling, then it can be accepted that
another might be. Perhaps, for devious reasons, the subject had
bent the spoon paranormally but had decided that she should conceal the fact, and disguise the event as fraud! Perhaps she did
not know what category of event it was herself!
    Thus, observation of instances of cheating required, firstly,
that some agreement was negotiated among the experimenters as

to which instances were consonant with genuine cheating and, secondly, that the experimenters would interpret or gloss that agreed set of movements as cheating. The whole of this discussion so far has been cast in terms of the glossing practices involved in classifying some set of movements as signifying fraud. This slant to the discussion is inevitable because the artifact that was finally produced out of these practices – the 'Nature' paper – claimed that the experimenters had seen fraud. But if the paper had claimed that they had seen the genuine phenomenon, then this discussion would have had the opposite slant, aiming to reveal the glossing practices involved in coming to that conclusion.

5 *The priority of the past*
At all the above stages it would have been possible to make other decisions or to refuse to go through with the glossing processes involved in the generation of the final conclusions that, first, fraud had been observed and, second, most or all cases of claimed paranormal bending were due to fraud. Probably, the stage of glossing that seemed most unrealistic to describe as 'glossing' was the last one. This was the stage at which, though all were agreed that they had seen movements consonant with cheating, they had to agree that 'this really was' cheating. Was it not obvious at this point that cheating had occurred, and is it not ridiculous to point to the glossing practices involved there?
For the purposes of a sociological view, the answer is no, and what is more, for the sake of completeness it is necessary to point out that, even to get to the stage of agreeing that there was something to be explained, prior agreements had to be entered into and prior procedures tacitly accepted. For example, it had to be accepted that what was seen from one side of the one-way screen was representative of what was happening on the other side – that, for instance, semi-silvered glass, not to mention glass of any sort, did not distort 'reality'. For example, the glass might have distorted our view in such a way that paranormal bending on one side appeared to be cheating on the other side.[3] In short, the experimenters were working with an implicit and tacitly accepted theory of glass. Without labouring the point, they were working also with unmentioned – and it would have been ridiculous to mention them – theories of camera lenses, TV tubes and film emulsions, electric lights, spoons, pens, tables and chairs, other peoples' upbringings, their intentions, and their comprehension of statements. In short, to have any confidence in observational procedures and procedures for coming to agreements about what had been witnessed, what has to be accepted is that version of the past that is part of our taken-for-granted reality.
Now it is easy to see that some of this past, the bits associated with the technological equipment, emerged through processes of negotiation akin to the processes that were pursued in deciding that cheating rather than paranormal bending had been witnessed in these experiments. For example, at some time or another, some-

one had to invent a film emulsion and agree that, when used in certain ways, it could produce an image of reality in which certain relationships were truly and permanently captured, so that they could be observed long after the original subject of the photograph had gone away. Further, it has to be accepted that the film image can tell the observer at any time in the future about relationships in the recorded event. (There is no reason to stick to procedures involving technical equipment in making this kind of point; it is just that it is easier to see in that context.)

Thus, the experimenters' glosses depended on the outcome of others' past glosses, and in the future others' glosses will depend on ours!

A major input to all these procedures is the way of thinking that led to the phenomenon under investigation being called 'paranormal', that is, not normally present and therefore not to be expected. This can, of course, explain to some extent the outcome of the glossing procedures that is found above. It should not be hard to imagine how the outcome of these procedures would have differed if the inputs had been different. If, for instance, fraud was almost unknown and 'paranormal' spoon-bending was the normal way to deform cutlery, then perhaps the experimenters would have understood what was happening to their spoons in a different way. In these circumstances, the absence of gross bending effects would not necessarily have been taken to signify the absence of psychokinetic forces at work (see next chapter) but, if it had been so taken, the experimenters would then have had to search for the conditions which made this subset of instances exceptional rather than normal. It would have had to be assumed that something was wrong with the experimental arrangements. The experimenters would look to see if, perhaps, one of the experimenters or technicians had a personality profile inimical to the production of psi. Alternatively, the subjects might be unwell. Certainly, the experiment would be counted as defective in some way and it could not possibly support the generalisation that there was no such thing as psi. If psychokinesis were normal, it is inconceivable that the observation of half-a-dozen instances when it did not appear could cast even a minute fraction of doubt on its existence.

Perhaps the value that the experiment would be seen to have would be in its discovery of the propensity of young people, when they believed themselves to be observed, to disguise their psychokinetic abilities as the use of physical force. Psychologists might make something of this. Perhaps they would say it shows that young people, around the onset of puberty, like to fantasise about amazing physical powers which make it unnecessary to use mental powers to manipulate the material world. In such circumstances, it would be difficult to design an experiment to reveal, unambiguously, the use of physical force!

In the next chapter it will be argued that it is because different scientists do see different phenomena as natural, and in particular because, for certain reasons, some see the paranormal

explanation as the natural one, it is possible for different interpretations to be produced, not only of Pamplin's and Collins's
experiment, but of other experiments. It will be argued that if
this possibility is understood then it can be seen why the Geller
enigma is not resolvable by the unproblematic application of a
routine scientific method.

OUR PRESENT AS OTHERS' PAST

A little of the future has happened since the report of the experiment was published, and one can now begin to see how it may
affect the glossing procedures of others in certain cases. Here is
first-hand knowledge of the method of construction of a little bit
of the present, and it is now possible to see how this fragile
tissue becomes a part of others' past.

The Editor of 'Nature', on receiving the manuscript, promised
to publish it prominently in the correspondence columns. He
commented, in his letter to Pamplin, 'What a fascinating experiment.
Why on earth haven't we done it before?' The BBC brought Collins
and Professor John Taylor together to talk about the experiment
on the programme 'Nationwide', on the day the letter was published, introducing the confrontation as follows:

> If you've always expected a touch of trickery in those Uri
> Geller spoon-bending feats, you could be right. A science maga-
> zine feature today reveals that a series of experiments amongst
> six children, who claim to be little Uri Gellers, showed that
> five of them had cheated anyway.

Several newspapers mentioned the experiment, responding in a
variety of ways. For instance, the 'Guardian' suggested that:

> Believers in the Uri Geller method of bending spoons by stroking
> them have received a nasty blow. Research at Bath University
> on children who claimed to be capable of the feat has revealed
> that they cheated.

Other papers gave more prominence to the reactions of parents,
Uri Geller and others who claimed the experiments were 'nasty'
or 'sneaky' for 'spying' on little children.

It was soon clear that the experiment was perceived as having
been intended to discover fraud, not the paranormal, and as having discovered fraud in an elegant and effective way. On 'Nationwide' Taylor went so far as to suggest:

> Well, I think the first question I would raise was why, in fact,
> was cheating encouraged? It was said just now and in the letter
> in 'Nature', that indeed the observers were required to relax
> when they were watching the child, to turn away. I suppose
> the problem is: how many children will cheat in a situation of

this sort where they think they can get away with it?

This view of the experiment was general among respondents, whether they viewed it with favour or not. When Collins explained that the initial intention really was to film paranormal phenomena with the cameras hidden so as to avoid disturbing the subject, one respondent replied 'I find that a bit implausible'.

Of course, respondents were entitled to draw these conclusions from the written account. Although, in 'Nature', Pamplin and Collins had stated that their intention had been 'to obtain a photographic or videotaped record of the actual moment of bending', this phrase could be interpreted in different ways. Later in the letter Pamplin and Collins wrote that 'We cannot, of course, conclude that all instances of the so called Geller Effect are due to cheating', but most respondents assumed that the experimenters were simply covering themselves. As one respondent put it, 'It's pure logic.' What is more, in later days, especially when Collins was being congratulated on doing such a good definitive experiment, he tended to forget that it hadn't been designed in that way from the beginning. If it had not been for the sociological cross-current running beneath the work Collins would probably now be happy to think of himself as 'one of the scientists who was instrumental in proving that the Geller effect was fraud'. As Collins's present slipped into his past, it could easily have become reified into the same sort of artifact for him as it was for sceptics.

The reactions of two other named respondents will be mentioned, for they were later to write about the experiment. Martin Gardner had already been told something of the initial motivation by other respondents by the time he was interviewed by Collins. However, he admitted that it had not occurred to him when he first read of the experiment that Pamplin and Collins were looking for anything other than cheating. Philip Morrison had come across the account of our experiment by chance while reading 'Nature'. Upon Collins introducing himself in Morrison's MIT office, he offered immediate congratulations on the experiment, saying that Pamplin and Collins had 'done a great job' and showed 'what we'd been hoping all the time was true'. He thought of it as a careful, 'second-by-second' experiment, and when Collins asked what he thought was the purpose of the experiment Morrison replied, 'I thought it was a direct test – challenge – to the accounts of Taylor.' Gardner and Morrison have written two of the three pieces to be found in the broadly scientific press which make reference to the experiment. All three are written by sceptics.

Gardner, in a long article in 'Technology Review' (1976) which reviewed the relationship between magicians and parapsychologists, wrote (p. 44):

Oddly, Taylor never actually *sees* anything bend, nor has he been able to capture the actual bending on video. He calls this the 'shyness effect'. Bending usually occurs only when nobody is looking. . . .

At Bath University, two psychologists [sic] designed a simple
test for six young spoonbenders. The observer was told to
relax his vigilance after 20 minutes. Rods and spoons Gellerized
all over the place while the unsuspecting children were being
secretly videotaped through one-way mirrors. In every case
where something bent, the children were seen doing the bending by 'palpably normal means'. One little girl had to put a
rod under her feet to bend it. Others held a spoon below a
table and used two hands. Taylor had not though it worthwhile
to design such a test because he had already decided that all
his children were honest.

Gardner had written a piece expressing similar sentiments in the
'New York Review of Books' of 30 October 1975 (Gardner, 1975a).
Morrison's review of a number of books in 'Scientific American'
(1976, p. 135) included the following passage:

Taylor, hopelessly misdirected by what he has 'seen', under-
takes to study metal-bending empirically. . . . His main discovery is a group of child metal-benders, who will do the Geller
bit willingly and repeatedly for Taylor. To be sure, they are
11-year-old innocents, and so he lets them go out of his sight
to bend their samples, even go home over the weekend. . . .
(as Randi quotes Taylor) 'this feature of bending not happening
when the object is being watched - "the shyness effect" - is
very common.' Common indeed! Lately a group from the University of Bath has published experiments with little volunteer
metal-benders, drawn like Taylor's from the great British pool
recruited by Geller over television. These small adepts, mainly
innocent young girls, went to work bending metal. The observer
did not see anyone cheating. But the sceptics from Bath had
taken one precaution: the room where the experiment was being
conducted was being carefully watched by several other observers through one-way mirrors from outside. Result: Five of
the six gifted youngsters cheated visibly. They hastily bent
metal by hand, tabletop and chair edge, presumably whenever
they thought the overt observer was distracted. (The sixth
subject bent no metal at all.)

Ray Hyman (1976, p. 79), reviewing Panati's book 'The Geller
Papers' in 'The Zetetic', castigates Panati for not including any
negative papers. He wrote:

The letter to *Nature* on spoon-bending experiments with six
children by Dr. Pamplin and Mr. Collins of Bath University
(4th September 1975) would certainly help to put Taylor's experiments with children and the Geller effect (i.e. the ability
of viewers of and listeners to a Geller performance to get their
broken watches to run and to bend metal) in a new light. Presumably their experiment is not mentioned because they were
able to catch each child on videotape in flagrant acts of cheating

when the min-Geller [sic] thought the observer was not watching.

All three of these authors use Pamplin's and Collins's account to persuade the reader that fraud is the most likely explanation of the Geller phenomenon. All wish to make sure that, as the 'Guardian' put it, 'Believers . . . have received a nasty blow.' Thus they juxtapose the experiment with Taylor's observations, writing of it as though it accounted for Taylor's observations as well as Pamplin's and Collins's own. Naturally, these sceptical authors include as fact the glosses used in Pamplin's and Collins's account but they have rather embellished the account for their own purposes. None of them mentions the stated reservations concerning the extent to which the conclusions could be generalised. Philip Morrison does not point out that Pamplin and Collins 'encouraged the cheating', or at least deliberately set up conditions conducive to it by 'ordering the dummy observers to avert their gaze after 20 mins'. (Collins and Pamplin did not actually do precisely this, of course, but Morrison was in no position to know that.) Hyman's comments make use of the account in a positively distorted way. He gives the impression that all of the subjects were caught cheating, not even five out of six, and, what is more, Pamplin and Collins are said to have caught the children in flagrant acts of fraud, whereas the published claim was only that they had been caught bending metal by 'palpably normal means'. The 'Concise Oxford Dictionary' defines 'flagrant' as 'glaring, notorious, scandalous' and 'palpable' as 'readily perceived by senses or mind'. Hyman also fails to mention that the experiment was designed to allow, or encourage, cheating.[4]

These accounts contrast starkly with Taylor's. As already mentioned, the point that Pamplin and Collins had encouraged, or at least allowed, their subjects to cheat was the lever used by Taylor, in his confrontation with Collins on 'Nationwide', to show that his results and those of Pamplin and Collins were not comparable. And none of the other commentators referred to what Taylor (1975b) said in a letter published in the correspondence columns of 'Nature' on 2 October 1975. There he pointed out that in his own experiments 'no more than one in six of those who claim metal bending powers . . . have been able to achieve the effect in a manner which I cannot explain by deception. This is consistent with the results of Pamplin and Collins.' Furthermore, on the basis of information provided by Collins on 'Nationwide', he wrote, 'Apparently some of the children still claimed they could spoon-bend without cheating after they had been caught' (ibid., p. 354) and he went on to suggest: 'They might still be able to do so, though only if the conditions are stringent enough will it be possible to get them to turn their attention to using any paranormal powers they possess' (ibid.).

By October 1975, probably all commentators would have agreed that Pamplin's and Collins's experiment did have some minimal impact - namely, raising the level of 'visibility' of the cheating hypothesis for young spoon-benders - but beyond that agreement stopped. Taylor pointed out the reservations and tried to gloss the 'Nature' artifact Pamplin and Collins had produced in such a way that it had little significance for the investigation of spoon-bending in general. The others treated the reservations as 'window-dressing' and took the artifact as fairly thoroughly discrediting the Geller effect. The latter manoeuvre seems to be the one that has had the widest impact.

CONCLUSION TO CHAPTERS 5 AND 6

In a sense, every human act is unique. Each time the 'same' act is performed it is performed in a slightly different way, in a different environment,[5] at a different time, by a different person, or one who is changed by virtue of being older. To point this out is to pose the problem of induction. That is, it is to ask about actors' warrants for assembling sets of these unique occurrences into generalisations. It is to ask how we see one thing as the 'same' as another (Wittgenstein, 1953). Naturally, the possibility of human discourse rests on our agreement to see sets of occurrences as the same as one another.

Experimental activity, as a species of activity in general, also consists of sequences of unique acts. To make sense of these acts it is necessary to see them as not unique. Seeing them as not unique requires that most of what could be seen as happening and most features of the environment be ignored. A scientific description is scientific to the extent that it is not anecdotal.

In these two chapters we have presented first the letter published in 'Nature', in which anecdote is almost entirely eliminated. Subsequently, we have gone some way to de-construct the 'Nature' account into its constituent acts. In chapter 5 the publication was 'unpacked' into parts described as activities in the laboratory. In chapter 6 these acts were in turn de-constructed. For example, the act of observing cheating was unpacked into the sequence of observations, assumptions and inferences out of which it was built.[6] Having unpacked this far, it was possible to see the 'Nature' paper as a certain kind of assemblage which ignored features in such a way as to support the generalisation that we had done an experiment which suggested that all cases of apparent PMB were due to cheating. Subsequently, we were able to see others repackaging the 'Nature' paper further so that it seemed to support this conclusion still more strongly. On the other hand, we were able to see Professor Taylor's repackaging of the same material to support a different conclusion.

Our general conclusion concerns the inability of experiments in themselves to legislate for the existence of any natural phenomenon. The conclusions that can be drawn from such activities depend, firstly, on a willingness to see them as generalisable and therefore as experimental[7] and, secondly, on the particular features of acts and their environment that are ignored in the generalisation process. Different conclusions will emerge from different agreements about these matters.

7 EXPERIMENT AND PARADIGM
Alternative interpretations of events and results

Outline of the argument over existence of paranormal metal bending - magicians' competence - working with apparently non-existent phenomenon - different interpretations of paranormal and orthodox experiments - objects bent inside glass vessels - retrospective psychokinesis - shyness effect - quark-detection experiment - gravity waves, psychic plants, high-energy physics - paranormal experimenter effects and their problems - theoretical solutions to experimenter-effect problem - pragmatic, working solutions - robustness of new programme of research in face of various difficulties

INTRODUCTION

In the first part of this chapter we compare normal and paranormal interpretations of a variety of experiments. The first sections of Part I concentrate on PMB while the sections which follow compare interpretations of a number of different experiments and findings. We find that self-consistent interpretations are available to support either the normal or paranormal 'world-view' in all cases.

In the second part of the chapter we discuss the problems that seem to arise as the paranormal interpretation is extended, and we look at some attempted solutions. At the end of the chapter we see that experimental activity in the new paradigm continues irrespective of these problems. Pragmatic solutions keep experimental activity going.

PART I NORMAL AND PARANORMAL INTERPRETATIONS

Criticism and response
The axes of the argument regarding the existence of paranormal spoon-bending are simple. No one disputes that spoons, forks, keys and other bits of metal have been bent by Uri Geller and others. The question is: Have they been bent paranormally? Probably all experimenters and interested scientists would now agree that on some occasions when Geller and others claimed that paranormal bending had taken place, the bending was in reality brought about by 'normal' means. As one respondent put it:

The problem we have in our discussions about Geller for

example, and in general, are, does he cheat, or does he have
real ability? And that's a false dichotomy, I think. People with
real ability will cheat to reach their goal. I can just hear the
rationalisation going on in their mind: 'Since I know I can do
it the fact that I'm faking a little bit here in order to prove the
principle of what it is I can do - there's nothing wrong with
that', and so on.

In addition, probably all observers would agree that on a further
subset of occasions, when bending was claimed to have taken
place by other than normal means, the circumstances were not
such as to *convince* a reasonable *disbeliever* that this was so, or
to *convince* a reasonable *believer* that it was not so. The argument
then devolves upon the question of whether there has been a sub-
set of occasions when it was claimed that paranormal spoon-
bending had taken place and the circumstances were such that a
reasonable sceptic would, in spite of his beliefs, be forced to
accept that paranormal bending had indeed taken place. In turn,
this argument reduces to a question of what such circumstances
would be like.
  The way that the argument has developed can be fruitfully
examined by looking at the responses to Joe Hanlon's (1974a)
critical article in the 'New Scientist', which was touched on in
chapter 2. It will be recalled that Hanlon had critically analysed
eighteen reports of incidents involving Geller's powers witnessed
by various scientists and reporters. Replies from scientists followed rapidly and were published in 'New Scientist' over a number
of weeks. On 31 October came replies from Hasted, Bohm and
Beloff among others. Hasted (1974) pointed out that his report on
the Birkbeck tests had not been intended for publication and that
it was inappropriate for a popular science magazine and a journalist to assume certain sorts of incompetence on the part of scientists on the basis of hearsay evidence: 'it might conceivably bring
into disrepute the whole process of laboratory training of the
experimental scientist at London University. Under certain circumstances it could become legally actionable.' He claimed also
that suspect performances on some occasions did not rule Geller
out as a suitable subject for laboratory investigation. Bohm (1974)
complained that Hanlon had used his informal telephone comments
out of context, in a way that misled the reader into supposing
that the Birkbeck team had sloppier controls than was the case.
  The issue of 7 November 1974 contained a letter from Ellison,
who had participated in the 'Sunday Mirror' transatlantic telepathy
test. Hanlon had claimed that Ellison had given Geller clues which
enabled him to guess the object being 'telepathically' transmitted.
Ellison (1974) said that Hanlon had misrepresented his views and
actions during the test. As far as he was concerned, he said, the
test had been a failure but at the time he had made positive encouraging remarks with the intention of setting up a friendly
atmosphere:

Experienced parapsychologists know that conditions of strong scepticism, whether overt or not, can completely inhibit the flow of material from the unconscious mind of the psychic. The investigation starts then in a positive encouraging way establishing a friendly atmosphere but without giving away information.

Ellison then pointed out that the fact that he gave guiding comments to Geller during the test, far from demonstrating the incompetence of the experimenters involved, proved nothing about experiments where success is claimed.

In the same issue Targ and Puthoff also replied and, among their comments, complained about Hanlon's use of anecdotal material to make his case, especially where such material was judged equally against the evidence of 'researchers who over a period of weeks set up carefully controlled experiments, sometimes find evidence for certain paranormal phenomena and with great caution examine the data for a year before publishing' . . . (Targ and Puthoff, 1974b).

The issue of 28 November 1974 contained long letters from Edgar Mitchell, Brendan O'Regan and Ted Bastin. The latter particularly questioned the impression of innuendo given by Hanlon's comments regarding the failure of Geller to present himself for the 'New Scientist' panel test. He claimed that 'New Scientist' could give him no evidence that its panel was better qualified to test Geller than any of the other groups of scientists engaged in such work, and suggested that in the light of the evidently biased subsequent reporting in 'New Scientist' Geller was probably right to refuse to participate.

Hanlon replied to many of these criticisms in detail, though not to the general point concerning the use of hearsay and anecdotal evidence. A sustained plank of his defence concerned the necessity of the presence of magicians to spot fraud: 'the fundamental difference between the *New Scientist* panel and those that tested Geller was that ours was the only group to include a professional magician and thus the only one that could spot possible fraud' (Hanlon, 1974b).

These exchanges by no means exhaust the debate, but typify many of its major aspects. The 'rigorous scientific testing' that had been set in train in late 1972, amid a feeling of certainty that a speedy end to speculation would soon be available, had run into a morass of claim and counter-claim. Regarding PMB, no rigorous claims had been published through the refereeing system, though one at least had been submitted (later to be turned down). What some groups of scientists considered to be rigorous conditions were not considered rigorous by others. The sceptics continued to draw analogies between laboratory testing and informal demonstrations, whereas the believers pointed to the differences between these occasions and stressed that events observed in the former could not be extrapolated to the latter. Above all, the critics continued to insist that any 'rigorous scientific testing' must take place in the presence of professional magicians in order to be worth while. A situation which seems to be typical of controversial scientific areas arose. The same experimental work was viewed differently by critics and believers, as regards its rigorousness, or demonstration of competence. In simplified terms, these views can be represented on a 'two-by-two' table (Table 7.1).

Table 7.1   Scientists' views regarding PMB experiments

| | | Scientist believes in PMB | |
		YES	NO
Experiment Claims	YES	Competent	Not
PMB	NO	Not	Competent

This state of affairs was maintained very simply in the early days of the Geller affair, since critics demanded the presence of a professional magician at any experiment which was to be counted as competent, while believers pointed out that the presence of sceptics, such as the magicians on offer, would destroy any likelihood of the appearance of the effect. To be a good experimental test of PMB an ambience had to be created which would foster the production of the effect, but the creation of this ambience required conditions that rendered the experiment inadequate for the sceptics. Later, one or two professional magicians endorsed the effects, and Targ and others pointed out that they were themselves trained in stage magic. However, at this point, the critics questioned the magical competence of Targ and the others, refusing to accept them into their category of 'magician licensed to legitimise a spoon-bending experiment'. (See the letters from and pertaining to 'Artur Zorka' in Panati, 1976.) Another similar table could be drawn up dividing critics' and believers' views as to the competence of magicians (Table 7.2).

Table 7.2   Scientists' views regarding magicians

| | | Scientist believes in PMB | |
		YES	NO
Magician claims PMB	YES	Not	Competent
is fraud	NO	Competent	Not

The paths into which the believers were led are nicely illustrated in a contribution to 'Nature' which appeared in the issue of 10 April 1975. This piece, written by Hasted, Bohm, Bastin, O'Regan and Taylor, included the following comment (p. 471):

> We have come to realise that in this domain the experimental situation is different in certain crucial ways from that which has been common in scientific experimentation. This is because the phenomena under investigation have to be produced from the minds of one or more of those who participate. Relationships among the participants therefore play a much more crucial role than is usual in traditional scientific fields. These relationships have to be taken into account in a way that is somewhat similar to that needed in the disciplines of psychology and medicine. . . . [In addition to being careful experimenters] we have also to be sensitive and observant, and not to react with a preconceived pattern of tough-mindedness that will interfere with our perception and that may destroy the very possibility of the phenomena that we wish to study.

There follows a technical argument denying the competence of magicians to spot all possibilities of fraud and the comment (loc. cit.) that:

> It has been our observation, however, that magicians are often hostile to the whole purpose of this sort of investigation so that they tend to bring about an atmosphere of tension in which little or nothing can be done.

Thus, the decision which faced scientists who wished to prove the existence of PMB concerned the extent to which they would accede to the conditions demanded by extreme critics. Agreeing to stringent conditions would help them to maintain their scientific respectability, but – and this is not entirely a matter of chance, because to some extent critics' demands are determined by the assumption of normality – it would eliminate the set of (potentially) scientifically acceptable cases of PMB. Refusing to accept the full set of conditions demanded by sceptics lays the scientist open to charges of sloppiness, bias, ineptitude, senility, etc. This choice is a difficult one. This kind of problem and the solutions adopted will be discussed more fully in the next chapter, where the idea of 'authenticity' will be shown to have a role.

Life goes on
Setting this problem aside for the moment, we will explain how a scientist who believes in PMB can proceed with scientific work in the face of what could be interpreted as an absence of any phenomena at all. In other words, how is it that puzzles can continue to be solved where apparently there is no natural substance to be manipulated in experimental circumstances? As Beloff (1977) has put it, 'until we have a replicable situation, we have not got a

science, by which I mean that we have only a set of claims but no established phenomenon or effect.' The answer to this is quite simply that, so long as the existence of the phenomena is taken to be more natural than their non-existence, measurements can be continued and hypotheses tested in the absence of gross manifestations of the phenomena.

One of our respondents put the point succinctly. He remarked:

> Naturally, one's judgment about these things is strongly altered by one's knowledge that there are some effects that he [Geller] has produced that are not done by trickery. That's to say you are in a very different position if you are already convinced that he has these powers sometimes. That makes your judgment of other occasions quite different from what it would be if you hadn't that conviction. . . . You are then interested in getting a feel for the phenomena and what happens, rather than this everlasting pursuit of the ultimately unbreakable case.

Within this philosophy the route to establishment of the effect moves away from repeated demonstrations of the existence of the phenomenon toward a search for its characteristics. The need for continued verification disappears. As another respondent put it:

> Any experiment that does not yield scientific insight to the phenomena isn't worth doing. If you develop only validation experiments - to me that just ends up in more controversy. The important thing is to do experiments to discover a new phenomenon that goes beyond either a particular individual, or a particular controversy.

Not only does verification cease to be important, but once it is accepted that the phenomenon is not sufficiently well understood to allow for its gross manifestation to be repeated at will, direct observation of the phenomenon ceases to be important also. This will be the case if it is believed that at this state of the art it is only highly gifted subjects who can readily produce the effect at a level where the gross effects are visible. Perhaps early outcroppings of highly visible phenomena were just exceptionally fortunate happenings which brought scientists' attention to what is an extremely subtle and reticent effect. However, if some physical correlate of the effect is known - some physical correlate which can be measured - then the problem of the dearth of gross effects disappears. A parallel example from 'normal science' may make the point more clearly. Dreaming is such an example. It is a subtle, and non-observable, effect.

The existence of dreaming is accepted naturally because of our own experiences. The problem of doing experiments on this nonobservable effect has been solved by the correlation of rapid eye movement with dreaming. Nowadays rapid eye movement (rem) is taken by sleep researchers to signify that the subject under investigation is in fact dreaming, and so the various other correlates of dreaming behaviour can be measured and their associated puzzles can be solved. But, of course, this correlation was only established by observing rem during sleep and then waking the subject and asking whether dreaming were taking place. The association is - in the last resort - dependent on experimental subjects' claims as to whether they were dreaming or not. No such research could possibly be done if dreaming itself had to be 'observed' every time some measurement was to be made. Now only rem has to be observed. (Imagine the difficulties that would be faced by dream researchers if only a few gifted individuals ever claimed that they dreamed, and magicians were interested in showing that their claims were fraudulent!)

In the same way as with dreaming and rem, if the existence of PMB is taken as unproblematic, then the subject's word, that he or she is attempting the feat, signifies there is a good chance that any associated effects will be present, even if gross metal bending is not manifested. For example, Professor Taylor worked with the theory that the phenomena are produced by some form of electromagnetic radiation. In the laboratory Taylor's attention only needed to be on his radiation detector. The subject was asked to try to bend metal paranormally while an aerial fed electromagnetic information into the detector. Any unusual radiation could be ascribed to the metal-bending phenomenon whether or not any metal was seen to bend under tight conditions.

Professor Hasted too had used such a philosophy (at least implicitly) in reaching a stage at which he was testing complex theories. Hasted was,[1] at the time of our discussions, no longer interested in verification experiments but used complex set-ups, without any special safeguards, to measure characteristics of the wave front of the conjunction of universes by which he explained the phenomenon (see chapter 4, p. 79). As he put it:

> If he [a theoretician] can give a sheer force at a universe boundary I can map it out in detail. And I think the mapping has got to be done. I'm abandoning a lot of the more old-fashioned experiments - you know - with specimens and validation and so on, and really concentrating on mapping. I think this is what I will have to do.

Thus Hasted observed only the temporal relationship of chart recorder plots taken from an array of strain gauges hung in various positions across a laboratory room. Strain gauges can record minute effects far below the level of force that would be required to bend the metal keys, and the like, in which they were embedded. It seems - and this is the logic of the situation - the emphasis was not on safeguards against cheating, such as filming, observation or other sorts of control of the environment. There was no special need to make certain that no conceivable normal cause could be responsible for the strain-gauge readings that were used in the universe boundary-mapping operations.

Hasted was also able to learn the characteristics of the phenom-

enon from experiments done in the subjects' own homes under no
supervision whatsoever. Thus the shapes into which pieces of
metal had been bent revealed further characteristics of the wave
front. For example, a spiral effect in the bent specimens would
confirm a view that the conjunction of wave fronts, hypothesised
by Hasted, rotates in space. These experimental artifacts may be
produced under no supervision because supervision is unnecessary
where there is no reason to suspect fraud or artifice, and there
is no reason to suspect fraud or artifice if the existence of the
paranormal phenomena is natural to the scientist. In these ways,
normal science can continue with puzzles internal to the field being
pursued and solved, though to an outsider there is no science
taking place at all.

To a philosopher of science who follows Karl Popper's views the
events must seem to reveal a classic case of unfalsifiability akin
to the case of astrology. Proponents cannot agree on a procedure
that will render falsifiable the existence of the phenomenon in
which they are interested. Reasons or excuses are always provided
to explain away failures of subjects to perform in any set of circumstances. Yet, the scientists involved would not want to say
that they were not doing science. It is difficult to see what they
are doing if it is not science. The Kuhnian notion of puzzle-
solving does seem far more relevant here. The existence of the
phenomenon is not at issue to the scientists working on the problems. They do not concern themselves with this type of question.
What they do is to solve puzzles, puzzles which, from the point
of view of the outsider, are the same whether there is 'really
any phenomenon there' or not.

The foregoing descriptions should have conveyed the nature
and style of work and argument between investigators and critics
involved in the spoon-bending controversy. The last section,
describing the puzzle-solving activities available to the investigator, in spite of what would be perceived by the critic as complete
absence of phenomena, may begin to suggest the appropriateness
of certain of Kuhn's descriptions of scientific revolutionary activity
to this area of endeavour. Here indeed would seem to be a candidate for description in terms of scientists talking through each
other. Imagine the scene in a laboratory if an experiment involving
no visible effect were to take place in front of sceptics!

In the sections which follow, this theme of alternative perceptions of the same experiment will be developed. The discussion
will not stay rigidly within the boundaries of PMB but will also
show how the problem manifests itself in the wider clash between
the parapsychological community and orthodox science. Many of
the examples could very well be described in Kuhnian terms, as
showing how 'old manipulations become indices of quite different
natural regularities'.

Glass envelopes
To begin with, a recent example familiar to the authors will be
discussed. It concerns the rival interpretations of the outcome

of experiments on metal specimens enclosed within glass envelopes. One response of experimenters to continued accusations of cheating, and to the failure of subjects to perform adequately in the presence of sceptics, was to design cheat-proof experiments that could be carried out in the subjects' own homes. This requirement was fulfilled by giving the subjects specimens sealed within glass tubes, or other containers, so that the specimen could not be bent by direct application of force. The results of these tests were either that the metal did not bend or that the tubes broke. Naturally, and quite understandably, these results were interpreted by critics as demonstrating the cheating hypothesis. Indeed, one such experiment of ours was reported to the local newspaper by Dr Pamplin, our colleague, in the following sarcastic terms (Pamplin, 1976):

> Young [subject] was most annoyed at the newspaper publicity following the appearance of our article in Nature [Pamplin and Collins 1975]. 'I am not a cheat,' she claimed. 'Yes, I did cheat, but only to please you in that laboratory. It wasn't bending so I had to cheat, but I really can do it.'

> We have had several subsequent, inconclusive trials with [subject], a little girl aged eleven. At the end of one I gave her a rod sealed in a glass tube.

> 'Take that home and try and bend the rod', I said.

> A month ago her mother rang. 'You won't believe this,' she said. 'That rod in the tube has bent.'

> 'That's most exciting', I replied. 'When may I see it?'

> 'Well, unfortunately it bent so much that it smashed the tube containing it!'

On the other hand, believers in the phenomena availed themselves of the subsidiary hypothesis that glass was in some way impervious to, or at least violently strained by, the unknown force involved in bending metal and this explained the frequency and distribution of breakages associated with the experiment. As one respondent put it, 'I think, when people think about glass [vessels] they break them. I've seen Geller break a glass container "just like that" - bang!'

The next step was to conduct experiments with metal objects sealed in containers with small holes in them to render them pervious to the unknown forces. Under these circumstances the subjects were able to bend the metal, but critics complained that the holes were sufficiently large to enable the bending to be done by normal means, through the use of specialised tools and techniques (see Hasted, 1976b, for a discussion).

Later, experiments were conducted with the holes sealed with a

non-glass film. It was found that subjects could not then bend
the specimens. For the critics this was final proof of their cheating hypothesis, whereas for (at least one) believer it demonstrated
the significance of psychological variables in the experiment. The
complete closure prevented the subjects from believing that they
could succeed, and therefore prevented them from succeeding.
Within this development the same experimental procedures did indeed indicate the existence of quite different natural regularities
to critics drawing on orthodox explanations and to believers in
PMB who had adopted the revolutionary course.

Retrospective psychokinesis

A still more striking example from the world of statistical psychokinesis can be given. One such experiment performed by Schmidt
(1976) involved the attempt by a 'subject' to influence the output
of a random-number generator. The random-number generator
produced a series of random binary digits and the subject was
asked to make it produce (say) significantly more ones than zeros.
This experiment has been carried out (apparently) successfully
in real time. The experiment has also been done in a precognition
mode, where the task was to predict the random-generator output,
rather than influence it.

In a new variation Schmidt recorded the binary digits and stored
them on tape for a period before anyone looked at them. After a
time (it might be months) the subject was asked to affect the
relative numbers of ones and zeros as the tape was run through a
transcribing service.

Success in these experiments has been interpreted in different
ways by parapsychologists and critics. For Schmidt, the experiments (may) show evidence of the existence of 'retroactive psychokinesis' - the power of mind to act now on a machine which operated
months previously (with the corollary that the signal on the tape
was not properly in existence until it had been observed, an idea
drawn from certain interpretations of quantum theory; see chapter
4). For at least one critic, the last experiment was seen as an
excellent control, demonstrating the spuriousness of previous
claims for this type of experiment performed in real time. When
the two Schmidt experiments were described to this respondent,
first, the experiment in which the PK effect was to take place in
real time and, second, the experiment in which the effect was
apparently retroactive, he remarked:

> We could consider the latter experiment a very good control of
> the first. .... How do you make the effect go away? . . .
> [Retroactive PK] is certainly a phenomenon that's very interest-
> ing; it's certainly as interesting as PK itself. If it didn't exist,
> and you couldn't get the subjects to [change the recorded tape],
> then I would consider that good evidence that there is something
> going on in the first experiment. The fact that they do it in both
> experiments makes me wonder - maybe there's something going
> wrong with the experiment . . . if the effect is always there no

matter what you do, then one wonders what is going on.

Another respondent would accept neither the 'retroactive' interpretation of the Schmidt experiment nor the results in the case
where precognition had seemed to be the operative mode. This
respondent did not trust the randomisation procedures involved
and, though he was prepared to accept that the Schmidt apparatus
might in principle demonstrate PK in real time, for him the precognition experiment was the control which demonstrated the actual
failure of the PK experiment:

> Since the precognitive results are so successful, I would say
> that there must be something going wrong in the randomisation
> and that will then flow over into the PK test. I'm very strongly
> against the possibility of precognition from an a priori argument.

Here, then, the 'same data' precipitate different readings
appropriate to the existence of different sets of natural regularities. The data consist of apparently successful interactions
between humans and a random-number generator, which took
place in three modes - simultaneous, prospective and retrospective.
For Schmidt, the data precipitated, respectively, psychokinesis,
precognition and retroactive psychokinesis. For the first critical
respondent, the existence of the data from the third mode precipitated the non-existence of any of these phenomena. For the
second critical respondent, the existence of data from the second
mode precipitated the non-existence of any of the phenomena.

Reticence of paranormal phenomena
Alternative perceptions of the same experiment were still more
evident in some generalised responses to the apparent lack of
success of experimenters in managing to produce an experimental
demonstration with a tight protocol. Naturally, critics felt that
this failure supported the fraud hypothesis, but two respondents
had systematic explanations drawn from the psi hypothesis.

  One respondent believed that events suggested that experimenter
sloppiness was systematically related to attempts to observe PK
phenomena. He described experiments performed at Stanford
Research Institute, where a materialisation phenomenon had been
witnessed by several observers, but all the three movie cameras
set up to record the event had failed simultaneously for different
reasons. He went on:

> Guys who are very precise at recording data suddenly get very
> sloppy, or they say that they are going to do things and they
> don't do things. Or people who can read meters very precisely
> suddenly don't see what's there. Observational defects suddenly
> turn up. A person who's a highly trained integrative head sud-
> denly doesn't operate with high integration and precision - that
> sort of thing. Or they will argue about things that actually
> happened - five different people will see five different things -

good trained observers who normally wouldn't have any trouble
agreeing, if they were doing a chemistry experiment or a biology
experiment, what the data was. They disagree and it's very
evident if you see some of these situations.

This respondent is suggesting, not that the sloppiness which
seems to be associated with parapsychological experiments signifies the non-existence of parapsychological phenomena, but that
the sloppiness is itself a natural regularity associated with the
phenomena and is itself evidence for the existence of the phenomena.
  Another respondent believed that psi experiments involved the
audience of potential readers of accounts of the experiment (see
below, p. 146) and that, until such potential readers became
generally sympathetic through a change in intellectual climate,
their scepticism would react back on the experimental situation.
Thus he explained

  one circumstance reported by [mentions some names at a con-
  ference]. They had a TV monitor with a closed loop of magnetic
  tape, with an image on that tape, and a TV monitor of Geller,
  and the whole works, and Geller was supposed to affect the
  equipment. Geller does affect the equipment, and [the experimenters said to Geller], 'Now open your hand and show that
  you don't have a magnet in your hands and we will have an
  experiment which proves this effect.' Well, if Geller were a
  magician, a rank amateur magician, he could palm a blasted
  magnet - that's a most trivial thing. I could do it, there are
  dozens of tricks for doing it. Instead, for a half-hour they had
  Geller on videotape struggling - I saw it - struggling to open
  his hand - he wouldn't open his hand, they couldn't get him to
  open his hand [laughter] - for a half-hour mind you. . . . I
  really felt that if I accept that Geller can do any of these things
  at all then I would tend to feel that this particular event was
  not staged by Geller trying to be a magician, because it would
  be too easy to pull it off as a magician. So it may be an example
  . . . of this type of thing that I'm talking about. So it was
  possible to pull this off, but not completely so that it would
  confront, and so to speak defeat all the opponents [the potential
  audience] of this idea.

For this respondent the appearance of extremely crude fraud
tended to confirm certain wider theories of psi manifestation.[2]
Rather than precipitating disbelief it confirmed the existence of
other associated phenomena.

Quark-detector experiment
The reinterpretation of experiments does not stop at the boundaries of experiments within the ambit of psychical research. In at
least one case both PK and orthodox experiments have been conducted on the same piece of apparatus, built at Stanford University.

In 1973 Arthur Hebard reported the design of a superconducting suspension for small metal spheres in connection with an experimental search for 'fractional charges' (fractions of the charge on an electron) which may indicate the existence of free 'quarks' - a type of elementary particle, (Hebard, 1973). Experiments had been in progress since at least 1970 under the general direction of Professor William Fairbank of Stanford University, and success in finding fractional charges was reported amid some publicity in 1977 (Sharrock, 1977; LaRue et al., 1977). Thus in the 'Sunday Times' of 1 May 1977 Bryan Silcock (1977) wrote:

They [quarks] have been sought for fifteen years without success, until last week that is, when a team from Stanford University in California announced that they might have found one: a genuine unfettered quark - the basic building block of matter. If the claim is confirmed it will be one of the major scientific discoveries of the century.

The same apparatus had featured in an experiment which took place in 1972. The following long quotation is from a letter sent (in June 1972) to interested parties by Hal Puthoff, one of the researchers later to do tests on Uri Geller and others at the Stanford Research Institute. He describes an experiment conducted by himself and others with the 'subject' Ingo Swann:

At the suggestion of Russell Targ, I am writing to you about an observation in the laboratory involving one Ingo Swann, a New York artist. To introduce myself, I am a laser physicist at SRI and co-author of the book 'Fundamentals of Quantum Electronics', by Pantell and Puthoff, a Wiley publication.

In order to eliminate the possibility of trickery, I decided on an experiment where if trickery were successful, that would be nearly as important as any direct effect he could produce. At the suggestion of Dr. Little (Stanford Physics Dept.) I made arrangements to use the superconductor shielded magnetometer being used in the quark experiments of Dr. Arthur Hebard, Stanford Physics Dept. This magnetometer is located in a well in the Varian Physics Building and is shielded by an aluminium container, copper shielding, and, most important, a super conducting cannister. Dr. Hebard assured me that in tests with large electromagnets no signals have been induced in the shielded magnetometer from the outside. The magnetometer is of the SQUID variety.

Prior to the experiment a decaying magnetic field had been set up inside the magnetometer, and its steady decay with time provided a background calibration signal which registers as a sine-wave output on an x-y recorder, the frequency of the sine wave corresponding to the decay rate of the calibration field. The system had been running for something of the order of an hour with no noise. Ingo was shown the set-up and told that if he were to affect the magnetic field in the magnetometer it would show up as a change in the output recording. He then placed his attention on the interior of the magnetometer (his description), at which point the frequency of the sine wave doubled for a couple of cycles (see output), or roughly 10 seconds. As you can imagine, we were quite amazed, and Art then said, 'Well, maybe it's noise - it would really be something if you could stop the sine wave altogether.' Ingo proceeded to do just that, as can be seen in the graph, for a period of roughly 10 seconds. He then said, 'Let go', at which point the output returned to normal. We asked him to describe what he had done, and he explained that he could see the apparatus inside and that looking at different parts created the effect. As he described what he was doing, the recording traced out a cycle as had occurred originally (double frequency). A rather peculiar dip in the recording took place then, and upon questioning him as to what was happening, he said he was looking at a new part, the niobium ball sitting in a cup which was inert for now in the magnetometer experiment (it is used in the quark experiment). We asked him to refrain from thinking about the apparatus, and the normal pattern then traced out for several minutes while we engaged him in conversation on other subjects. At one point he started to discuss the magnetometer again, at which point the tracing went into a high-frequency pattern. At our request he stopped, and we terminated the observation as he was tired from his effort. We then left the lab., and Art Hebard then continued to run the apparatus for over an hour with no trace of noise or nonsinusoidal activity. At various times during this and the following day where similar data were taken, the experiment was observed by numerous graduate students, and also by Dr. Little of the Physics Department, and by Dr. Martin Lee from SLAC [Stanford Linear Accelerator], the designer of the electron storage ring.

An interesting sidelight of the experiment was that Ingo was able to describe rather well what the interior of the device looked like, apparently with some form of direct observation. I am quite certain that he would not have had a chance to look at a diagram beforehand, as he did not know that we were going to use this particular piece of apparatus until we arrived in the laboratory.

At this point I wish to state that I consider this an observation, not a controlled experiment. There are variables I would want to check if we had time and money, such as whether it was the recording itself that was tampered with rather than the field being recorded. This could be tested by a disconnect of the apparatus from the recording equipment to see if the recording would continue to change on command. [See also Targ and Puthoff, 1977.]

Neither of the two experiments done on this apparatus was un-problematical. The quark experiment depends upon the elimination of other forces which might produce the same result. As Silcock wrote in the 'Sunday Times' (1977), 'Could the fractional charges measured be the result of some kind of experimental error? Per-haps, but Fairbank is an outstanding experimentalist, and spent months searching for possible sources of error before announcing his results.' The 'New Scientist' made a similar point: 'Fractional charges can be mimicked by a number of different small forces to which the ball is subject, and everything depends on eliminat-ing, or measuring them. Fairbank and friends claim to have done that ...' (Monitor, 1977; see also Patterson, 1977). Indeed, the account in 'Physical Review Letters' (LaRue et al., 1977) and other reports did spend some time discussing and discounting the other sorts of possible cause for the observations which would not imply the fractional-charge hypothesis.

As regards the PK experiment, Puthoff's reservations in the final paragraph of his letter must be taken seriously, and Fairbank and the other experimenters would think it appropriate to have still more reservations about the experimental protocol. As one of the parties suggested to Collins, 'That experiment wasn't care-fully done, because no one anticipated that anything was going to happen.' Now, in this case, though both experiments were done with the same apparatus, no connection between the quark exper-iment and the PK experiment has been drawn. Certainly none of the accounts of the quark experiment mention - among their qualifications - that the apparatus may have proved permeable to PK forces but that no evidence of PK influence was discovered during the experimental runs that support the fractional-charge hypothesis. (What would such evidence look like?)

It is important to make clear that no suggestion is being offered to the effect that Fairbank and his colleagues have been remiss in not discussing the possibility of psi influence on their appar-atus. The Swann experiment was far from conclusive and, what is more, Collins has been told that Swann later tried to move the suspended ball without success, so that there is not even a prima-facie case that he could have affected the main part of the exper-iment, let alone affected it in exactly the ways required to mimic a fractional charge, or a free quark. Fairbank acted as a physicist should in ignoring an unlikely disturbing influence that does not fall within the ambit of physics. But imagine what would happen were the possibility of this kind of PK mimicking to be taken seriously. It would lead to a marked decrease in confidence in the validity of this experiment, and others of its general type. The experiment is typical of that class of experiment near to the frontiers of research where the effects looked at are very small and are difficult to separate from various sources of noise, and where the experiment as a whole is difficult, delicate, time-consuming and requiring great dedication.

Already, other laboratories have tried to repeat the work with-out success. A pattern rather like patterns that have been reported

before (e.g. Collins, 1975, 1976) is emerging, and it is likely
that arguments concerning the adequacy of the various competing
experiments with their associated competing results will emerge.
If PK were taken seriously, then Fairbank's claims could be made
to collapse much faster in the face of the opposition. His positive
results could be explained away quite simply and quickly in terms
of a psychic experimenter effect, and little more than one quick
refutation of his findings would be required. Indeed, if PK were
taken just a little more seriously, it is difficult to see how this
experiment, or any other delicate experiment, could be done at
all, barring the invention of some sort of shielding for PK effects.
Perhaps parapsychologists at least will soon come to see the
Fairbank experiment as a classic case of parapsychological experimenter effect in the way that they do see certain other results.

Gravity waves, psychic plants, high-energy physics
Most respondents were asked about two other areas of experimental
work, and several respondents mentioned a third candidate for
reinterpretation without being prompted.[3] Fifteen respondents
were asked about their interpretation of the Weber 'gravity-wave'
story (Collins, 1975). This was an experimental series which
started towards the end of the 1960s when Joseph Weber, Professor
of Physics at the University of Maryland, claimed to begin observation of the effects of cosmic gravitational radiation (an effect
predicted by Einstein's General Theory). He used a very sensitive
antenna consisting of a large mass (tons) of aluminium delicately
suspended in a vacuum. This apparatus is sensitive to such tiny
inputs of energy that even the impact of the photons from a flash-
light will produce an easily measurable effect. Weber's results
were of such general interest, importance and contentiousness
(in so far as he claimed to find far more radiation than theory
would seem to allow) that a number of other laboratories set out
to test them. None of the other half-dozen or so experiments confirmed his findings. Nevertheless Weber remained certain that his
detector did find some genuine disturbance.
    Of the respondents that were asked about the Weber effect, all
but one had thought about it beforehand. Eleven of these could
be classed as believers in the possibility or actuality of some
psychic effect or another, and eight of the eleven thought that
the effect was a prime candidate for the operation of psychokinesis.
They thought that Weber's results were the outcome of his intense
desire to find the waves affecting his immensely delicate apparatus.
For example, one of the respondents remarked that one of his
interpretations was that 'Weber did the most sophisticated PK experiment ever run'. He went on to add:

> The signals are real . . . and are just about the right level for
> a PK experiment with a good PK subject - and most first-rate
> physicists are good PK subjects if they believe in something,
> but they all disbelieve so that they give significant negative
> results. Only when you con them into believing that they are

doing a real physical experiment will they roll out for you the
very great capability that they have. . . . I don't think that
he [Weber] would be charmed by the idea [that his effect was
due to psychokinesis] at all . . . physicists - if they enter-
tained it - would think that it was a terrible thing. 'Here he
was fooled by a PK effect!' and, furthermore, 'We don't believe
in PK effects!'

Naturally, the 'sceptics' did not reinterpret Weber's results as
the product of psychokinesis, preferring the explanation of fraud
or mistake. They tended to stress the negative results of the
other laboratories and one suggested that 'this is a perfect case
for illustrating how well modern physics is really operating'.
Thus, in this example too, it can be seen that a collection of data
which is taken to signify one thing to one set of observers signifies something different to other observers. The Weber experiments, along with the negative replications, signify errors of
some sort to the majority of orthodox scientists, but correlate
with the psychokinesis hypothesis for those predisposed to see it
that way.
The other experiment that respondents were asked about is a
more complex case drawn from the borders of parapsychology
itself rather than orthodox physics. It is, what is more, an experiment that most parapsychologists distrust (see Collins, 1976)
and critics are not likely to have thought about seriously. It concerns the ability of plants to respond emotionally to their surroundings. This responsiveness was claimed to be established in
polygraph (lie-detector) tests on plants conducted by Cleve
Backster in 1968 (Backster, 1968). None of the respondents who
were asked about this project accepted that Backster's findings
were correct, but parapsychologists were ready to reinterpret
his results in terms of other sorts of psychic functioning. Thus
one respondent remarked:

... to my mind, proving the consciousness of plants by
some technique is overlooking the very simple possibility
of PK. Which I think is already more well reported than
consciousness experiments ...
Q: Do you mean PK on the plant or PK on the apparatus?
A: Take your choice . . .

Another said:

I think they are poorly designed experiments and clearly mis-
interpreted [Backster did not control the electrodes properly.]
. . . He didn't take into account the possibility that instead of
measuring primary perception in plants he's measuring his own
PK, which I think is a much more likely hypothesis. . . . I
think that plants are probably sensitive to human PK - I'm not
sure how you could design an experiment that would rule that
possibility out.

Here, then, even where parapsychologists are critical of others' experimental work, their explanations of experimental mistakes include overlooked possibilities of psychic effects, not simple fraud or bad design. (Some respondents reacted to the Schmidt retroactive PK experiment in the same way, preferring to interpret the results as Schmidt's contemporaneous PK acting on his apparatus.)

Half-a-dozen respondents volunteered reinterpretation of the phenomena of high-energy physics without being asked. Two of these had written of their beliefs in print. Brian Josephson, the Nobel Laureate and Professor of Physics at Cambridge University, has written (1975):

> We may ask therefore whether the observer's intentions can influence the outcome of an experiment. Quantum mechanics only tell us the probability distribution of observed values of physical quantities. If the observer was emotionally involved in the outcome of the experiment and particularly wanted one result to come out rather than another, perhaps that would shift this probability distribution. Physicists normally have a degree of detachment and probably wouldn't influence the results of experiments in just that way (if they did they would end up in some other job). They might, however, have an influence in causing the experimentally determined probability distribution to come out just as they expected it ought to be.

> Currently in physics there's the strange phenomenon that the laws of nature seem to keep on changing. New symmetry violations are being discovered, the velocity of light is found to be different from what people thought it was, and so on. An odd thing, which may or may not be significant, is that sometimes when a new observation is made different people get different results. In one instance a particular symmetry was broken on one side of the Atlantic, but not on the other; however, after a while everyone got the same results. The conventional explanation would be that errors were being made on one side of the ocean, but conceivably the true explanation is that the discrepant results were genuine, and that it was the process of communication of knowledge from one side of the Atlantic to the other which caused a kind of phase transition or ordering process, as a result of which identical results were subsequently found in both places. One might speculate that perhaps one can control not only the state of the system but the Hamiltonian itself. That is to say, perhaps one can modify the laws of nature This may be the way in which psychic phenomena take place. One could make a force to act on something merely by modifying the Hamiltonian which determines the equations of motion in a system. Perhaps also some kinds of psychic phenomena can be considered as establishing a coupling energy between oneself and the thing one wants to influence.

This idea has been picked up by Jack Sarfatti (1975, p. 291), who, after suggesting that Weber's experiments are a candidate for Josephson's speculation, goes on to say:

Still another candidate for psychokinetic physics, illustrating Josephson's suggestion, is the simultaneous discovery of the long-lived 'charmed' particles seen at both Brookhaven and SLAC (Stanford Linear Accelerator). These discoveries received great publicity in the popular press which was very convenient for the economic survival of these laboratories because the federal government has seriously cut back on their grants. High-energy physicists are working under the sword of Damocles and have been experiencing great emotional stress. These same conditions also obtain in poltergeist phenomena. The manifestation of psychokinesis increases with threats to survival.

Another respondent picked on the high-energy physics example to illustrate a more general point about the impact of parapsychological findings upon the world of orthodox science:

What it really boils down to - and I think this underlies a lot of the emotionality over the acceptance of these phenomena - is deep down somewhere the realisation that if this stuff [Psychokinesis, etc.] is real it could change the very nature of science. Is science a process of discovery, or is it a process of creation? What's happening in these microphysics experiments where some theoretician comes up with a new theoretical particle and generates a lot of enthusiasm on the part of the subcommunity in physics that this particle should occur? They start looking for it, and eventually they find it. Is it really there?

Here the seeming endlessness of the elementary particle 'chinese box' fits neatly in with the psychokinetic interpretation. The natural regularities being looked at are not the laws of high-energy physics but, for the parapsychologists, the laws of mind, creating matter.

PART II CONSEQUENCES AND PROBLEMS OF PARANORMAL INTERPRETATIONS - SOME SOLUTIONS

Paranormal experimenter effects
What for parapsychologists is speculation with respect to orthodox work is a pressing problem with respect to their work in parapsychology. If experimental 'failings' can be explained away by reference to 'psi' hypotheses, how can parapsychological experiments be designed in the first place? As one respondent who despaired of ridding parapsychological experiments of the 'experimenter effect' put it:

[Experimenter effect, where the experimenter is himself the

'psi source'] is a potential problem in all of these experiments, as long as you've got an experimenter who has some motivation to make the experiment work - that's more motivation than the subject [in a psi experiment] has, usually. I think that this whole question of experimenter effects has been treated in the field as something sort of, like, paranormal cheating I guess you might call it. There really is logically no way that we can pin down any of these effects to a given organism - in a rigorous way - and it may be that we are just going to have to concede that we are dealing with something that is intrinsically transpersonal.

Further, some respondents had thought through the problem in terms which included not only immediate experimenter effect, but also what one might call 'observer effect'. Some theoreticians who based their reasoning upon ideas related to the collapse of the wave function (see chapter 4) believed that observer effect would be very important. For example, one respondent suggested:

You also see that this shows very clearly, where if you have many sceptics in an audience where some psychic is trying to perform - if there are many sceptics they will block the phenomenon because they are reducing the wave function against that man.

Another respondent included all observers of an experimental result into the experiment, though these observers may not be present at the time of the experiment and may not 'observe' until some time in the future. Notions of retroactive PK are here invoked, leading not only to problems for psi experimentation but also to a radical reassessment of all previous orthodox work:

You have the problem of how do you terminate this sequence? Here you have a subject who produces an effect and then the experimenter supposedly can also affect it and then some other observer standing around can be involved. The reader of the journal article could be affecting it and so forth. [Explains a detailed quantitative theory of effect on experimental results of various numbers of journal readers.] . . . So what I really feel is needed is to educate folks - scientists - that there is something in the quantum-mechanical theory of all this which is compatible with most of their notions. . . . There are a number of different things that are quite hard to understand about this particular [idea]. For example, . . . if you have an experiment and a thousand read about it, an attitude is generated . . . the new readership has their whole medium shifted. . . . There is a kind of consensus develops among the observers that bias the observers. And this is where a miraculous sort of thing comes up. A wild idea. All of a sudden I could see that, that could be the basis for physical laws. All physical laws could be that way!

At a less abstract level, the problem occurs in the day-to-day design and interpretation of experiments. In the case of the work done at Bath, the experimenters occasionally experienced doubts about the security of the one-way mirror system for observing the 'mini-Gellers' in the laboratory – 'Do they have some psi faculty which lets them know we are watching them even though they cannot know of our presence through normal sensory channels? Are they, then, just as much put off by the presence of 'hidden' cameras (perhaps subconsciously) as they would be by visible ones?'

Again, two respondents, discussing an experiment – performed by John Taylor – that used a letter balance as a crude and simple way of measuring the force being applied to a test object clamped to it, remarked that it was difficult to be certain that the balance was reading properly. One of them commented:

> You have the side problem – which may not be a side problem at all, it may be [the] central problem – Is the balance functioning normally? If you find [as I understand occurred] that the needle has bent ninety degrees, well, it's not capable of registering zero pressure because it has been damaged psychically.

The other pointed out:

> It's full of a lot of problems. For instance, people seem to think that if a camera photographs a thing like that, that shows something, then it must be alright. But if people do have odd powers, why should they not change the refractive index of the air locally? *I've got no way of dealing with it, you see. . . .* It's much easier to change the refractive index of the air than it is to soften a piece of metal (italics added – see our chapter 6!).

Theoretical solutions to the problem of experimenter effect
Theoreticians and 'methodologists' have attempted to offer solutions to these problems. At the most abstract end of the spectrum, the theoretician who developed the theory of the effect of readership on experimental results offered a solution, based on his theory, which could predict the size of possible psi effects in experimental apparatus by reference to the sources of quantum noise in the system. By 'calibrating' the subjects, the possible contributions of subjects to the readings of measuring apparatus could be calculated and this would enable experiments to be done. As he put it:

> In the long run, when we know the parameters to control, and these parameters include the readership, the things will become much easier to handle. You have to calibrate the observers as well as the subject. You have to deal with a subject that's good enough to match up with the readership that you are going to have.

A more general attempt to deal with certain of the problems of experimental design has been made by Robert Morris (1975). He has tried to separate out the different modes of psi operation that could give the same experimental results, in the hope of being able to design less ambiguous experiments. Some idea of the approach and its problems can be seen in the following example, where Morris discusses the problem of designing an unambiguous precognition study. (Bear in mind that precognition is probably the most complicated case.) Morris discusses an imaginary subject 'Fred' attempting precognition of a deck of five-symbol ESP cards:

Example: Fred is asked to guess the order a deck of ESP cards will have two days later. He is given pencil and paper and makes his guesses while he is alone. He then seals his guesses inside an opaque envelope and dates the envelope. This is done on 12 separate days, at 10 p.m. His targets are then determined in four separate ways, three days for each way: (a) The experimenter throws a dice to determine each card individually; (b) The experimenter takes a fresh deck and, without looking at the cards, gives the pack ten dove-tail shuffles; (c) The experimenter looks in the next day's morning paper to obtain the temperature highs for six predesignated cities during the day of Fred's responses. The last digits of these highs, taken as a six-digit number, key an entry point into a table of random digits which through a simple code then determines the exact order of the deck of cards; (d) The experimenter takes the same weather information from the paper two days later and uses them in the same way to determine the order of the deck.

We can model each of these methods in different ways. In each case, the deck of cards in its finally determined order is the designated source and Fred is the designated psi receiver. For Procedure (a) the experimenter makes no additional decisions in the determining of the target, but he does put in motion a set of environmental events not in themselves rigidly determined but which do in turn determine the message content in the source. Thus one could argue that these events themselves or any representation of them at any future time could serve equally well as the true source, since the message would be constant. One could also devise a complex alternative path of information flow as follows: Fred's guesses were in fact not due to receiving any information from the future. Once made, they became a source, with the experimenter as psi receiver. The experimenter then became in turn a psi source for the dice as receivers, such that he influenced them to correspond with the order of Fred's guesses. Thus the designated source (the card order) and the designated receiver (Fred's guesses) would in fact correspond, indicating that tacit communication had taken place, but would not necessarily indicate that the information had flowed along the path conceptualized by the experimenter.

Procedure (b) has similar problems. Instead of throwing dice to determine the designated source order, he shuffles cards. Thus, he might serve as psi receiver for Fred's guesses, as before, and then serve as psi receiver a second time, as he shuffles the cards. Their order after the ninth shuffle would be the source, such that he would then, by subtle unconscious hand movements during the tenth shuffle, affect their final order. There are other ways the shuffle could be influenced, but the example cited will suffice to illustrate.

Procedure (c) presents a different sort of problem. The experimenter has no further effect on the deck's final order and is thus eliminated as a psi component. However, the final order of the deck is already in fact determined by the time Fred makes his guesses, in that by 10 p.m. all the highs for the day for the cities involved will already be on record. Fred may thus be the true psi receiver, functioning at the time he makes his guesses, but receiving information from a complex set of non-psi sources – the separate temperature records (and, if he doesn't already know it, the code for converting those numbers into card symbols).

Procedure (d) appears relatively free of such complexities. No experimenter decisions or choices lie between the designated receiver response and the designated source, nor do any tidy, small random events. The critical events are temperature recordings made a day after Fred's guesses. It is possible that the individuals reading the temperature recorders might on rare occasions have to make a decision (and therefore be potential psi receivers, with Fred's guesses, the existence itself of the study, the other temperature recordings, the appropriate entry in the random number table and the conversion code all as necessary sources). It is also possible that Fred or the experimenter or any other interested party may have served as psi source to influence the weather recordings themselves, with the recording device or the air around it serving as receiver. These two possibilities are considerably more unlikely, in terms of the results of other studies, than the alternatives posed for Procedures (a) (b) and (c) but any complete modelling of the study should probably take them into account.

This example gives some idea of the complexities of the problem.[4]
  Some parapsychologists have tried to solve part of the technical problem by suggesting that all physical measurements associated with psi effects should be made on multi-channel recorders, which measure the same effect in a variety of different ways. Thus, if some positive effect is found it will be possible to locate the point in the train of measurement at which the effect was manifested. For example, if all the channels confirm each other, it can be assumed that the effect manifested itself within the experimental object or apparatus, but if the channels give contradictory read-

ings, then it can be assumed that the effect manifested itself in the instruments of those channels which produce a positive reading.

A similar solution involved the redesign of instruments:

> The thing that everyone assumes is that when you use a scientific instrument in these kinds of experiments you are also assuming that it is behaving, or going to behave, in the same way that it was intended to in a normal milieu. But the milieu of a psychic experiment is by no means equivalent to the situation for which the instrument was designed. You could take a very crude analogy and say, if you had some weird theory that time passed at a different rate under water, and you had a crude alarm clock from Woolworth's to measure time, sitting on your desk, you don't drop it into a tank to measure the rate of passing of time under water because you know it will leak and it won't work. Similarly, you take a scientific instrument such as a Geiger counter or a pan-balance . . . and you drop them into another milieu - a force of some kind - you don't know whether it's giving you good readings at all . . .

Q: What sort of protocol do you adopt to get over this problem?

A: [Mentions ways in which multiple videotapes and other controls can get over the verification problem] . . . and another thing . . . if you are going to use sophisticated instrumentation you need multiple read-out on multiple recorders from the same point. So, say you had a Geiger counter. You need it to be reading out into several different strip-chart recorders in several different locations, because you want to know: 'Where is the source of the interference? Is it at the strip-chart level?' Also you need to re-rig that instrument so that every available, or possible, change within it that could cause an ultimate signal is also being monitored. So a complete redesign of an instrument, I think, is necessary if you are really going to do it.

One other theoretician held to a somewhat less abstract theory of the limitation of experimenter effect:

Q: Would the existence of PK require reinterpretation of previous experiments?

A: I'd have thought that there wouldn't really be any major effect in most cases. One would guess that normally the effect of the experimenter is very small. . . . Perhaps in special cases it could have a big effect. I don't know whether in situations like the existence of elementary particles it might have an effect. . . . The fact that results are usually obtained suggests that normally the effect is small. As I mentioned at [names a conference], perhaps some observers are psychokinetic and they don't get good results for their experiments in schools, and they don't become physicists. So, perhaps

there's some automatic selection going on [laughter].
[Mentions the supposed negative effect of Wolfgang Pauli.]

Another respondent hoped, and thought, based on his experience,
that the problem would not be great:

Q: How can people treat meter readings as unproblematical
when they are doing experiments which accept such un-
orthodox events as spoon-bending?

A: The kind of person who can go and manipulate physical
objects is going to have the power to louse up your experimental result - you just can't get away from that. . . .
But the hope is that the kind of energy you're playing
with, with the spoon, is sufficiently localised . . . so that
when you get, say, a foot away from the spoon, things
start being normal and the meter will be normal. . . .
Everything I've seen, and I've seen some pretty hairy
phenomena, is consistent with the hypothesis of localisation.

Some pragmatic solutions
Perhaps the most interesting replies to questions on experimenter
effect came from four active experimenters, who had to find
solutions to the problem in order to continue their day-to-day
work. The first three quoted were relatively innocent of theoretical advances in parapsychology, and their pragmatism is un-
disguised.

Q: Can you now rely on meter readings that you have done in
the past in connection with your orthodox work in physics,
if you take seriously the possibility of PK?

A: No [laughter]. But if a lot of other people have also repeated them and if PK is rather rare, then it becomes very
unlikely that the results were unreliable. . . .

Q: How does PK affect meter readings?

A: You won't get PK effects on meters if you are in the right
frame of mind, and you don't want them, and all scientists
always are in the right frame of mind. Therefore, unless
they have very bad luck, it's unlikely that their meter
readings have gone wrong. Now, against that there are
some scientists who are known to have PK effects, and the
famous example, historically, is Pauli. This is an illustration
of scientists getting to know when the meter is wrong. You
only distrust the meter when Pauli is in the neighbourhood.
. . . I can stop [this effect] in myself, obviously. . . .

Q: Does PK require one to reinterpret meter readings in orthodox physics?

A: First of all, there are very few subjects who may be effective at it [PK]. If there's only one in ten thousand in the
population it makes it very unlikely that scientists will have

this power. Secondly, scientists in particular have this power ironed out of them - filtered out by their process of learning and intellectualisation. Now, if we accept that there are some people with this power, it is possible that they have affected some of their meter readings. But if you take the way science goes, by consensus, then you would need to have a number of experiments which you can repeat and which duplicate each other before they are accepted, it's even less likely that the same effects of PK will result from different groups of experimenters. [Though non-repeatability due to PK effects may have slowed science down in the past. Nowadays] . . . with large machines that require automatic data taking - people won't get into the way of those! - I think the other point is that you have to ask 'Well, what is it that has to be done in order to achieve psychokinesis?' As far as we understand, it's got to be done by [fear?], reason or attitude, and scientists don't usually think about changing the data they're trying to get, they're usually trying to be honest about it.

The final response is from an experienced experimentalist who had made contributions to theory himself. His pragmatism emerges in response to being presented with a consequence of his own theory:

Q: Wouldn't PK involve changes in laboratory practice?
A: Actually, since generally these effects are so small under normal conditions, and since when you're not working to-ward a psychokinetic effect, probably your whole thought processes are so random that in most experiments it isn't going to make any difference. . . . Maybe when there is a sensitive experiment here or there, and there is some controversy, then it may be worth taking a look at. That's in physics . . . in psychological experiments . . . such as involve running rats through mazes, then it's probably a worse problem. You might actually be affecting the outcomes of experiments.
Q: But aren't most new effects in physics dealt with at the level of noise precisely because they are so new that no one knows how to control them sufficiently to get the signal much above the noise? Isn't this going to be true in most important, that is brand-new, areas?
A: That's not a bad argument [laughter]. . . . I guess I'm schizophrenic on it myself. On the one hand I follow along that argument - noisy systems, that's where physics is done and so on. It sounds reasonable. On the other hand, I know, and I myself have been involved in lots of exper-iments near noise levels hoping for certain outcomes and so on, and haven't actually, so far as I know, seen it arise to be a problem. So, you know, for that reason I'm inclined to sort of go middle of the road, I guess.

This last set of responses seem to show that pragmatism is the experimentalists' response to the problems associated with shifting conceptual ground. Again, life goes on, more or less regardless.

What has been shown in this chapter is that once the existence of paranormal effects is taken for granted - that is, once they are seen as normal - the apparent absence of effects is no bar to the development of a programme of puzzle-solving. Many interpretations of this seeming absence of effects are available. The acceptance of the new paradigm does precipitate problems of another kind, however. These emerge from the necessary reinterpretation of orthodox physics and therefore the newly perceived unreliability of many formerly unproblematic techniques involving instrumentation. Complex theoretical solutions to this problem have been offered, but scientists who are determined to continue with their experimental work solve the problem in a pragmatic manner. Theoretical and methodological niceties are not allowed to stand in the way of the new programme.

8 EXPERIMENT AND PARADIGM
Symptoms of a scientific revolution

New ways of life and transitional symptoms – antagonism and resistance to antagonism – 'challenge test' at Bath – concern with replicability – inauthenticity as a symptom of transition – concern with credibility – inauthentic appearance of 'EM hypothesis' – inconsistency suggests inauthenticity – enthusiasm for work – problem of sceptical approach to paranormal – professionalisation of psychics – curious extrapolation of paranormal research – Appendix: protocols for the challenge test

Throughout this work the idea that the social and the cognitive are inextricably entwined in human action has been developed and illustrated. In chapters 3 and 4 it was shown that a purely 'cognitive' approach to the analysis of the relationship between paranormal and orthodox 'paradigms' is not fruitful. In chapter 7 experimental activity and theoretical activity were shown to interact in a complex fashion; experimental possibility may be the master of acceptable theory.

Winch's formulation of one of the ideas which drive this analysis will now be presented for a third time. It will be recalled that Winch (1958, pp. 121-2) says that the development of the germ theory of disease was a

> radically new departure, involving not merely a new factual discovery within an existing way of looking at things, but a completely new way of looking at the whole problem of the causation of diseases, the adoption of new diagnostic techniques, the asking of new kinds of questions about illnesses, and so on. In short it involved the adoption of new ways of doing things by people involved, in one way or another, in medical practice. An account of the way in which social relations in the medical profession had been influenced by this new concept would include an account of what that concept was. Conversely, the concept itself is unintelligible apart from its relation to medical practice.

Informed by this idea, we will look in more detail at the way that social relations in the PMB laboratory may change as they become coextensive with new concepts. The extent to which they do change will be the extent to which the new concepts become an authentic part of scientific society. The scraps of new potential community life that were observed during the field study will be recorded here.

As Gellner (1974) has revealed, Winch's analysis cannot deal with the period of transition between old and new 'ways of looking at things' in communities. The temporary juxtaposition of different sets of ideas would seem to precipitate, in those temporarily exposed to both, no actions that could be described coherently. Kuhn's struggles to characterise the transition between one paradigm and another are equally problematic. We can, however, say some rudimentary things about scientific revolutions.

If one were present during a revolution one would expect to see two broad types of innovatory actions. One would expect to see actions that were characteristic of the new way of looking at things - this is what Winch does talk about - and actions typical of the transition period only. These are a general feature of revolutionary periods. For a participant in the revolutionary episode it would not always be easy to separate one sort of action from another. However, one sort of action that would be ascribable unambiguously to the transitional stage would be an action which was overtly antagonistic to the new ideas and an action designed to resist this antagonism.[1] Again, unambiguously belonging to the transition period would be actions and feelings which appeared to grow out of the very newness of the ways of thought pertaining to the new paradigm and actions relating to lack of certainty that it was really 'the way to go'. Also unambiguous are actions which involve crossings between the two camps, for it is only at a time of transition that two camps are there. These features of the transitional period should be generally found in all revolutions, whether in science or in the broader field of politics.

Actions which are unambiguously characteristic of the new way of looking at things will, of course, be different in different revolutions. Here, as characterising the psychokinetic revolution, we will cite the changing relationship between scientists and subjects, the discrediting of scepticism as part of scientific method and the professionalisation of psychics. In between these unambiguous cases we will discuss the need to persuade others that the new ways of thinking are sensible ways of thinking - sensible enough to be maintained and sensible enough to work with. This appears to be a feature of revolutionary transitions and also a potentially permanent feature of the potential psychokinetic revolution.

ANTAGONISM AND RESISTANCE TO ANTAGONISM

Throughout the earlier chapters the views of critics and believers have been compared, so there is no need to reiterate the point that the claims of the 'psychokineticists' did not go unchallenged. However, only in chapter 2, where the 'vigilantes' were described, was it made clear that resistance to paranormal claims is an organised activity, an activity which is, apparently, endorsed by many well-established and prestigious scientists and philosophers.[2] The Committee for the Scientific Investigation of the Claims of the

Paranormal comprises about forty 'fellows', whose names are printed on the cover of the 'Skeptical Inquirer', the Committee's organ. They include Carl Sagan, B.F. Skinner, Anthony Flew, Richard Hull, Ernest Nagel and W.V. Quine. One of the strangest things that these fellows seem to endorse is the activity of professional magicians and journalists, who move from one location to another debunking the activities of psychics in the name of science. The scientific antagonism to the new phenomena is strong enough for scientists and philosophers to accept even non-scientist outsiders as their allies in their effort to maintain the current view.

We can give an illustration of the magician's approach through our experience of conducting a challenge test of a young spoon-bender in our own laboratory. The stage magician James ('the Amazing') Randi, following in the footsteps of Houdini, had offered $10,000 to anyone who could produce the PMB effect in his presence and under satisfactory protocol.[3] It was Professor Hasted's wife, we understand, who suggested that one West-Country spoon-bender take up the challenge, and Professor Hasted suggested that the test be conducted in our laboratory. Those present at the test were Joseph Hanlon and Farooq Hussain, journalists with 'New Scientist', Mr Hutchinson, who is connected with the British arm of the Committee, and one of Randi's young assistants. These four accompanied Randi to the test. Professor and Mrs Hasted brought the subject to the laboratory and Bob Draper, a senior technician in Bath's physics department, helped the authors with the experiment.

The test was adjudged by all not to have produced any positive results, but the 'scientific' spirit in which the test was carried out is worth recording, as it exemplifies the antagonistic quality of the argument in this transitional stage. The authors had produced a written protocol for the experiment, as had the Randi group. (Both are reproduced in the appendices to this chapter.) In the end, all parties agreed to the Bath protocol and signed accordingly but before this there was quite a heated argument over a particular aspect of procedure. Randi demanded that those designated 'judges' should sign the following agreement:

> We the undersigned agree that the experiment involving [subject's name] on June 12, 1977, at the University of Bath laboratories will be considered definitive evidence as to whether or not this person is able to paranormally effect the bending of simple metal utensils under satisfactory experimental protocol. We agree that the procedure set forth in the accompanying document titled 'Protocol' is acceptable to us and that these experiments are satisfactory in all respects.

Randi also insisted that the subject sign a long declaration, including the following passage:

> In the past, during demonstrations of this sort I have not used

methods of trickery or subterfuge to bend or break utensils. I
agree to abide by the decisions of the judges at the termination
of the experiment as to whether or not significant paranormal
events took place, and I agree to allow the use of my name and/
or likeness in subsequent reports of these experiments by any
interested parties without recompense or hindrance. Signed
by me, and by my mother on my behalf as my legal guardian.

It is clear that Randi and those with him - who supported his demands - were not only interested in carrying out an experiment
on one subject on a particular occasion. Should the effect not
be reproduced on this occasion Randi wanted to generalise this
to all occasions. He wanted official approval, as it were, for a
major 'inductive adventure'. He was concerned to win a victory
in the crusade against the PMB effect and anyone, including the
subjects, who professed its existence. Indeed, crusade is not an
inappropriate term, as can be seen from the transcript of the
discussion which preceded the experiment. This concerned the
use of the subject's name in any report. Randi explained that he
was concerned not to be sued by the subject should he report
that she failed in her attempts:

Collins (C):	Well, why not do it anonymously?
Randi (R):	Well, results have been published before in her name. [This is perfectly true; the subject's name has appeared frequently in the popular press.]
C:	I really don't think we need to crucify this girl.
R:	Why not? Is she a liar or is she . . .
C:	Because she's just a girl - you know - she's just a little girl.
R:	. . . No, not at all. She's not just a little girl, she's the subject of a scientific experiment. And if she's a liar, she's a liar. She's a little-girl liar instead of a grown-man liar.
C:	Subjects, I don't think . . . Experimenters have responsibility and experimenters can be accused of lying, cheating and everything else.
R:	If she wants to cross it out, she can cross it out, but she can be assured that I will use her name.

The experiment went ahead, and no positive results were forthcoming. In the reports that were published by Hanlon in 'New
Scientist' and by Randi in the 'Humanist' and the 'Skeptical
Inquirer' the subject's name was mentioned.
   Response to this type of antagonism involves a degree of attention to laboratory protocols and security quite foreign to the
normal run of experimentation. The experimenter in this area
knows that any mistakes he makes may be exploited without charity
in the attempt to describe the area in its worst possible light.
Various new kinds of expertise have to be acquired. Books on

confidence tricks and stage magic have to be read and the com-
pany of friendly magicians has to be sought. All manner of
strange instructions have to be given to subjects, technicians
and experimenters. Details of experimental protocols must be
prepared as though they were legal documents. Nothing on the
security front can be taken for granted. The exact procedure of
experiments becomes a topic for heated debate not only between
scientist and scientist, but between scientist and magician.

To illustrate the problem further: on one occasion Randi entered
the office of John Taylor under false pretences and tampered
with equipment. Later Randi claimed that this had demonstrated
Taylor's gullibility when faced with fraud of this sort (Randi,
1975). This means that unknown visitors to the laboratory must
be suspected. Doors and cupboards must be hurriedly locked,
should visitors appear, in order to safeguard experimental specimens. On one occasion an Italian TV producer visited the Bath
laboratory early in the day of a projected visit by Randi. It
transpired that the producer knew Randi but claimed to know
nothing of his impending visit to Bath. In spite of this disclaimer
we felt that we must be very careful not to reveal too much to
the producer until it was certain that he was not an accomplice
of Randi's who had come with the intention of 'setting us up' in
some way. (For example, he might pass some experimental material
to Randi so that he could prepare it beforehand and thus demonstrate the permeability of the Bath protocols.) When Randi was
left alone in Collins's office on that very day he did 'prepare'
the latter's afternoon teaspoon in order to bend it, apparently
miraculously, later in the afternoon. (So far as the authors know,
Randi has not made any capital out of this particular incident.)
On a previous occasion, when Randi was kind enough to treat
Collins to a pizza lunch during an interview at his New Jersey
home, Collins was offered a doctored fork to eat with. (Rapid
bending backward and forward will soon fatigue most spoons and
forks to the point of breaking.)

Presumably a certain degree of 'security consciousness' might
be typical of new areas where phenomena are scarce and easily
faked. A large number of cases of fraud immediately spring to
mind in this connection. The most well-known of these is the injection
of ink into the 'midwife toad' to support the Lamarckian theories of
Kammerer (see Koestler, 1975, for a fascinating description). A
more recent case is Summerlin's fraudulent experimentation on
mouse cancer (Culliton, 1974a, 1974b; Hixson, 1976). However,
the case with the most interesting parallels to magicians' recent
efforts is the 'disproof' of the existence of Blondlot's 'N-Rays' by
Wood in 1904. Wood went to Blondlot's laboratory and secretly removed a vital part of Blondlot's apparatus during an experimental
run. When Blondlot continued to 'see' the manifestations of his
claimed 'N-Rays' in spite of the indisputable, but unnoticed, temporary defectiveness of his apparatus, Wood was able to claim to
have demonstrated beyond doubt the spuriousness of the whole of
Blondlot's case (see Watkins, 1969).

We would claim, then, that security consciousness, together with the ways of thinking and new ways of acting that this involves, is typical of revolutionary periods. It is a response to the antagonism which is manifested in the ruthless exploitation of any weaknesses of protocol or security which experimenters expose. In the absence of this degree of antagonism - after the transitional stage if the revolution is successful - it would be silly to spend time worrying about security. No one is antagonistic enough to normal science to be willing to put in the effort required to discredit a piece of loosely conducted work. No one would break into a laboratory to tamper with equipment in order to reveal the unscientific quality of the work in progress. In a transitional period, though, ways of acting consistent with security consciousness are to be expected.[4]

THE SALIENCE OF REPLICABILITY

Another set of concerns typical of transitional periods only are related to replicability and non-replicability of phenomena. In the normal way, scientific phenomena are not reproducible with great reliability, but this is usually explained as being a consequence of scientists' mistakes, or 'anomalies', or some anodyne formulation such as 'gremlins' or the 'fifth law of thermodynamics'. Confidence in the correct way to describe and manipulate nature survives her manifest intractability. In periods of transition, where there is less concrete social support for the new ways of looking at things, each failure to reproduce an effect seems to reveal the fragility of the new world view. Critics will, of course, make the most of non-reproducibility and this highlights the problem still further. A great deal of scientific work in the transitional period is then likely to be expended in trying to improve the reproducibility of effects, in trying to 'explain away' instances of non-reproducibility, in trying to determine the boundaries between what counts as legitimate reasons for non-reproducibility and what counts as ad hoc manoeuvering. The worrying feeling that scientists' solutions to the problem of non-reproducibility and solutions to theoretical difficulties (as discussed in earlier chapters) are ad hoc rather than 'scientific' will disappear after the transitional period. This type of pragmatism will then become just another invisible component of the taken-for-granted knowledge about the way to do experimental work in the no-longer-new area. Activity associated with replication and reproduction is typical of the transitional period.

INAUTHENTICITY

One other characteristic of scientific transitions, and this seems never to have been remarked upon before, is the prevalence of accusations of 'inauthenticity'. These might reflect a prevalence

of inauthentic actions since, where two world views are juxta-
posed, an opportunity for 'sitting on the fence' arises which is
no longer present when the ultimate victory of one side or the
other removes the fence. The special quality of revolutionary
transitions arises out of the all-inclusive quality of paradigm
commitment. As Kuhn (1970a; pp. 203-4) suggests, being persuaded of the possible value of a new paradigm is not the same as
internalising it. New paradigms have to be internalised 'all of a
piece', not a step at a time. Also, as Weimer puts it (1974, p.
382):

> . . . there can be no 'simultaneous' research in conflicting
> paradigms: once the world is seen from a new point of view, it
> will take the 'Gestalt Switch' to retrieve the old perspective
> and like the alternative perceptions of the Necker cube, they
> cannot both be had at once.

Not surprisingly, where the usual agonising choices among professional strategies are combined with such total, and almost
irreversible, commitments, scientists may be tempted to try to
accommodate rather than revolt.[5]

Such a state of affairs makes for confusion and for suspicion.
A number of what one might call 'half-baked' positions are bound
to develop, involving being persuaded but not internalising; doing
one's best with limited cultural resources; demonstrating or not
demonstrating one's preparedness to accept certain consequences
of certain positions. In the case of parapsychology in particular
the professional risks are exacerbated because of the exaggerated
status asymmetry of the available options. This asymmetry arises
out of the historical connotations of the whole field of parapsychology and its association with seances, fraud, popular belief,
gimmickry, showmanship and crankiness in general. The 'cranky'
image is fostered by the critics in every possible way (see Collins
and Pinch, 1979). In short, the immediate choice facing the
scientists in our study was between a comfortable life in the bosom
of the physics community - especially comfortable in the case of
some of the principal actors discussed here as they were already
the holders of chairs in London colleges - and identification as
scientific cranks caught up in the spoon-bending fad. It is hardly
surprising, then, that those scientists who are prepared to take
risks in public might distrust the motives of those who are not.
They might think of them, in the words of Warnock (1967, p. 35),
as:

> the kind of character . . . of whom it would be impossible to
> answer simply whether they were sincere or insincere, whether
> their professions of enthusiasms or interest, for example, were
> genuine or derived from some picture of themselves which, for
> the time being, they were making real.

That is, they might think of them as characters who, to use

Sartre's terms, act in-authentically, or in bad faith. Warnock is writing of bad faith in the context of a book entitled 'Existentialist Ethics' and is interested in the concept because of its moral overtones. The notion of bad faith seems to imply a moral imperative: 'act in good faith'. However, it must be stressed that the moral content of the notion is not relevant to the issue discussed here. No morality is automatically forced upon the authors by the use of the term. It is important not to misunderstand this point. The authors are condemning nobody, but have not been surprised at finding some respondents condemning or 'suspecting' some others of acting in bad faith. This, we claim, should be an observable consequence of the incommensurability of paradigms around the time of the beginning of a potential revolution. Scientists must experience the temptations of professing interest in the new area without making the irrevocable decision to be embraced by it. If temptation is experienced, it must be natural to assume that others have succumbed.

One respondent, Professor Hasted, had thought through aspects of this problem and had published some comments upon the necessity of avoiding the temptation of disowning the more incredible aspects of the paranormal. In the 'Journal of the Society for Psychical Research' he wrote (1976b, p. 382):

> Reliance can be placed on the motive of a researcher to maximise his credibility. It is therefore with reluctance that he reports an incredible event. . . . One therefore might be tempted not to report the anomalous, particularly incredible paranormal events in large proportion. Yielding to such temptation of course makes the pursuit of experimental science impossible; one therefore does not admit to yielding to it, one deceives oneself into actual disbelief of the evidence for the event. . . .
>
> The contradiction is overcome if one accepts the situation that one's own credibility is relatively unimportant. . . . I am . . . very conscious of the temptation to maintain a high level of credibility and even to build it up as capital; and of the importance of resisting this temptation.

Again, when the matter was discussed with Professor Hasted he was horrified at our suggestion that the appropriate way for an investigator to maximise the chance that his findings would be taken seriously was to maintain a 'credibility budget', that is, developing credibility through association with negative results - which disprove some of the wilder hypotheses. Against this he stressed that 'it is the moral duty of the scientist not to worry about his credibility'. On another occasion he affirmed that he would be quite prepared to sacrifice his credibility and dignity in order to create chances to do experiments on Geller himself (though his opinion may have changed on this point).

This issue of sincerity also came up during interviews. Respondents were naturally cautious about endorsing any of their more wild ideas in front of relative strangers and were concerned to

'feel the interviewers out' before committing themselves. Both of
the following extracts occurred within the first five minutes of
interviews. The first is a warning about the interviewers' possible
inadequacy. The respondents are suggesting that the interviewers
will need personal experience and commitment if they are to make
adequate judgments.

> *First respondent to us:* Do you have any personal experience
> with Uri Geller - have you been in his presence?
> *Us:* No, never.
> *Second respondent:* It must be an interesting project for you -
> sort of picking up the pieces [laughter].
> *First respondent:* Yes, right, because to me this whole business
> seems rather unreal and difficult to deal with without having
> personal experience, because some of the phenomena are so in-
> explicable and puzzling that you tend just not to believe in it.
> That's a normal instinct, I think, when you're presented with
> all these reports.

The second extract is warning the interviewers that the respondent is quite aware that some of the things he may say might
seem a little strange. Again, commitment and adjustment are required to accept the phenomenon:

> I find myself occasionally with this problem - do you really
> believe this kind of strange stuff? I'm sure that you encounter
> this in a very strong way - most people do. I guess this is one
> of the aspects that gives rise to this accusation of people who
> work in this field being believers, or not being believers. If
> you go through the literature you just can't help, at some point,
> throwing up your hands and saying, 'This is nonsense.' A per-
> son can accept some of the minor types of phenomena. . . . The
> mind-reading type thing has an analogy with radio, and one can
> imagine how that may be occurring, in a physicalistic sort of
> sense. And then one comes to more and more of the phenomena -
> precognition is very, very difficult. If he's not a physicist it
> may not bother him too much, and if he's a wild-eyed theoretical
> physicist then he can imagine weird things there too, in an
> analogy with relativity . . . but clairvoyance is a really difficult
> . . . but with regard to all of these you will see at some point
> in the literature something that occurred and this is just non-
> sense. In particular when you get to the metal bending [laughter].
> So that you have to be almost a rabid believer in order to con-
> sider it. Even when you see such a thing occur, people go into
> a funny psychological state because their value system has been
> destroyed. It takes a couple of weeks to re-establish that value
> system.

On another occasion, a respondent warned that he was a bit
'starry-eyed' about 'all this', before launching into a complex
explanation of what would seem to the non-believer to be poorly

verified data. It is as though the respondent realised that endorsement of the theories he was about to expound would give him
the appearance of madness, but he wished to reassure the interviewers that this appearance was not to be taken seriously for
he was sane enough to recognise what the appearance was. Mad-
men think that they appear sane was the implication.

Consciousness of the dangers and temptations associated with
bad faith is thus likely to influence the assessment of the motives
of other scientists. This can be exemplified in respondents'
assessments of the work of Professor Taylor and Dr Sarfatti. It
is important to stress again at this point that the authors are not
interested in condemnation, nor are they competent to deal with
notions such as inauthenticity in any absolute sense. Firstly,
inauthentic actions might be appropriate means to authentic ends.
Building up a balance of credibility by appearing 'sane' as long as
possible in order to make one's final pronouncements credible, is
a possible example. Secondly, the authors are not psychologists
or psychiatrists, and are not therefore concerned in any absolute
sense with the motives of named individuals. Thirdly, it must be
said that on all occasions but one – an occasion when an appointment made with the authors for the purpose of scientific experimentation was abandoned without notice for the sake of an
appointment with a film crew (neither Taylor nor Sarfatti was
involved) – respondents' actions and discussions were entirely
consistent with an authentic and enthusiastic approach to the
positions they endorsed. Nevertheless, respondents' accusations
about other respondents must be documented if the social atmosphere of this type of science is to be understood.

Broadly, Professor Taylor was thought by many to be insincere
in his endorsement of the electromagnetic (EM) hypothesis – the
notion that PMB must be caused by some mechanism mediated
through electromagnetic radiation. Taylor had changed his mind
about this. In 1971 (p. 221) he wrote:

> If . . . various phenomena are accepted as valid and not fraudu-
> lent . . . these various paranormal experiences may then be
> taken as evidence of a new field of force, generated by this new
> faculty, of a different nature from the four basic ones of the
> physical world: electromagnetism, gravity, nuclear, and that
> causing radioactivity.

However, in a series of talks and lectures in the years following
his involvement in the PMB controversy, he took the stance that
any effect must be explained by one of the four forces and,
furthermore, that the only one of these that could possibly do
the work of explanation was the electromagnetic force. In his
book 'Superminds: An Enquiry into the Paranormal', published
four years later, he discussed the possibility of a 'fifth force'
and what he calls a 'psi-field' but dismissed them along with the
other three known forces of nature. He concluded, 'We have to
return then to electromagnetism, our only hope, as the intention-

ality field' (Taylor, 1975a, p. 127). More recently still, Professor Taylor has seemed to move in the direction of suggesting that those paranormal phenomena that could not be explained in terms of electromagnetism must be assumed not to exist.[6]

Some respondents felt that Taylor did not act in the manner of a sincere scientist, since his books, particularly the glossy 'Super-minds', seemed to demonstrate the operation of interests other than purely scientific ones. One respondent suggested that Taylor was just 'making a living' and nearly all respondents thought that the book had done great damage to the overall credibility of the field. Taylor himself thought that all popularisers suffered the same sort of criticism. More interesting, however, were the comments of respondents upon Taylor's endorsement of the electromagnetic hypothesis. These three quotations from different interviews typify the situation:

> The trap that Taylor is getting himself into is trying to make an electromagnetic model. Because he daren't . . . he knows that once he moves out of ordinary physicalistic explanations he's in very deep water. So he's really sticking his neck out for an electromagnetic hypothesis. . . . I know that his model can't explain some of the things he's claimed to observe.

> Q: What do you think of Taylor's EM hypothesis explanation of metal bending?
> A: I hardly think he's serious. I mean, I know he says this in public, and I've the feeling that he's carrying it on because if he went for a more way-out theory, people really would throw stones at him. So he's . . . saying, 'Well, it's quite a normal part of physics – we all accept this, it's just that metals bend in some way.' But, I hardly think that deep down he's very serious about it.

> Q: What do you think of Taylor's EM hypothesis?
> A: This I really don't believe at all. I wonder if he truly believes it himself. . . . You know that very influential people in the physics community are a priori strongly prejudiced against parapsychology, so it has been dangerous to speak of it for sociological reasons. Right or wrong, my feeling is that Taylor is very aware of this and is trying to be as conservative as he can.

What these respondents had seen was the obeisance of the EM hypothesis to the status quo of orthodox science. If the phenomenon is not explicable in the terms of orthodox science, then the evidence of the senses must be set aside in favour of the dogma of orthodox science. The phenomenon can be pursued in safety, without danger of the scientist being caught up in the revolutionary net; that is, without danger of the scientist finding himself defending the phenomenon further than it can be defended within

the legitimate cultural range of orthodox science. In times of difficulty the hypothesis will ease its supporter back into, rather than away from, the bosom of science, whereas other hypotheses, as has been seen, have the opposite effect.
The case of Sarfatti is different: Dr Jack Sarfatti was criticised by respondents for changing his position with regard to the spoon-bending phenomenon from active believer to disbeliever. Sarfatti had been present at one of the early demonstrations at Birkbeck College and, by all accounts, had been one of those most excited by the extraordinary events. He was responsible for alerting the press widely to what had taken place. Subsequently Sarfatti changed his mind as a result of a demonstration of spoon-bending by the magician James Randi. Sarfatti's two positions are contained in the following two quotations.

My personal professional judgement as a Ph.D. physicist is that Geller demonstrated genuine psycho-energetic ability at Birk-beck, which is beyond the doubt of any reasonable man, under relatively well controlled and repeatable experimental conditions. While the experimental conditions were not perfect, the events at Birkbeck do represent a major step forward in the new field of experimental psychoenergetics (Sarfatti, 1974b, p. 46).

On the basis of further experience in the art of conjuring, I wish to publicly retract my endorsement of Uri Geller's psycho-energetic authenticity. In particular, I retract my statement in *Science News:* 'My personal professional judgement as a Ph.D. physicist is that Geller demonstrated genuine psycho-energetic ability at Birkbeck, which is beyond the doubt of any reason-able man . . .'
I have witnessed the Amazing Randi fracture metal and move the hands of a watch in a way that is indistinguishable from my observation of Geller's 'psycho-kinetic' demonstrations. Also, I am advised of Randi's demonstration of causing bursts in a Geiger counter and of deflecting a compass needle as reported in a letter from King's College University of London (11 July 1975), signed by Maurice Wilkins FRS and four other faculty associated with the Department of Biophysics. . . . I do know that Geller's report of the Birkbeck tests in his book *My Story* is distorted to Geller's advantage (Sarfatti, 1976a).

The opinion of many respondents was that Sarfatti's change of mind was not to be taken too seriously as he was inclined to en-dorse positions for reasons of expediency and on the basis of too little hard evidence. As one respondent put it:

I've seen him [Randi] convince people that he could do that [reproduce Geller's feats]. Sarfatti really got taken in by him. . . . Sarfatti is another story - you could do another story just on Sarfatti alone. He's a brilliant theor-

Q: etical physicist, but in terms of his opinions of what's
going on in experiments - they change from day to day.
He's influenced a lot by political considerations.
Q: You mean what he thinks it is good to believe at the time?
A: Yeah! I don't know if he'd admit it to you. . . . You know,
him changing his mind is just giving the field a bad name.
None of his opinions were ever very substantial to begin
with, so if he changes his mind . . .
Randi came and did a little trick with him at lunch. I was
able to see through that when Randi did it but Jack got
swept up by that. . . . He had this idea that [a journalist]
was going to write a lot about him and make him popular -
which in fact [the journalist] did. So he wanted to kind
of butter up to [the journalist], so he went along with
Randi - again based on very insubstantial information.

On the other hand, Dr Sarfatti suggested to the authors that,
as many important people now believe in Geller's abilities, if he
were interested in political expediency he would endorse these
abilities, not deny them.

It is important to point out that criticisms of scientists for
perceived inauthenticity came from believers and sceptics alike.
Perceptions of inauthenticity did not vary noticeably according
to the respondents' categorisation in these terms. Only one case
was encountered where 'mixed motives' were openly admitted by
a respondent himself. One of our respondents told us that he
had been discouraged from doing this type of research by the
professors within his department:

The main sort of comment that people have made is, 'You
could lose your credibility like [another scientist] has if
you spend too much time doing things like that.'
Those sort of discouraging remarks [have come from]
colleagues and supervisors.
Q: And those sort of remarks have affected your approach
to the subject?
A: Yes - yes. One likes to do things that are approved of, I
suppose.

This respondent also commented that his handling of the experiment was motivated, in part, by other than purely scientific
considerations.

Q: Why did you send preprints of your scientific publication
on spoon-bending to the newspapers?
A: I think, probably, if I hadn't been a political animal I
would not have done that. . . . Being a political animal,
getting one's name in the papers and keeping one's name
in front of the public is of some small importance. . . .
I thought I'd get . . . a kick out of the local paper's version of what I saw to be a serious scientific article which

was of popular interest as well as serious interest.

These comments, however, are the only evidence that would lead the authors to say that any of the scientists in the field did act in less than scientific good faith. All else is other scientists' opinions.

Inauthentic actions, and more certainly accusations of inauthenticity, are transitional symptoms of paradigm conflict, it has been argued. Inevitably, few accusations of inauthenticity will be committed to paper, so it may not be possible to recapture this phenomenon in the evidence that survives from historical episodes. In the case under discussion, the extent to which scientists demanded that their colleagues take up committed positions had ironical consequences. It will be recalled that Professor Taylor first claimed that PMB could not be explained by science in response to a Geller demonstration on the David Dimbleby TV programme. Also Dr Sarfatti's response to Randi's demonstration of fake spoon-bending has been discussed. In these two cases, the scientists concerned altered their allegiance in opposite directions. Yet both scientists were thought by their peers, believers and sceptics alike, to have acted inauthentically. Evidently, committed scientists are not expected to change their minds easily on issues such as this.

ENTHUSIASTIC ACTIVITY

It is probable that a kind of artificially fostered enthusiasm will be associated with any development where an essential element in the winning of acceptance of the claimed new natural phenomena is (in Kuhn's terms) persuasion (Kuhn 1962, p. 94). This enthusiasm will be necessary to keep up the spirits of co-workers, potential recruits, technicians, funding agencies (if things get that far) and the innovating scientist himself. This is so because it is likely that when a radical innovation is being pursued the phenomenon in question will be scarce, marginal, and 'not really there at all', according to the researcher's most distinguished peers. In our own series of experiments, we found ourselves working at being cheerful in order to keep up our own spirits and to keep the technicians from becoming unco-operative from sheer boredom and the growing conviction of the futility of the whole exercise. At times we were grateful for the experimental subjects' confidence in their ability. This helped when we, the experimenters, experienced moments of doubt. Mutatis mutandis, we found it necessary to express our confidence in the experimental subjects.

This type of fevered enthusiasm is likely to drop away if the revolution succeeds and work of the once-revolutionary nature takes on a matter-of-fact or 'nine-to-five' quality. In the particular case of parapsychology enthusiasm may be a more lasting phenomenon.

PERMANENT FEATURES OF POST-REVOLUTIONARY LIFE

Object into subject. The demise of scepticism
In the normal way it is the physicist *par excellence* whose work
demands that he be completely detached and distanced from the
world of objects which are his business. Such a relationship does
not seem to work in the case of investigation of psychokinesis for
three reasons. Firstly, overt, friendly and faithful relations must
be maintained with the experimental subject if he or she is to
continue to be willing to work in the laboratory. This requires a
change in experimental style for the physicist. A second reason
for the necessity of this kind of change is more fundamental. It
is said that certain extrovert qualities are required of the scientist if the psychokinetic subjects are to be able to perform in the
laboratory, irrespective of whether or not they are willing to
perform.

Thirdly (and this is potentially most significant as a determinant
of the future style of laboratory life), it may be said that the
mere presence of sceptics in the laboratory could inhibit the
appearance of the effect through covert and ill-understood
channels. This suggestion has been widely canvassed and might
well become part of the new paradigm if it ever develops.

The necessity of changed relationships required on the first
count came home to the authors very clearly in their own experiments. From the beginning, our philosophy had been one of
treating experimental subjects as objects without name or identity
as far as the media and the journals were concerned. Furthermore, these objects were to be called into the laboratory for tests
at well-spaced intervals which suited the experimenters, their
programmes of teaching and their other research projects. It was
soon found, however, that the subjects could not be handled in
this way. Subjects sought publicity and the excitement (and
possible financial gain) that came with it. The legitimacy conferred
on subjects' wonderful powers as a result of being involved in
experiments at a university was used to advantage by them in
their relationship with the media. The experimenters' statements
regarding their abilities were therefore carefully scrutinised by
the subjects themselves. If they were found to be unsatisfactory
this would lead to recrimination. Thus, on one occasion it was
demanded that one of the experimenters telephone a local radio
programme and insist that they announce over the air that some
statements just made about the subject's abilities were too negative.
This demand was made under threat of resignation from the project. Eventually the project was nearly terminated when a subject
refused to be involved in further laboratory work because a
magazine article had stated that he had not managed to bend
spoons under certain stringent conditions.

Now, a little foresight would have made it clear that such
problems were bound to arise unless the experiments were an
unqualified success. When public attention is drawn to the wonderful powers of a named individual, these powers will become the

central element in the local community life of the subject and his
or her family. Presumably their identities in the neighbourhood,
school and work become intimately tied up with the new powers
and any suggestion that the subject was anything less than
genuine would become a major source of problems in all these
arenas. The pressure on the experimenter to withhold negative
or inconclusive results therefore becomes intense if any positive
results are ever to be discovered.

As well as demands for public affirmation of abilities, the
authors experienced demands for faithfulness to our experimental
subjects. Frequently the authors were accused by one subject
of testing other people during the long gaps between requests
for experimental services. Without wanting anything other than
a cold, objective relationship we found ourselves involved in a
warm, subjective relationship, with all the restrictions on action
that this involved. It was as though meters or magnetometers
had suddenly demanded the right to exclusive contracts with the
right of veto over experimental results.

The need for 'extrovert' qualities, required on the second
count, seems to be emerging from the parapsychological world in
general as it is noticed that different experimenters have differential success in producing results. The most celebrated case
here is undoubtedly that of John Beloff, who, though a firm
believer, is notorious for his ability to 'extinguish' the fine performances of subjects from the United States. Beloff himself, in
one publication (Beloff and Bate, 1971), has conceded that personality variables might account for the difference between his
negative results and those of another parapsychologist who had
performed a successful and celebrated experiment. Throughout
such experiments, then, it must be borne in mind that results
may be, in part, a function of some as-yet-unspecifiable relationship between experimenter and subject. What may emerge from
this is a new class of scientist, who has some natural capability
that fits him for this sort of experimental work but which is independent of normal academic ability or even normal experimental
skills.

It is difficult to think of an equivalent case in orthodox science,
though the existence of certain types of experimental ability is
jokingly referred to as the 'Pauli principle'. It is said that Wolfgang Pauli was not only incapable as an experimenter but actually
had a negative effect on others' experiments, so that all experiments in progress broke down in any town he was visiting as
soon as he stepped off the train. Such a notion of experimental
skills has not, however, been accepted to the extent that, for
example, manipulative skills are directly measured at the outset
of a scientist's career to determine whether or not he or she
would be capable of pursuing a career as an experimentalist.
Perhaps the closest analogy within orthodox science would be a
case of colour-blindness in an analytical chemist. Not to be able
to see the changes in colour of indicators would perhaps be a dis-
qualifying factor equivalent to not being able to encourage psychic

subjects to perform. This leads on to the third point under this heading – the suggestion that the mere presence of sceptics may inhibit manifestation of the phenomenon.

This point has been noted in parapsychological circles for a considerable time and indeed the 'sheep-goat' effect – the correlation of belief with ability – is claimed to be one of the most well-established parapsychological generalisations. Thus in the laboratory it is important that those present not only act in a confident, extrovert way, but also actually believe in the existence of the phenomena themselves. This may not always be difficult as, for most scientists, extended experimental work is associated with firm belief in the existence of the phenomena under investigation. However, as the experimenter effect here is likely to extend to anyone in the laboratory environment, including those not committed to the experiment, a problem arises. Either the scientist must work alone, dispensing with technicians and other assistants, or he must somehow manage to persuade his assistants and technicians that the effect is genuine. He cannot order them to believe it! Again, the very presence of 'unbiased observers', surely a reasonable demand in all orthodox experiments, may affect the outcome of the experiments in a negative direction. On the other hand, other observers may affect results in a positive direction. For example, one observer who many claimed had a positive effect on subjects was an American psychologist, Melanie Toyofuku.

Thus, new classes of person may be created to enter or be deliberately excluded from the experimental situation. In the physics laboratory the only thing that need disturb the cool, objective, sceptical loneliness of the physicist is his personal enthusiasm for his research, and perhaps the modern 'big physics' requirement of working in a team. In the spoon-bending laboratory, life is all false bonhomie and genuine bonhomie; smiles, congratulations, intimate relationships with experimental subjects, no longer seen as objects; persuasive rather than authoritarian relationships with technicians and others; exclusion of sceptics from contact and inclusion of individuals who do nothing but amplify the effect by their presence; and, finally, agreement between scientist and subject regarding what can be published. These new social relationships can only be understood as the social locus of the new theories and concepts of psychokinetic research. These concepts and theories themselves will take on meaning and acceptability and will become 'taken for granted' only as they are embedded in the continuing forms of life sketched out above. The exclusion of certain classes of scientist from the laboratory scene is only comprehensible if the new theories are understood and believed. They can only infuriate the critic. To him they will seem to be lame and pathetic excuses. Conversely, the new theories only become true if the revolution succeeds, if the conventional categories of scientists become changed and if the critics' viewpoint ceases to be tenable.

There are wider possibilities, too. Certain theories (discussed

above) suggest that the participants in a parapsychological experiment are not restricted to those individuals within the four walls
of the laboratory, but include all potential observers of the
experimental results. That is, they include all the potential
readers of the journal in which the results are published. That
means that the numbers of believers and sceptics among the
eventual readership determine the outcome perceived by the experimenters themselves.

One respondent made this point after describing the failure of
an experiment because of the refusal of Geller to submit to appropriate controls. He suggested that this apparently senseless behaviour may have had a significant explanation:

> It may be an example . . . of the type of thing I've been talking
> about . . . so that it was possible to pull this off, but not
> completely so that it would confront and, so to speak, defeat
> all the opponents of this idea. So what I really feel is needed
> is to educate folks - scientists - that there's something to the
> quantum-mechanical theory involved that is compatible with
> most of their notions. And then, when they are a different kind
> of audience - an audience that could accept it - this stuff could
> occur.

Conceivably, if these ideas come to be, then a part of experimental
life would come to be involved with persuading the public at large
of the possibility of these phenomena.

Professionalisation of psychics
Finally, another wider change associated with the growth of
acceptability of these phenomena may also be beginning. This is
the growth of professionalisation among psychics. There are now
definite stirrings among certain groups of psychics over their
rights. One group prepared a petition on 'Psychic Freedom as an
Inalienable Human Right' for the United Nations Commission on
Human Rights.

A new problem, which began to trouble some groups of experimenters, is the organised refusal of psychics to work with
scientists whom they do not consider sympathetic and ipso facto
successful in evincing their abilities. The resultant difficulties
for the design of replications which would satisfy a sceptical
scientific community can be imagined! Critics would be delighted
to be able to say that 'as experimental subjects were determining
the appropriate credentials for competent replicators, they would
naturally accept only those who (by whatever means) produced
positive results'! Such a situation would, however, be quite
acceptable should the existence of these phenomena become
routine.

CONCLUSION TO CHAPTER 8

In this chapter we have begun to show what laboratory life would look like if a psychokinetic revolution were to grow out of the new wave of experimentation of the early 1970s. We have not simply extrapolated from our observations, since we think that much of what we observed during our field study was a feature of the transitional period rather than a likely feature of post-revolutionary scientific life. The transitional features may be of greater sociological interest than the permanent since variants of them are likely to apply in any revolutionary period. However, our major thesis, which has to do with the relationship between cognitive life and social life, is better illustrated in the permanent features.

Winch writes that the concept of 'germ' is unintelligible apart from its relation to medical practice. We suggest that if the psychokinetic revolution took place the concepts pertaining to the new form of scientific life would not be properly comprehensible except in their relation to the corresponding new scientific practice. In a way this chapter must fail because we cannot embed the reader in this, currently almost non-existent, practice in order that he or she may properly comprehend the concepts that have been mentioned. What we are suggesting is something like this. The concept of germ is given to us in activities pertaining to hygiene and antisepsis. The ritualised, almost fetishistic, scrubbing procedures of surgeons before they enter the operating theatre are comprehensible only in terms of the concept of germ, and the concept is given meaning every time these procedures are performed. If we imagine the parapsychology laboratory of the future we can make some guesses about what we might see that would correspond with, and make available, the concepts discussed in this chapter.

What we would not expect to see is any special concentration on the design of foolproof protocols, on security or on replicability. All those aspects of experimentation would proceed in the relaxed fashion which is typical of most of science. What we would expect to see is a great air of enthusiasm and bonhomie, and some concern that the general public share in the local enthusiasm. We would expect to see groups of cosseted psychic subjects around the laboratory whose status would appear to be higher than that of the scientists that they worked with. They would be highly sensitive of their rights and rather well paid. A time traveller, cast into this scientific world from out of our own, might think himself in, say, a high-class showroom, or a beauty parlour, or a health farm, or an American Express advertisement rather than in a scientific laboratory. These sets of social relationships, strange though they would appear to the time traveller, would make the equally strange concepts of psychokinetics routinely available, as a matter of course, in a completely natural way, to those who shared in them.

APPENDIX 1

Protocol brought to Bath for the 12 June 1977 experiment by the Randi group

Protocol
1 The purpose of the experiment shall be to determine whether or not the subject is able to cause the bending and/or breaking of simple spoons and/or forks of the type normally in domestic use. By 'bending' is meant a significant deviation from the normal profile amounting to a displacement of more than 1 cm. at one end.
2 The subject is allowed to hold the utensil in the accustomed manner, without applying pressure that could be expected to bend the utensil by normal means.
3 Only one utensil will be subjected to experiment at any one time and before being touched by the subject it will be checked for profile against an identical utensil kept for reference only. Following any handling by the subject the profile of the utensil will be compared against the reference.
4 The experiment is deemed to be in progress only while video-tape monitoring is performed and an announcement of 'experiment in progress' is made officially. Upon the utensil leaving the control of the subject and having passed through the terminal profile check an announcement of 'experiment suspended' will be made.
5 A carefully delineated area to be known as the 'test area' will be constantly monitored on videotape, and reference utensils, test utensils, and a running clock shall be constantly in view to the video camera.
6 Should the above protocol be broken for any reason the experiment is automatically terminated just prior to that point. Utensils, profiles and all standards will be re-established to the satisfaction of the judges.
7 Copies of the videotape of the experiment will be made available subsequently to any of the judges or experimenters for reference purposes.

Description of experimental materials
There are four utensils, common kitchen spoons and forks designated A, B, C and D. A duplicate set is also supplied, for use only as profile comparison standards. These latter are marked, in addition to black-and-white paint marks as here described, with red stripes as well.

A: Teaspoon, stainless-steel, plain design, imprinted on obverse 'STAINLESS KOREA', 14 cm. long, 2.9 cm. at widest point of bowl. Weight approx. 17 gms. Marked: two white patches at tip of bowl, two white stripes at neck.
B: Teaspoon, stainless-steel, fluted design, imprinted on obverse 'STAINLESS STEEL EMPIRE MADE', 13.4 cm. long, 2.9 cm. at widest point of bowl. Weight approx. 20 gms. Marked: white patch at tip of bowl, white stripe at neck.

174 Symptoms of a scientific revolution

C: Soupspoon, stainless-steel, fluted design, imprinted on obverse as specimen B, 18.3 cm. long, 4.7 cm. at widest point of bowl. Weight approx. 45 gms. Marked: white patch at tip of bowl, white stripe at neck.
D: Fork, stainless-steel, fluted design, imprinted on obverse as specimen B, 192 cm. long, 2.6 cm. at widest point of bowl. Weight approx. 37 gms. Marked: white tips on two centre lines, white stripe at neck.

NOTE: Comparison standards are not to be handled at any time by subject. Only ONE test utensil will be available for experiment at a time. Other test utensils will be used only after proper announcement by the judges, and each will be tested before and after each use, according to rules outlined in 'Protocol' sheet.

Statement of judges
We the undersigned agree that the experiment involving [subject's name] on June 12, 1977, at the University of Bath laboratories will be considered definitive evidence as to whether or not this person is able to paranormally effect the bending of simple metal utensils under satisfactory experimental protocol. We agree that the procedure set forth in the accompanying document titled 'Protocol' is acceptable to us and that these experiments are satisfactory in all respects.

Statement of subject
To whom it may concern:
I [subject's name] understand that I am not required to bend or break the utensils but only to attempt to do so and therefore am under no obligation to cheat. I agree to comply with the rules set down for the experiments to be performed at the University of Bath on June 12, 1977. I will at no time attempt to use any trickery or subterfuge to accomplish the bending and/or breaking of spoons and/or forks supplied to me during the experiment and that any deformation of the supplied utensils will be accomplished without the application of ordinary pressures that might normally be expected to bend or break the utensils.
In the past, during demonstrations of this sort I have not used methods of trickery or subterfuge to bend or break utensils. I agree to abide by the decisions of the judges at the termination of the experiment as to whether or not significant paranormal events took place, and I agree to allow the use of my name and/or likeness in subsequent reports of these experiments by any interested parties without recompense or hindrance.
Signed by me, and by my mother on my behalf as my legal guardian.

APPENDIX 2

Protocol produced by Collins and Pinch for the 12 June 1977
experiment

Protocol
Everyone must agree to written protocol before experiment starts.
A signature on these sheets signifies that the signer believes
that protocol covers all reasonably foreseeable eventualities. If
any observer thinks that the protocol has been broken during the
experiment he should make this known immediately and all observers should note the time, the reasons given, and whether
they agree that it has been broken or not.
    If the protocol is broken, the run is void and a new run must
be started.

Observers
A panel of observers must be agreed to before the start of the
experiment. These are:-

At the termination of the experiment the observers should state
whether or not they think paranormal bending has taken place,
and give their reasons. All discussions will be tape-recorded.

Spoon
All observers must agree that the spoon is appropriate for the
test, being neither abnormally strong or weak, but of roughly the
standard of a stainless-steel teaspoon that can be purchased from
Woolworth's, such as have been used in tests at Bath University.
Spoons should be marked in ways agreed by the observers and
sealed in a container placed in the observation room.

Layout
The subject will work in the 'experimental room', separated by a
one-way-mirror screen from the 'observation room'. In order not
to upset the subject, observers must stay within the observation
room from a time before the subject arrives until the termination
of the experiment. Professor Hasted will deliver subject. Observers
must not talk loudly except for Collins, who may shout instructions
into the experimental room. No smoking or lights will be allowed
in the observation room. Pinch will act as the 'experimenter' and
will have access to either room. Others, excluding [subject's
mother], may stay in the same room as subject with her agreement, and the agreement of all observers, but apart from Pinch
(and Hutchinson) all others should stay away from the immediate
experimental area.
    Those present in the experimental room are:-

Others (with the agreement of the observers) who are not observers may enter and leave observation room, but may not enter
experimental area during the course of a run.

Start of run
Spoon inside sealed container will be taken by Pinch (who will not
be privy to the spoon-marking arrangements) from the observation
room to the experimental room as quickly as possible. Container
should be opened in sight of camera. Pinch will then coat inside
of bowl of spoon with lampblack from a candle left burning in
camera shot. Subject will show clean hands to camera and un--
marked black surface will also be shown. Subject will then rub
spoon, holding it in one hand only.

Termination of experiment
Subject should show clean hands to the camera and unmarked
lampblack surface. If spoon has not bent Pinch will demonstrate
to the camera than it can be bent with reasonable force.

(Termination of run
Spoon to be replaced in container in view of camera, then restart
as before.)

Template
If there is doubt over whether spoon has bent or not, Pinch may
compare spoon with identical 'template' spoon, which will be
treated with similar security precautions as experimental spoon
and must stay in camera shot continuously.

Duration of runs
Two runs of approximately 50 mins. each will be attempted, but
breaches of protocol may necessitate a larger number of shorter
runs. One hour and 40 mins. of videotaped experiment should be
the overall target.

Typical breakdowns of protocol
   Spoon goes out of frame, or camera breaks down.
   Subject touches spoon with both hands at once.
   Subject presses spoon against table.
   Anyone other than Pinch touches spoon in camera shot.
   Any foreign body not mentioned above touches spoon.

Agreement of protocol
Those who have signed below agree with the above protocol:

[NOTE: items in parentheses were added immediately before start
of experiment. The flickering candle, apart from serving as a
means for blacking the bowl of the spoon, was also intended to
serve as a check on film continuity should any doubts arise outside or later. Our theory is that such a random and uncontrollable
datum cannot be reset for editing purposes. Observation between
the two rooms was through the one-way mirror. The only addition
to the protocol suggested by Randi was a second mirror placed
behind the subject's hand to give a back view as well as a direct
view to the observer.]

CONCLUSION

*Restatement of aims – not an attack on science – outline of
argument and conclusion of each chapter – work is neutral to
the existence of paranormal metal bending – experimental evidence always ambiguous – future studies should relate scientific
and political revolutions – empirical study of philosophical problems is possible and rewarding – sociology of knowledge has
wide scope*

Our aim throughout this book has been to show the relevance of
empirical investigation to the conceptual and epistemological issues
at the centre of recent sociological and philosophical debate.
Though we have focused our empirical attention on an area of
modern scientific endeavour, we have taken our findings to bear
upon what has become known as the 'rationality debate'. We have
argued that when certain current ideas about the nature of scientific progress are interpreted in a radical way, they make for a
striking parallel between traditional problems of historical and
sociological research and the newer problems of the history and
sociology of science. These parallels suggest a new way of approaching the old problems – through the study of modern science.
Given the peculiar visibility and accessibility of modern science,
this approach is beset with far fewer obstacles to empirical research than previous approaches.
    In the first chapter of the book we have set out the interpret-
ation of the current ideas about the history of science which make
it possible to treat scientific rationality as an example of the wider
problem. The catalytic figure for the new treatment of science is
Thomas Kuhn. His book 'The Structure of Scientific Revolutions'
(1962) gave rise to a widespread re-reading of scientific history.
The impact of the book has been less or more radical according to
the background of its readers. It now seems that the book was
not intended to be taken as a particularly radical statement. Kuhn
would not appreciate the parallel that we have drawn between the
radical discontinuities in rationality to be found between, say,
Western societies and primitive tribes and those to be found between scientific paradigms. If our interpretation is taken up, then
'Kuhn n'est pas Kuhnist'.
    The radical interpretation arises out of a reading of Kuhn's
book informed by the philosophical views associated with Wittgenstein, Winch, Collingwood, the phenomenologists and the ethnomethodologists. For Collingwood, the ways of life of epochs in

history are informed by different sets of 'absolute presuppositions'. Understanding the actions of participants in a different epoch requires an approach founded on their absolute presuppositions rather than those of the historian. In Wittgenstein's later philosophy it is shown that meanings of terms cannot be separated from the social activity in which those terms are embedded. In Winch's interpretation and application of Wittgenstein's ideas the inextricability of ways of acting and ways of thinking is drawn out further and applied to whole societies and, sketchily, to scientific developments. The phenomenologists stress the importance of the taken-for-granted, unquestioned, social base of action and the ethnomethodologists, at least the early ones, point to the variation in members' methods of making sense of their local social environment. Within the context of these philosophical views, Kuhn's ideas about paradigms and their incommensurability seem like a natural and full-blooded extension of the social framing of meaning into scientific endeavour.

Unsurprisingly, the extension of the notion of radical discontinuities in the framework of thought to scientific thought and action - usually taken as the canonical example of rationality - has been widely resisted. Writers have suggested that this view is self-refuting, or absurd, or otherwise unacceptable. In chapter 1 we looked briefly at these arguments, concluding that they do not present an obstacle to empirical research. Indeed, these arguments often rest on supposedly self-evident premises which are, in reality, themselves a matter for empirical investigation. For example, the extent of the discontinuity between ways of thought has been said to have been overstated, and the extent to which scientists argue rationally one with another has been said to have been ignored. In truth, there is little evidence available on either matter - a state of affairs which we hope to have partially remedied in this book.

Perhaps the major mistake of those who resist the arguments put forward here is to think that the invasion of the heartland of science by sociological thought entails a prescription for scientific anarchy. This, however, is far from the case. Our analysis makes the basis of scientific authority more clear rather than less. Scientific authority is socially negotiated and socially sanctioned. In this respect it is like moral and legal authority. Scientists are experts on the natural world in the same way as lawyers are experts on the law. In both cases the most valuable opinions are to be had from, respectively, scientists and lawyers. But neither lawyers nor scientists are immune from criticism from their colleagues by virtue of their access to some extra-social realm of pure reason or pure fact.

Having argued that aspects of scientific thought and practice can be looked at as examples of thought and practice in general, we set out our claim that the area of science we had chosen for our research exemplified a scientific discontinuity. With hindsight, it seems that the events that took place in the early 1970s in connection with Uri Geller were not to bring about a scientific revol-

ution. Though isolated scientists are still actively researching
the problem, the Geller brand of large-scale psychokinesis now
has less credibility in the scientific community than at any time
since Geller first appeared.[1] This makes no difference to our
analysis. We argued only that we had located an example of potentially revolutionary scientific activity, not one that would lead to
a successful revolution. We argued that to locate the beginnings
of a successful revolution would require not science but *prescience* - an ability which neither author would claim to possess.
Our claim that the Geller-associated scientific activity had the
qualities of revolutionary activity rested on criteria other than
the success of its outcome. It rested on criteria such as its potential conflict with orthodox science - which can be seen through
the conflict with parapsychology in general - and its location
within science rather than outside it. The study of paranormal
metal bending does not oppose science from the outside in the way
that, for example, various 'anti-science' movements oppose it.
On the contrary, most of the researchers involved were active,
'orthodox' scientists.

In chapter 1, then, we argued that the area of science we chose
as a potential revolutionary area might come to be seen as a
spurious area, but we argued that this was no disabling handicap.
This is because the relativist viewpoint consonant with the radical
interpretation of Kuhn cannot distinguish between true and false
science. The methods precipitated by this viewpoint are neutral
with regard to the truth and falsity of the science under investigation. The view of the investigator who works from within this
perspective is the same as the view of the scientist engaged in
trying to find out what is true and false. Neither investigator
nor scientist can know what will turn out to be counted as true
or false until it has 'turned out'. It is this which makes it possible
to talk of revolutionary activity in the absence of a consummated
revolution. Here again we find ourselves opposed to Kuhn, who
does not seem to count activity which has no fruit for the development of science as properly scientific.

The major methodological problems thrown up by any attempt
to study scientific revolutionary activity in practice were discussed in the last part of chapter 1. The problems are, firstly,
to do with the difficulty of generating understanding of one or
more scientific cultures which are not familiar and which perhaps
stand in a relationship of incommensurability. Secondly, there is
the problem of conveying that understanding in words. The first
problem we do not think is insuperable, given sufficient access to
the various communities in question. We do our best to show our
warrant for thinking that we achieved success in this regard. The
second problem seems a priori insuperable, since the readers of
this book do not share our access to the native communities.
Doubtless, our feeble efforts of presentation will not begin to do
justice to the experiences that we try to describe. Nevertheless
in spite of this philosophical impasse, we hope there is enough
to make the excursion worthwhile.

Though the major theme of the book is the problem of rationality we hope that some of the descriptive material will be interesting in its own right. The second chapter describes the parapsychological communities in Britain and the USA, into which paranormal metal bending entered as an unexpected and not entirely welcome guest. The emergence of Geller and his sponsors, the rapid growth of scattered scientific interest and the development of the 'mini-Geller' phenomenon are set out. The hopes of a speedy resolution of the Geller affair, through a programme of rigorous scientific research, were to be disappointed. Those who believed that the publication of positive results would itself be enough to establish the scientific reality of the paranormal were as disappointed as those who thought that a small set of negative demonstrations would quickly discredit it. A 'vigilante' group arose, which still regularly publishes debunking articles. Paranormal research continues in roughly the same way as it did before Geller arrived on the scene.

This lack of clear and definitive outcome is, however, unsurprising in the light of the analysis in the rest of the book. Since the settling of a major scientific dispute is like the settling of any other major dispute, there is no reason to expect that it should happen quickly and efficiently. Indeed, there is reason to expect scientific disputes to be resolved less quickly than others. To take up the legal analogy from an earlier paragraph: judges and juries terminate debates according to a prescribed timetable, otherwise, one may be sure, the advocates themselves would rarely agree a verdict. In the case of science there is no agreed judge or jury or timetable.

Disputes in science are supposed to be unlike other disputes because the grounds of argument can be set out clearly and because unambiguous evidence can be brought to bear on the issues. In chapters 3 and 4 we looked at the way that scientists and philosophers argue in the abstract about the existence of parapsychological phenomena. In chapters 5, 6 and 7 we looked at the way that evidence is brought to bear on these arguments. The parapsychological debate has been carried through from a range of stances. Paranormal phenomena have been said on the one hand to contradict orthodox science, or, on the other, to be a necessary part of the modern scientific world view. Others have dismissed the very idea that a new phenomenon could contradict science – since science must encompass all new natural phenomena. Alternatively, it has been said that science is full of contradictions anyway. Even where arguers have agreed that the paranormal does contradict science, they have disagreed about the consequences of this view. For some it shows that the paranormal claims must be mistaken, for others it shows that paranormal phenomena are of vital importance. For still others, it means that even if they do exist they are fundamentally unimportant. All of these arguments were set out and exemplified in chapter 3. One set of arguments – to do with the relevance of the quantum theory – was saved for the next chapter.

In chapter 4 we explained those aspects of quantum theory that have brought it to prominence in the debate over the existence of paranormal phenomena. It is the paradoxical nature of quantum theory itself which seems to allow for happenings such as paranormal events. The strange nature of quantum theory was brought out by examination of the 'measurement problem' and the 'Einstein-Podolsky-Rosen' (EPR) paradox.

A closer examination, however, shows that the variety of interpretations of quantum mechanics makes possible a range of arguments about its compatibility with the paranormal. Both the measurement problem and the EPR paradox have resolutions which can seem to leave no room for paranormal phenomena, or can seem to make paranormal phenomena possible, or can seem to make the strangest of paranormal phenomena - such as retrospective psychokinesis - actually necessary! Both chapters 3 and 4 show the failure of all the deductive arguments that have been deployed so far in the attempt to settle the debate about the existence of paranormal phenomena. If this debate is an instance of paradigm-conflict or discontinuity of some sort in rational processes, then the deductive arguments which have been deployed so far cannot resolve it. We *induce* that no such arguments could ever bridge such a gap.

The debate about the existence of the paranormal subsumes a broad range of phenomena. Indeed, the description 'paranormal' is open-ended; it defines by excluding the normal rather than by setting a positive boundary on what is to be included. Of course, the description is conventionally applied to a fairly restricted range of phenomena, as we explained in chapter 2. However, even this range is too wide to make it feasible to undertake a detailed study of all the evidence for and against. In chapters 5 and 6 we described our investigation of the way evidence is brought to bear on the particular argument about paranormal metal bending. In these chapters we worked through our own development of evidence. In chapter 7 we looked at some others' deployment of evidence on the broad question of psychokinesis.

Chapters 5 and 6 described a series of experiments done by the authors in collaboration with others. The experiments were set out in some detail so that the processes which led to the production of the published account could be followed. The experiments were then reanalysed and the underlying assumptions and taken-for-granted expectations of the experimenters were brought out. It turns out that the experimental methods used and the interpretation of results were specific to presuppositions consonant with the world being 'normal'. Though the experimental evidence seemingly pointed, in an unambiguous way, to fraud as the explanation of spoon-bending, the same experiments, interpreted under the expectation of regular and normal manifestations of psychokinetic abilities, could have provided evidence for the further positive study of those abilities.

Rather than casting doubt on the existence of paranormal metal bending, the experimenters would have had to explain the paucity of data as being the result of deficiencies in their work. All cases of bending, however slight, would be naturally explained as the result of the action of psychokinetic abilities. Pamplin, Collins and Pinch all accepted fraud as their favoured interpretation because of their fundamentally orthodox predispositions.[2]

Thus, the conclusion of these two chapters is that experimental evidence is not unambiguous. It may appear to be unambiguous so long as the assumptions upon which it is based are not examined too radically. One might say that experimental evidence appears unambiguous within a taken-for-granted set of rules of induction but that different rules of induction operate in different scientific paradigms. A fortiori we may expect different rules of induction to operate in radically different societies, yielding different, but self-consistent, pictures of the world.

This conclusion is given further weight when the use of other scientists' experimental evidence is examined. In chapter 7 we saw that opponents in the debate about the existence of paranormal metal bending and other psychokinetic phenomena actually have put alternative interpretations on the same data. This happens in the most straightforward way when different groups have different definitions of competence, when the term is ascribed to whole experimental set-ups. Thus different groups were able to claim that the same completed experiments demonstrated either the existence or the non-existence of psychokinetic phenomena. Furthermore, those who believe in the phenomena can continue to do what appears to them to be sensible cumulative scientific work - solving new puzzles as they come along - whereas those who do not believe would not see anything being worked on. This is not a difference of physiology, psychology or optics, but a difference in the taken-for-granted rules of interpretation of experiments.

These differences have a tendency to extend 'back' into 'orthodox' physics. Some of our respondents found themselves reinterpreting the past as though psychokinesis were a natural explanation for familiar scientific experiences or previously puzzling results. The new rules for inductive generalisation suggested that certain old experiments had always exhibited previously unnoticed psi effects. This could account for previously ambiguous results in a parsimonious way.

The process of reinterpretation did, however, pose problems for scientists who wished to continue to use techniques that they had acquired within their orthodox careers. Conventional reasoning seems to suggest that the reinterpretation process must be extended to routine measurements. These could no longer be taken as unproblematic. As we saw, experimenters actually solved these problems by recourse to a variety of ad hoc pragmatic theories. Again, a purely cognitive approach to the relationship between forms of scientific life does not capture the picture. New habits of mind present new technical problems, yet pragmatic approaches to practice can solve the problems even when logical extrapolation in certain directions would seem to make them a priori insoluble.

The coextensive nature of ideas and social actions can also be seen outside those actions which pertain to narrowly defined experimental activity. In the final chapter broader changes were examined. Certain types of activity, it was suggested, are typical of revolutionary periods whether in science or in politics. These types of activity are related to antagonism, to uncertainty and to divided loyalty. In the case of research on paranormal metal bending, antagonism between camps was very evident - even organised. Uncertainty was manifest in the ritualistic demands for reliability and replicability. Consciousness of the possibility of divided loyalty was manifest in the accusations of inauthenticity which characterised the episode under examination. Each of these manifestations of revolutionary activity was documented.

Finally, the traces of what might have become permanent features of post-psychokinetic life were described and examined. The Zande way of life (Evans-Pritchard, 1976), coextensive as it is with the operation of the poison oracle, must include what would be for us an unusual interest in chickens and in witches. The psychokinetic way of life would seem to have its counterparts. New categories of individuals, such as gifted psychics and those who can enhance or extinguish psychic performance, began to develop. The very flavour of laboratory life began to change from one of austerity and objectivity of relationships to one of bonhomie and communality between scientist, technician and experimental subject. Acceptable 'healthy scepticism' - which lies at the heart of scientific method according to many philosophies of science - would disappear if certain experimental interpretations were taken up. Fortunately, or unfortunately, this state of affairs does not seem likely to come about in the near future. Meanwhile, we can live comfortably with our taken-for-granted, and therefore unnoticeable, 'normal' ways of acting.[3]

The reader who has persisted this far will realise that an unusual exercise has been attempted in this book. There may be many readers who have been surprised at, or disappointed with, what has been done. There will be those who expected a 'debunking' exercise aimed at spoon-bending 'pseudo-science'. There will be others who are disappointed in not finding scientists' beliefs in these paranormal phenomena explained by their wider religious, philosophical or political predilections, or even their positions in the social structure. Again, there may be a group who expected to see some sort of defence of paranormal research against unfair repression. Experience suggests that some readers might even see the work as a defence of aspects of parapsychology in so far as it does not do an outright job of debunking.[4]

With the evidence at hand, any of the above types of analysis could have been pursued. Evidence has been collected that would suggest, on the one hand, that paranormal metal bending is a 'genuine scientific phenomenon that is being unfairly repressed', and (see above p. 23) there have been times when such phenomena seemed, to both authors, to be a necessary part of their world of ideas. On the other hand, attention could be drawn to the well-documented cases of subjects cheating, the large sums of money made out of this episode by certain of the proponents of Geller, their moments of apparent insincerity and their more trans- parent mistakes.[5] Some examples of the range of possible inter- pretations of the whole affair were given at the end of chapter 2.

The authors do not know whether paranormal metal bending is 'real' or not - nor, as sociologists, do they care. It would make not one jot of difference to the analysis. Doubtless, however, the scientific fate of the phenomenon will affect what will be looked for in this work. If, as seems almost certain, it is to fade away as just another fad, the authors will probably be accused of missing the whole point. Views such as these would be inappropriate, how- ever, because what has been done here is neutral to the existence of psychokinesis. The question of its existence is a non-question from the point of view of this research and its analysis. As we have stressed throughout, conventional opinion as to the quality of scientists' work, or the motives for it, must not be unthinkingly adopted by the sociologist of scientific knowledge, if a sociologi- cally debilitating ethnocentricism is to be avoided. That is why the work and ideas of some unprestigious scientists have been quoted alongside the work of others whose opinion would be con- ventionally taken to count for much more. Sociologists are not hyenas waiting for the rotten meat to be abandoned by the scien- tific lion.

If the analysis has been convincing then it will have shown, through an empirical study, that philosophies of science that de- pend heavily upon the invocation of experimental evidence to decide between major differences in theoretical perspective are not tenable. It would seem that evidence is so bound up with the society or social group which gives rise to it that theories held by members of radically different scientifico-social groups cannot be adequately tested against each other by experiment. It matters not whether the evidence is intended to corroborate, 'prove' or refute the theories in question. Similarly, these differences can- not be settled by logical argument. If this is accepted for science - the 'locus classicus' of modern rationality - then, a fortiori, it must be accepted for relations between other culturally divided social groups. More detailed understanding of the relationships between such groups must arise from further study of the ideal- typical case of science. Our hope for this study is that the detailed analysis of an attempt to change what counts as scientific knowl- edge will shed some light on the process, not only of scientific revolution, but also of social revolution. Both sorts of revolution involve changes in what counts as true knowledge about the world.[6]

As we have stressed, one overall aim of this work has been to present the social study of science as a peculiarly straightforward and empirical way of studying the construction of knowledge. What we have looked at here, is knowledge at a time of revolution. What has been demonstrated, with specific reference to science, is that the idea of paradigm incommensurability, even when interpreted in its most radical Winchian/Wittgensteinian sense, has a part to play in the understanding of contemporary science. Sociologists should not be afraid of taking such philosophically contentious and apparently intangible ideas into the field.

To return again to our main theme, a major problem, perhaps the major problem, for the sociology of knowledge is the question of the nature of 'rationality' and the extent to which a universal rationality must be assumed. The answer to this question defines the limits of the sociology of knowledge. One way of approaching the question is to look at the universalistic claims of science. If evidence of radical cultural discontinuities can be found in contemporary science, and that is the claim of this work, then the scope of the sociology of knowledge is very wide indeed.

NOTES

INTRODUCTION

1   The work of Ludwick Fleck (1979; first published in German in 1935) represents an astonishingly early attempt at a full-blooded sociology of scientific knowledge, though Fleck would not have called it that. He appears to have anticipated Kuhn's analysis in many respects. Still more remarkably, Fleck was an active researcher in the very field of science that he took as a case study. See Mulkay (1979) for a discussion of the reservations regarding science in the work of Mannheim (1936), who wrote at the same time as Fleck.

2   This may be the particular importance of the sociology of science for sociology in general.
    Of course, to use rationality as discovered within science as an exemplary case of rationality in general is to take the view at the outset that scientific culture is not a special case. This is a view which has been well argued, most notably by Barnes (1974), and we do not intend to go over the old argument again. At the same time whether it is a view which can be held consistently in the face of the practice of modern empirical science is one of the questions on which this study sheds light. The answer, we believe, is an affirmative one. For a discussion of recent work on the sociology of science in the context of sociology, see Overington (1979).

3   See Pinch (1979a) for a comparison of Kuhn's latest work with his earlier position.

4   See Wittgenstein (1953, 1956); Winch (1958, 1964); Berger and Luckman (1967); Collingwood (1967); and Krausz (1972, 1973).

5   Even recent ethnomethodological studies do not seem to have gone as far as this, though the degree of commitment to the study of science of researchers currently associated with Professor Garfinkel is laudable indeed.

6   There is some danger that fragmentary evidential artifacts may be taken to be substantially revealing of the process of scientific discovery. Would one be able to learn much from a tape-recording of Archimedes in the bath shouting 'Eureka'?

CHAPTER 1   THE IDEA OF SOCIO-COGNITIVE DISCONTINUITY AND ITS PROBLEMS

1   For four components of scientific change see Weingart (1974).

2   For a discussion of the application of Wittgensteinian ideas to the sociology of scientific knowledge see Bloor (1973) and Collins (1974).

3   'Chamber's Twentieth Century Dictionary' (New Edn, 1972).

4   The work of Paul Feyerabend (e.g. 1975) is highly germane to this debate. See also Hesse (1974).

5   Note that the discovery of apparently ordered 'rational' debate, based on manifest mutual comprehensibility between members of different paradigm groups, would only bear upon the question of incommensurability under certain circumstances. This may have been overlooked because of the prevalent confusion of incommensurability with incomparability. To argue metaphorically, the side and diagonal of a square are incommensurable but they can be compared: one is longer than the other; they always point in different directions, etc. In the same way there are dimensions along which incommensurable paradigms could be compared without conflict.
    For example, the notion of deity and teleological explanation might be common to paradigms which in other respects constituted quite different natural worlds. Presence or absence of deities might then be unproblemati-

cally agreed upon and might be taken as an indicator of progress even though the deities and teleology might be explaining different things in different theories. What is being suggested here is that, if members of different paradigm groups agreed that their paradigms contained more or less deities and teleology, they might agree that a criterion of progress could be fashioned upon such a comparison. But this is not to say that the members would have to agree that one paradigm was better than another on this basis. Perhaps one group would consider presence, and one group would consider absence, of these concepts as signifying progress. Thus the notion of incommensurability is not outlawed by its incompatibility with rational talk, or the possibility of cross-paradigmatic acceptance of a notion of progress.

To give a more relevant example, certain of our more orthodox respondents would agree that the non-materialist elements in parapsychological research represented progress over currently available world views in physics, even though they might not accept a shred of the experimental evidence so far amassed.

6   For example, if the undoubtedly revolutionary ideas of the actors involved become subverted, once they have seized power, by the pragmatic necessities associated with holding on to it.

7   This is not quite true. Parapsychologists have taken to Kuhn with something of the same avidity as sociologists once did. Nevertheless it seems unlikely that any parapsychologists ever 'set out' to revolutionise science in the Kuhnian sense, though many now rationalise their rejection in these terms.

8   Kuhn himself, in conversation, has suggested such an approach.

9   The difficulty here is that the archives represent a slice of activity that may be entirely inappropriate for the type of investigation in hand. What is more, historical sources must be subject to particularly vicious distortion in science, where earlier cultural resources are suppressed because of the prevailing myths of continuity, progress, cumulativeness, and rationality within the discipline. The definition of current knowledge as truth, and past knowledge as mistaken, is a central article of faith for practising scientists and teachers of science - the transmitters of scientific culture across the generations.

10   David Bloor's (1976) 'strong programme in the sociology of knowledge' comprises four tenets which include 'symmetry' and 'impartiality' of explanation of true and false beliefs. Bloor's other two tenets - causality and reflexivity - tend to confuse an otherwise clear prescription (Collins, 1980a). Empirical work precipitated by the strong programme has a rather different emphasis from that presented here, in particular in its stress on the notion of 'interests' as a causal explanatory variable.

11   He suggests that science can expand into 'areas of ignorance' and thus not engender opposition (Mulkay, 1975).

12   We believe that our extrapolation tells us that PMB does (did) have revolutionary possibilities. Naturally, these possibilities would only be realised if PMB was taken up in a certain way, for example, after the manner of Hasted, rather than Taylor (see chapter 8). Nevertheless, we are claiming more than that problems of cross-paradigm communication emerge entirely out of the way that scientists take up the options open to them. Such a view seems to be suggested by Barnes and MacKenzie (1979, p. 64, note 11). There are also questions about what options are realistically open, and the answers to these have something to do with what currently counts as coherence within available traditions of thought and practice.

Travis (1980), in a study of the memory-transfer phenomenon, shows how different options may render a new view apparently contradictory or apparently continuous with an old one.

13   Another example is the activities of some sceptics who, before attempting an exposé, befriend parapsychologists under the guise of wishing to repeat their experiments and use the experimental details gleaned as evidence of the parapsychologists' sloppiness.

CHAPTER 2   PARANORMAL METAL BENDING RESEARCH:
ITS BACKGROUND AND ITS GROWTH

1   Recent authors include Gordon (1975), Allison (1973), McVaugh and
Mauskopf (1976), Nilsson (1975, 1976), Wynne (1979) and Palfreman (1979).
Gauld (1967) has written an instructive history of the early days of parapsychological research. McVaugh and Mauskopf (1980) have recently completed a history of parapsychology up to the 1940s.

2   In addition to the American and British communities there are other 'out-
posts' of parapsychology in Europe and the Third World. Their work has
had less impact in general. Rumours abound as to the size and significance
of Soviet and eastern block efforts. It would seem that highly sensationalised
reports of a concerted Soviet attempt to lead the West in psi research have
little basis (Pratt, 1971).

3   Recently the eminent physicist John Wheeler (1979a) has attempted to remove
the Parapsychological Association from the AAAS. This disaffiliation attempt
was unsuccessful and Wheeler (1979b) eventually admitted that some of his
specific charges against parapsychology were incorrect.

4   By contingent forum we mean the forum in which are set those actions
which – according to old-fashioned philosophic orthodoxy – are not supposed
to affect the constitution of 'objective' knowledge. We would expect to find
there the content of popular and semi-popular journals, discussion and
gossip, fund raising and publicity seeking, the setting up and joining of
professional organisations, the corralling of student followers, and everything that scientists do in connection with their work, but which is not
found in the 'constitutive forum.'

5   The true cost of the research has, of course, been far higher. The figure
does not include the salaries of the researchers, the time of technicians,
who in the early days controlled the videotape equipment and later set it
up and dismantled it, and the use of space and equipment. Fortunately, all
these could be provided within the 'infrastructure' of Bath University. In
Britain it is not usual to charge the basic infrastructural items to research
grants, for they are seen as being paid for through the University Grants
Committee without specific 'earmarking'. In the USA a large 'overhead' is
charged on each research project to cover these items.

6   See Westrum (1976) for an excellent critical review of this article. Westrum's
review was, ironically, published in 'The Zetetic', causing, so we understand, a considerable rift among the editors.

7   For an examination of scientology by a sociologist see Wallis (1977).

CHAPTER 3   IS PARAPSYCHOLOGY COMPATIBLE WITH SCIENCE?
SCIENCE, PHYSICS, PSYCHOLOGY

1   Thus in Figure 4.1 the lines which link the 'base of the tree' to its
finer branches are not our deductive links, nor do we argue for their
deductive validity. To argue for the validity of each individual link would
itself be the work of a book or a paper and we cannot present that work
here. Our presentation of argument 'fragments' is meant to give a taste of
the larger debate and to form the foundation of an inductive argument.
This inductive argument is that, since all these deductive arguments and
counter-arguments are viable to the extent that they are reasonably publishable, no deductive argument is likely to be decisive.

2   We rely on Burt's quotation here since, in spite of careful perusal of
Hansel's writings, we have been unable to find the original.

CHAPTER 4   IS PARAPSYCHOLOGY COMPATIBLE WITH SCIENCE?
THE QUANTUM THEORY

1   For early examples of how physicists attempted to connect quantum mechanics with parapsychology see Jordan (1951, 1955) and Margenau (1956).
The possibilities of forming links between the two areas were critically
assessed by Chari (1956) and Whiteman (1973) before the current upsurge
of interest.

2   Interestingly enough it is the fundamental statistical nature of quantum

mechanics which is at the basis of the random-number generators used in many modern parapsychology experiments. The suitability of the randomness of quantum-mechanical events for parapsychology experiments seems to have first been suggested by Beloff and Evans (1961). The best-known experiments using such random-number generators are those of Schmidt (1969a, 1969b, 1970, 1971, 1973, 1975, 1976). The possibility of using such a set-up to test experimentally various interpretations of the quantum theory was first noted by Klip (1966, 1967).

3   A further conference was held in Reykjavik, Iceland, in 1977 (Puharich, 1979). Several of our respondents presented papers on quantum mechanics and parapsychology.

4   The Fundamental 'Fysiks' Group was organised by Elizabeth Rauscher, a theoretical physicist at the Lawrence Berkeley Laboratory. Its 1975/6 seminar programme reads as follows:
Organizational meeting and comments by Jack Sarfatti on 'Thermodynamics and information transfer', 7/5/75; Fritjof Capra, 'The Tao of physics' and 'Eastern thought and Western particle physics', 16/5/75 and 21/5/75; Fred Wolf, 'Quantum potential and causality', 28/5/75; June and July, Setting up remote viewing experiment no. 1 to replicate SRI work of H. Puthoff and R. Targ; Group discussion on 'Twin paradox', EPR, Young's double-slit experiment and the Michelson-Morley experiment (led by Fred Wolf and E.A. Rauscher), 23/7/75; meeting was called off due to Buford Price's announcement of the magnetic monopole find (one of them), 30/7/75; general discussion of the implications of physics for paranormal phenomena, 6/8/75; Jack Sarfatti, 'Topics in the foundations of the quantum theory of measurement', 12/7/75 (Bell's theorem and the necessity of superluminal quantum information transfer); John Clauser, 'Why I don't believe in quantum mechanics and objective local theories' - motivation from the 'Bell's theorem test', 19/9/75; Saul-Paul Sirag, 'Godel's incompleteness theorem and its relation to the Copenhagen view of quantum mechanical completeness', 3/10/75; Nick Herbert, 'Bell's theorem and superluminal signals', 10/10/75; E.A. Rauscher and G. Weissmann, 'Information transmission under conditions of sensory shielding and the EPR paradox', 24/10/75; Henry P. Stapp, 'Implications of Bell's theorem (what does it tell us about nature?)', 31/10/75; John F. Clauser, 'Counter efficiencies and the consequences for the "Bell theorem" experiment (the nature of photons)', 14/11/75; Fritjof Capra, 'Bell's theorem, bootstrap and the one-universe model', Part 1, 24/11/75; Fritjof Capra, 'Bell's theorem, bootstrap and the one-universe model', Part 11, 5/12/75; J. Sarfatti, E. Rauscher and S.P. Sirag, 'Time, space-like quantum signals, quanta and entropy and quanta of action', 12/12/75; report on the Esalen January Symposium on 'Physics and consciousness' (organized by J. Sarfatti and Mike Murphy), S.P. Sirag, J. Sarfatti, Fred Wolf, Nick Herbert, E. Rauscher and Laura Margolis, 6/2/76; Geoffrey Chew, 'S-matrix, bootstrap, and models of physical reality', 13/2/76; Philippe Eberhard, 'Quantum physics, external reality and tests of quantum theory', Part I, 20/2/76; Hal Puthoff and Russell Targ, 'Remote perception of natural targets - survey and current research', 27/2/76; Lesley Lamport, 'Everett-Wheeler many-universe theory and the quantum formalism for Young's double-slit experiment', 5/3/76; Philippe Eberhard, Part II, 12/3/76; George Weissmann, 'The Copenhagen pragmatic interpretation of quantum theory', 19/3/76; J. Sarfatti, 'Quantum logic and "Space-time code" of David Finkelstein', 26/3/76; N. Herbert, 'Quantum logic systems and quantum language - is it fundamental?' 2/4/76; F. Capra, 'David Bohm's view of reality - report on his return to the U.S.A.', 19/4/76. N. Herbert, 'Quantum Logic', Part II, 16/4/76; E.May, 'Maimonides research on psychokinesis', 23/4/76; B. Sparks, 'Are UFO's a physical or psychological phenomena?' 30/4/76; J. Harder, 'Exploring the unknown: possible evidence for UFO's', 7/5/76; S. Hubbard, 'History of parapsychology, methods and results', 14/5/76; E. May, 'Research methods in parapsychology: "Can you believe what you see?"', 21/5/76; E.A. Rauscher, 'Views of reality: Einstein special and general relativity and application to paranormal phenomena',

28/5/76; E.A. Rauscher, 'General relativity, cosmological models and multi-dimensional geometries', (Part II), 4/6/76; G. Weissmann, 'Propagation, S.-matrix and the Copenhagen interpretation of the quantum theory', 11/6/76; E.A. Rauscher, 'Results of my remote perception experiments', 17/6/76; G. Weissmann and H. Stapp, 'Copenhagen pragmatism and the S-matrix', Part II, 25/6/76.

5   For a more detailed account of this solution see Ballentine (1970).
6   For further details see d'Espagnat (1976).
7   The connection between mind and quantum theory has been pursued as an issue independently of parapsychology. Apart from the writings of Wigner, see Mills (1976) and Stapp (1968); see also Shimony (1963) and Freudlich (1972) for critical reviews. The connection between mind and quantum theory has also been pursued into neurophysiology; see, for example, Bass (1975). The neurophysiological connection between quantum mechanics and consciousness is an important element of Walker's theory of parapsychology (Walker, 1975, 1977). For an attempted experimental test by quantum physicists of whether consciousness reduces the wave packet, see Hall et al. (1977). The negative result of this experiment causes little trouble to those who draw on this solution to the measurement problem to explain parapsychology, since non-psychic subjects were used in the test (see Mattuck and Walker, 1979, p. 126).
8   See Costa de Beauregard (1975, 1976) and Walker (1970, 1971, 1972, 1974a, 1974b, 1975, 1976, 1979). For an extension of Walker's ideas see Mattuck (1979) and Mattuck and Walker (1979). For related views on consciousness, quantum mechanics and parapsychology, see Sarfatti (1974a, 1975, 1976a, 1976b) and Wolf (1975, 1976). See also 'Nous Letter' (1976).
9   See Dewitt (1970, 1971), Dewitt and Graham (1973b), Everett (1957), and Good (1975).
10 For another idea as to how tests of Bell's theorem may be connected to parapsychology, see Werbos (1973, 1975).
11 Other theories of quantum mechanics and parapsychology which seem to entail a radical break with present conceptions of quantum theory are those of Bastin (1975) and Whiteman (1975). For another approach altogether see Capra (1976).
12 The philosophy of parapsychology continues to flourish. For an interesting recent contribution see Braude (1980).

CHAPTER 5 PARANORMAL METAL BENDING AT BATH:
INVESTIGATING AND PUBLISHING
1   One argument that is gaining currency is that, since all accounts are unreliable, the only way to treat them is to look at the way they are constructed and read (Woolgar, 1976; Mulkay, 1980). In this work we are going to do much more than this with at least some of our accounts. For example, we are going to use Collins' account of the spoon-bending experiments to reveal something of the construction of the account published in 'Nature'.
    The philosophical/methodological stance of this work is 'interpretivism' (see chapter 1), a view which accepts that a participant in a social situation has a privileged understanding when compared with one who is not a participant. Thus, we would claim that Collins' account of the experiments is a better account than could be produced by one who was not present when the experiments were being performed.
    It seems to us that the belief that accounts should only be examined for their construction and reading rests on two fallacious arguments. Firstly, it rests on the reflexive argument: 'Since we discuss only the construction and reading of scientific accounts and eschew any mention of the relative validity of conflicting accounts, we should apply the same principle to our own accounts of social situations.' Such an argument can be drawn from, for example, Bloor (1976). We would argue that the reflexive argument rests on the prescription 'treat sociological knowledge as being like scientific knowledge', and this seems an arbitrary, unnecessary and undesirable prescription (see Collins, 1980a, for expansion of this point).

The second fallacious argument (very evident in Mulkay, 1980) rests on the claim that assumptions to do with the quality of (always unreliable) accounts can be entirely avoided if it is only their construction and reading that is attended to. (We will call this the 'judgmental neutrality argument'.) This claim is fallacious since, to pick on a set of accounts to study – for whatever reason – is to make a judgment about their quality. Otherwise, it would be possible to take any set of visual or aural stimuli as an account of anything. In these circumstances, for example, 'The Bluebells of Scotland' played on a comb-and-paper might well be taken as an account of the mechanisms of, say, oxidative phosphorylation. These would not be very productive circumstances in which to proceed. Thus all uses of accounts, including those that have no interest in the content of the accounts (such as purely conversational analyses), rest on judgments of quality even if it be native members' judgments that are adopted.

Given that such judgments have to be made somewhere along the way, the extent to which the analyst then wishes to use these judgments in his or her later analysis is a matter for choice. The decision is not forced on the analyst by the argument of 'judgmental neutrality'. It is then open to the analyst to do analyses of construction and reading of accounts, or to use these accounts in other ways.

What we have done is to select our set of scientific accounts via native members' judgments of their quality, e.g. they are published in sensible places or produced by responsible scientists. (We include ourselves as temporary native members of the scientific community.) We then concentrate only on the construction and reading of these accounts of scientific practice.

The accounts which we present as sociologists, we treat as being more correct than anyone else's accounts of the events in question. We are not particularly interested in the way we construct our sociological accounts or the way they are read. We are, of course, interested in methodology and in doing our work well according to the canons of (at least one section of) the sociological community.

2   All names are pseudonyms where they are given in inverted commas on first presentation. Throughout our work we have tried to conceal the identity of our child subjects (see chapter 8 for further discussion).

3   Running agitatedly, looking very close to tears, seemingly masturbating with the metal rod.

CHAPTER 6 PARANORMAL METAL BENDING AT BATH: USING THE PAST IN MAKING THE PRESENT

1   It should be added that H was a very firm believer in the phenomenon, and different reactions might be obtained from disbelievers. Indeed, one respondent took one of our photographs to illustrate cheating in a highly sceptical book that he was writing on the subject. Nevertheless, it is important here, too, not to fall into the 'cultural dope trap'. Some believers would be prepared to accept that the photographs do show cheating because cheating subjects were selected, and some sceptics might not think that the photographs made good evidence. Perhaps it would be possible to find a statistical correlation between belief and attitude to the photographs, but this is not the sort of point that is being made here. The point that is being made concerns the way that perceptions feed into beliefs; how artifacts are needed to maintain beliefs in certain perceptions but that the artifacts themselves are not unambiguous.

2   We feel no need to be apologetic about the interpretative comments contained in the square brackets in these transcripts. We can imagine that ethnomethodologists might raise their eyebrows at the licence we have given ourselves. We feel that we are in an interpretatively privileged position (see chapter 5, note 1).

3   Our physicist colleague, Dr Pamplin, read a draft of this manuscript. He wrote 'rubbish' in the margin opposite this section!

4   Subsequently a fourth account has been published in a book. Marks and Kammann (1980, p. 148) claim that:

Taylor's theory that metal benders don't cheat received a serious blow
when Harry Collins, a sociologist at the University of Bath, observed
young metal benders through a one-way mirror. In association with psychologist [sic] Dr. Brian Pamplin, Collins reported in *Nature* (vol. 257,
p. 8) that he observed six young benders, five of whom successfully bent
metal rods or spoons. This bending occurred, however, *only while the
observers in the room with the subject deliberately looked away.* (Shyness
effect?) In every case the subjects were observed cheating by the experimenters on the other side of the mirror. (See Fig. 20 for one typical
case.)
[Their Fig. 20 actually shows photographs of a Geller set-up.] Pamplin
and Collins asserted that 'in no case did we observe a rod or a spoon
bent other than by palpably normal means.' This was a bitter pill even
for Collins to swallow, as he'd fully expected to observe genuine psychic
spoon bending.

5   The 'environment' here includes the whole of the (changing) universe.
6   This is a rather similar process to that which led the positivists into what
     seemed to be the dead end of 'logical atomism'.
7   See Collins (1980b) for an expansion and application of this point.

CHAPTER 7 EXPERIMENT AND PARADIGM:
ALTERNATIVE INTERPRETATIONS OF EVENTS AND RESULTS
1   We do not mean to claim that Professor Hasted has never used controlled
     conditions in his experiments, nor that he does not use such conditions
     nowadays. Our remarks refer to a period within Professor Hasted's research
     career, and to the logic of his research programme at that time.
2   He believed that the potential audience of Geller's potential feat were so
     sceptical that they reacted – via a kind of retrospective psychokinesis – so
     as to make the feat impossible!
3   Collins had found on an earlier field trip that parapsychologists volunteered
     reinterpretations of the gravity-wave story and of Backster's plant phenom-
     ena. That is why these two incidents were made the subject of deliberate
     questioning. The voluntary reinterpretation of high-energy physics results
     was new.
4   Cleve Backster, whose work is discussed earlier in the chapter, had very
     severe problems with experimenter effects. His experiments required that
     plants be exposed to the death of specific living organisms while they were
     held in a controlled environment in which no other deaths were taking place
     (Backster, 1968). Since millions of microbes are dying continuously in the
     air, and in and on the human body, he had little chance of producing the
     controlled conditions he sought.

CHAPTER 8 EXPERIMENT AND PARADIGM:
SYMPTOMS OF A SCIENTIFIC REVOLUTION
1   This is not to say that antagonism is a sufficient indication of revolutionary
     activity. Resistance and antagonism are likely to be encountered in areas
     of science which it would be quite inappropriate to label as revolutionary.
     Barber (1961), for example, has considered the nature of resistance to
     scientific discovery of all types. Many other cases of resistance to new ideas
     have been discussed, where the potentially revolutionary nature of the
     ideas is less than clear (e.g. see Dolby 1979).
     Another set of reservations pertaining to this study involves the ambiguity
     of some of our respondents' actions and the ambiguity of others' responses
     to them. A subset of respondents (from both sides of the controversy) had
     histories of idiosyncratic behaviour (for scientists) long before they entered
     the PMB controversy. Both John Taylor and Christopher Evans (an active
     member of the Committee for the Scientific Investigation of the Claims of the
     Paranormal) were well known in the field of scientific popularisation – even
     scientific showbusiness! Taylor had written popular books, some might say
     irresponsibly speculative books, on the brain ('The Shape of Minds to Come',

1971) and the physics and 'philosophy' of 'black holes' ('Black Holes: The End of the Universe?', 1973). In addition he had appeared on television as a scientific 'authority'. In 1977 Taylor wrote a piece on the paranormal for the magazine 'Vogue'. Chris Evans (whose untimely death occurred recently) favoured frequent popularising appearances on the media, had a number of semi-academic sidelines and was known among psychologists as somewhat of a jet-setter. Inevitably (this is not necessarily to say 'justly'), such activities are viewed with suspicion and distaste by the mainstream scientific community, and any involvement by these men with new scientific 'media-bait' is likely to be credited with the basest motives, irrespective of the seriousness of the 'internal' socio-cognitive threat of their ideas.

A third reservation concerns the contribution of the media to this particular debate. The very intenseness of media coverage of the controversy - and it appears to have remarkably evergreen qualities - has had a distorting effect on the debate only a part of which could fairly be said to be related to the specific quality of community life associated with the new paradigm. The media must have contributed to resistance to the (potential) revolution directly and indirectly. Their direct contribution is in their substantive critical comments. Indirectly, they must have caused conservative scientists to shy away even further from 'Gellermania', as the press calls it, and they must have reduced the scientific legitimacy of the field by making it seem that the media rather than the journals have been the proper place to hold the debate (see Collins and Pinch, 1979, for expansion of these points).

2   Frankel's paper (1976) on the history of corpuscular and wave theories of light is refreshing in its attempt to treat a scientific revolution as involving organised political activities in the social world of scientists.

3   Randi's emulation of Houdini, in most of his activities, becomes clear on reading Milbourne Christopher's fascinating biography (1970).

4   Of course, in the case of parapsychology, with its long history of fraud, security consciousness is greatly exaggerated.

5   Bourdieu (1975) provides a very interesting analysis of professional strategies. He suggests that the dominant scientists in a field are committed to conservation strategies 'aimed at ensuring the perpetuation of the established scientific order to which their interests are linked' (p. 29). 'New entrants' may find themselves orientated towards the risk-free investments of succession strategies, which are guaranteed to bring them a predictable career and the profits awaiting those who realise the official ideal of scientific excellence through limited innovations, within authorised limits. Alternatively, new entrants may opt for subversion strategies which have infinitely more costly and more hazardous investments and will not bring them the profits accruing to the holders of the monopoly of scientific legitimacy unless they can achieve a complete redefinition of the principles legitimating domination. Newcomers who refuse the beaten tracks cannot 'beat the dominant at their own game' unless they make additional, strictly scientific, investments, from which they cannot expect high, short-run profits (in terms of recognition, etc.) since the whole logic of the system is against them (p. 30).

6   In what some critics would see as the final vindication of their views, Taylor has recently retracted his views regarding the existence of paranormal phenomena. In articles (Balanovski and Taylor, 1978; Taylor and Balanovski, 1980) and a book (Taylor, 1980) he explicates his electromagnetic theory and claims that, since no abnormal electromagnetic fields were associated with purported paranormal events, these events cannot be paranormal.

CONCLUSION

1   Professor Hasted is still working on the problem and a book of his is about to be published (Hasted, 1981).

2   That is to say, though we set out to look for psychokinesis, we did it from within a fundamentally orthodox viewpoint. To save misunderstanding, we

should add that, were we to change our professions and become parapsy-chologists, our first efforts would still be informed by this fundamentally orthodox viewpoint. It is a viewpoint given to us by our current locations within scientific society.

3   They are of course becoming noticeable nowadays in the 'New Sociology of Science' of which this book is a part.

4   Certainly, this was how an earlier piece of work of ours was interpreted (Collins and Pinch, 1979, p. 263).

5   One would not need to seek far! Hasted withdrew early claims about the production of wire 'scrunches' in glass vessels with holes in them (Alabone and Hasted 1977) and Franklin admitted a mistake as regards the apparent paranormal bending of a metal ring (Franklin, 1973, 1977).

6   The argument of this book goes against the grain of some Marxist ('old left') writings on science in which the claim is made that scientific practice tran-scends the boundaries of social revolutions (see Werskey (1978) for a dis-cussion of such writings). It seems that for such writers capitalist science and socialist science are the same animal (but possibly untethered within socialism). Clearly, if radical discontinuities can be found within science, then the appeal to the universality of scientific practice as a motor of social change or progress is not tenable.

BIBLIOGRAPHY

Alabone, R.P. and Hasted, J.B. (1977), Letter to the Editor, 'Journal of the
   Society for Psychical Research', 49, 558-9.
Allison, P.D. (1973), Social Aspects of Scientific Innovation: The Case of Para-
   psychology, M.A. dissertation, University of Wisconsin.
'Ariadne' (1972), 'New Scientist', 9 November, 360.
Ayer, A.J. (1965), Chance, 'Scientific American', 44-54.
Backster, C. (1968), Evidence of a primary perception in plant life, 'Inter-
   national Journal of Parapsychology', 10, 4, 329-48.
Balanovski, E. and Taylor, J.G. (1978), Can electromagnetism account for
   extrasensory phenomena?, 'Nature', 276, 64-7.
Ballentine, L.E. (1970), The statistical interpretation of quantum mechanics,
   'Reviews of Modern Physics', 42, 358-81.
Barber, B. (1961), Resistance by scientists to scientific discovery, 'Science',
   134, 596-602.
Barnes, S.B. (1974), 'Scientific Knowledge and Sociological Theory', London:
   Routledge & Kegan Paul.
Barnes, S.B. and MacKenzie, D. (1979), On the role of interests in scientific
   change, in Wallis (1979), 49-66.
Barnes, S.B. and Shapin, S. (eds) (1979), 'Natural Order: Historical Studies
   of Scientific Culture', Beverly Hills: Sage.
Bass, L. (1975), A quantum mechanical mind-body interaction, 'Foundation of
   Physics', 5, 159-72.
Bastin, E.W. (ed.) (1971), 'Quantum Theory and Beyond', Cambridge: Cam-
   bridge University Press.
Bastin, E.W. (1975), Connections between events in the context of the com-
   binatorial model for a quantum process, in Oteri (1975), 229-52.
Bell, J.S. (1964), On the Einstein, Podolsky and Rosen paradox, 'Physics',
   1, 195-200.
Beloff, J. (1970), Parapsychology and its neighbours, 'Journal of Parapsy-
   chology', 34, 129-42.
Beloff, J. (1974), 'New Directions in Parapsychology', London: Elek Science.
Beloff, J. (1975), Letter to the Editor, 'Journal of the Society for Psychical
   Research', 48, 154-5.
Beloff, J. (1977), Personal communication, June.
Beloff, J. and Bate, D. (1971), An attempt to replicate the Schmidt findings,
   'Journal of the Society for Psychical Research', March, 45, 21-31.
Beloff, J. and Evans, L. (1961), A radioactivity test of psychokinesis, 'Journal
   of the Society for Psychical Research', 41, 41-6.
Berger, P.L. and Luckman, T. (1967), 'The Social Construction of Reality',
   London: Allen Lane.
Billig, M. (1972), Positive and negative experimental psi results in psychology
   and parapsychology journals, 'Journal of the Society for Psychical Research',
   46, 136-42.
Bloor, D. (1973), Wittgenstein and Mannheim on the sociology of mathematics,
   'Studies in the History and Philosophy of Science', 4, 173-91.
Bloor, D. (1976), 'Knowledge and Social Imagery', London: Routledge & Kegan
   Paul.
Bohm, D. (1951), 'Quantum Theory', Englewood Cliffs, N.J.: Prentice-Hall.
Bohm, D. (1952), A suggested interpretation of the quantum theory in terms of
   'hidden' variables, I & II, 'Physical Review', 85, 166-93.
Bohm, D. (1957), 'Causality and Chance in Modern Physics', London: Routledge
   & Kegan Paul.

Bohm, D. (1974), Letter to the Editor, 'New Scientist', 31 October, 356-7.
Bohm, D. and Hiley, B. (1976), Some remarks on Sarfatti's proposed connection between quantum phenomena and the volitional activity of the observer-participator, 'Psychoenergetic Systems', 1, 173-9.
Boring, E.G. (1955), The present status of parapsychology, 'American Scientist', 43, 108-17.
Bourdieu, P. (1975), The specificity of the scientific field and the social conditions of the progress of reason, 'Social Science Information', 14, 19-47.
Braude, S. (1980), 'ESP and Psychokinesis: A Philosophical Examination', Philadelphia: Temple University Press.
Brier, B. (1974), 'Precognition and the Philosophy of Science', New York: Humanities Press.
Broad, C.D. (1937), The philosophical implications of foreknowledge, I & II, 'Proceedings of the Aristotelian Society', Supplementary Volume, 16, 177-209, 229-45.
Broad, C.D. (1949), The relevance of psychical research to philosophy, 'Philosophy', 24, 291-309.
Broad, C.D. (1960), Contribution to: Physicality and psi, a symposium and forum discussion, 'Journal of Parapsychology', 24, 16.
Brown, R. (1965), 'Social Psychology', New York: Macmillan and Free Press.
Burt, C. (1960), Contribution to: Physicality and psi, a symposium and forum discussion, 'Journal of Parapsychology', 24, 29.
Burt, C. (1966), Parapsychology and its implications, 'International Journal of Neuropsychiatry', 2, 363-77.
Burt, C. (1967a), The implications of parapsychology for general psychology, 'Journal of Parapsychology', 31, 1-18.
Burt, C. (1967b), Psychology and parapsychology, in Smythies (1967), 61-141.
Capra, F. (1976), Can science explain psychic phenomena?, unpublished paper, Lawrence Berkeley Laboratory, University of California.
Chari, C.T.K. (1956), Quantum physics and parapsychology, 'Journal of Parapsychology', 20, 166-83.
Chari, C.T.K. (1975), Parapsychology, quantum logic, and information theory, in Oteri, (1975), 74-90.
Chauvin, R. (1970), To reconcile psi and physics, 'Journal of Parapsychology', 34, 215-9.
Christopher, M. (1970), 'Houdini: The Untold Story', New York: Pocket Books.
Clauser, J.F. and Horne, M.A. (1974), Experimental consequences of objective local theories, 'Physical Review', 10, 526-35.
Clauser, J.F., Horne, M.A., Shimony, A. and Holt, R.A. (1969), Proposed experiment to test local hidden-variable theories, 'Physical Review Letters', 23, 880-4.
Collingwood, R.G. (1939), 'Autobiography', Oxford: Oxford University Press.
Collingwood, R.G. (1967), 'The Idea of History', Oxford University Press.
Collins, H.M. (1974), The TEA set: Tacit knowledge and scientific networks, 'Science Studies', 4, 165-86.
Collins, H.M. (1975), The seven sexes: A study in the sociology of a phenomenon, 'Sociology', 9, 205-24.
Collins, H.M. (1976), Upon the replication of scientific findings: a discussion illuminated by the experience of researchers into parapsychology, Paper presented to the 4S/I.S.A. Conference, Cornell University, 4-6 November.
Collins, H.M. (1980a), The radical programme as a methodological imperative, Paper presented to the Philosophy of the Social Sciences conference, Toronto (published, 'Philosophy of the Social Sciences', II (1981), 215-24).
Collins, H.M. (1980b), Comment on 'Seven evidential experiments', 'Zetetic Scholar', 6, July, 98-100.
Collins, H.M. (ed.) (1981), 'Knowledge and Controversy: Studies of Modern Natural Science', special issue of 'Social Studies of Science', 11, 1-158.
Collins, H.M. and Cox, G. (1976), Recovering relativity: did prophecy fail?, 'Social Studies of Science', 6, 423-45.
Collins, H.M. and Cox, G. (1977), Relativity revisited: Mrs Keech, a suitable case for special treatment?, 'Social Studies of Science', 7, 327-80.

Collins, H.M. and Harrison, R. (1975), Building a TEA laser: the caprices of communication, 'Social Studies of Science', 5, 441-50.
Collins, H.M. and Pinch, T.J. (1979), The construction of the paranormal: nothing unscientific is happening, in Wallis (1979), 237-70.
Colodny, R.G. (ed) (1972), 'Paradigms and Paradoxes', Pittsburgh: University of Pittsburgh Press.
Condon, E.U. (1969), UFO's I have loved and lost, 'Bulletin of the Atomic Scientists', 25, 6-8.
Costa de Beauregard, O. (1975), Quantum paradoxes and Aristotle's twofold information concept, in Oteri (1975), 91-108.
Costa de Beauregard, O. (1976), Time symmetry and interpretation of quantum mechanics, 'Foundations of Physics', 6, 539-59.
Culliton, B. (1974a), The Sloan-Kettering affair, a story without a hero, 'Science', May 16, 644-50.
Culliton, B. (1974b), The Sloan-Kettering affair (II): an uneasy resolution, 'Science', June 14, 1154-7.
Dean, E.D. (1969), 'The Parapsychological Association Becomes Affiliated with the American Association for the Advancement of Science', unpublished informal document.
d'Espagnat, B. (1976), 'Conceptual Foundations of Quantum Mechanics', 2nd edn, Boston, Mass.: Benjamin.
Dewitt, B.S. (1970), Quantum mechanics and reality, 'Physics Today', Sept. 30-5.
Dewitt, B.S. (1971), Dewitt replies, 'Physics Today', April, 41-4.
Dewitt, B.S. and Graham, N. (1973a), Resource Letter IQM-1 on the interpretation of quantum mechanics, 'American Journal of Physics', 39, 725-38.
Dewitt, B.S. and Graham, N. (eds) (1973b), 'The Many-Worlds Interpretation of Quantum Mechanics', Princeton: Princeton University Press.
Dixon, B. (1973), Science, religion and a broken spoon, 'New Scientist', 2 August, 256.
Dobbs, A. (1967), The feasibility of a physical theory of ESP, in Smythies (1967), 225-54.
Dolby, R.G.A. (1979), Reflections on deviant science, in Wallis (1979), 9-47.
Ducasse, C.J. (1954), The philosophical importance of psychic phenomena, 'Journal of Philosophy', 51, 810-23.
Ducasse, C.J. (1959), Causality and parapsychology, 'Journal of Parapsychology', 23, 90-6.
Ehrenberg, W. (1960), Contribution to: Responses to the forum on physicality and psi, 'Journal of Parapsychology', 24, 216-8.
Ellison, A.J. (1974), Letter to the Editor, 'New Scientist', 7 November, 444.
Evans, C. (1976), Geller effects and explanations, 'New Humanist', July/August, 50-3.
Evans-Pritchard, E.E. (1976), 'Witchcraft, Oracles and Magic among the Azande', Oxford; Clarendon Press.
Everett, H. (1957), 'Relative State' formulation of quantum mechanics, 'Reviews of Modern Physics', 29, 454-62.
Feinberg, G. (1975), Precognition – a memory of things future, in Oteri (1975), 54-76.
Festinger, L., Riechen, H.W. and Schachter, S.C. (1956), 'When Prophecy Fails', New York: Harper and Row.
Feyerabend, P.K. (1975), 'Against Method', London: New Left Books.
Fleck, L. (1979), 'The Genesis and Development of a Scientific Fact', Chicago: Chicago University Press.
Flew, A. (1953), 'A New Approach to Psychical Research', London: Watts.
Frankel, E. (1976), Corpuscular optics and the wave theory of light: the science and politics of a revolution in physics, 'Social Studies of Science', 6, 141-84.
Franklin, W. (1973), Teleneural physics, 'Physics Today', August, 11-12.
Franklin, W. (1977), Prof. Franklin retracts, 'Humanist', Sept./Oct., 54-5.
Frazier, K. (1976), Science and the parascience cults, 'Science News', 109, 346-8.
Freedman, S.J. and Clauser, J.F. (1972), Experimental test of local hidden-variable theories, 'Physical Review Letters', 28, 938-41.

Freudlich, Y. (1972), Mind, matter and physicists, 'Foundations of Physics', 2, 129-48.
'Fuller, U.' (1976), 'Confessions of a Psychic', available from Karl Fulves, Box 433, Teaneck, N.J. 07666,USA.
Gardner, M. (1957), 'Fads and Fallacies in the Name of Science', New York: Dover.
Gardner, M. (1975a), Paranonsense, 'New York Review of Books', 30 October.
Gardner, M. (1975b), Concerning an effort to demonstrate extrasensory perception by machine, 'Scientific American', October 1975, 114-8.
Gardner, M. (1976), Magic and paraphysics, 'Technology Review', June, 43-51.
Gardner, M. (1979), Quantum theory and quack theory, 'New York Review of Books', May 17, 39-41.
Gauld, A. (1967), 'The Founders of Psychical Research', New York: Schocken Books.
Gellner, E. (1974), The new idealism: cause and meanings in the social sciences, in Giddens, A. (ed.), 'Positivism and Sociology', London: Heinemann.
Giddens, A. (1976), 'New Rules of Sociological Method', London: Hutchinson.
Good, I.J. (ed.) (1963), 'The Scientist Speculates', New York: Basic Books.
Good, I.J. (1975), And Good saw that it was God(d), 'Parascience Research Journal', 1, No. 2, 3-14.
Gordon, J.E. (1968), 'The New Science of Strong Materials', London: Penguin.
Gordon, M.D. (1975), The Institutionalisation of Parapsychology: A Study of Innovation in Science, M. Sc. dissertation, Manchester University.
Gwynne, P. (1973), Diets and psychics, 'New Scientist', 22 March, 666-7.
Hall, J., Kim, C., McElroy, B. and Shimony, A. (1977), Wave-packet reduction as a medium of communication, 'Foundations of Physics', 7, 759-67.
Hanlon, J. (1974a), Uri Geller and science, 'New Scientist', 17 October, 170-85.
Hanlon, J. (1974b), Replies to Bastin, Mitchell and O'Regan, 'New Scientist', 28 November, 682.
Hanlon, J. (1975), Can MoD prevent Taylor from using its money to study 'Geller Effect'?, 'New Scientist', 13 February, 400.
Hansel, C.E.M. (1959), Experiments on telepathy, 'New Scientist', 26 February, 457-9.
Hansel, C.E.M. (1960), Experiments on telepathy in children, 'British Journal of Statistical Psychology', 13, 175-8.
Hansel, C.E.M. (1966), 'E.S.P.: A Scientific Evaluation', New York: Charles Scribner's Sons.
Harvey, B. (1981), Plausibility and the evaluation of knowledge: a case-study in experimental quantum mechanics, in Collins (1981), 95-130.
Hasted, J.B. (1974), Letter to the Editor, 'New Scientist', 31 October, 356.
Hasted, J.B. (1976a), 'My Geller Notebooks', revised and redrafted as Hasted (1981).
Hasted, J.B. (1976b), An experimental study of the validity of metal bending phenomena, 'Journal of the Society for Psychical Research', 48, 365-83.
Hasted, J.B. (1979), Relation between psychic phenomena and physics, 'Psychoenergetic Systems', 3, 243-57.
Hasted, J.B. (1981), 'The Metal Benders', London: Routledge & Kegan Paul.
Hasted, J.B., Bohm, D.J., Bastin, E.W., O'Regan, B. and Taylor, J.G. (1975), Report on approaches and philosophy of work, 'Nature', 254, 470-3.
Hebard, A.F. (1973), A superconducting suspension with variable restoring force and low damping, 'Review of Scientific Instruments', 44, 425-9.
Herbert, N. (1975), Cryptographic approach to hidden variables, 'American Journal of Physics', 43, 315-6.
Hesse, M. (1974), 'The Structure of Scientific Inference', London: Macmillan.
Hixson, J. (1976), 'The Patchwork Mouse', New York: Doubleday.
Hoagland, H. (1969), Beings from outer space - corporeal and spiritual, 'Science', 163, 625.
Holt, R.A. and Freedman, S.J. (1975), Test of local hidden-variable theories in atomic physics, 'Comments on Atomic and Molecular Physics', 5, 55-62.
Honorton, C. (1975), Error some place, 'Journal of Communication', 25, 103-16.

Horton, R. and Finnegan, R. (1973), 'Modes of Thought', London: Faber and Faber.
Hyman, R. (1976), Review of 'The Geller Papers', 'Zetetic', 1, 73-80.
Hyman, R. (1977), Psychics and scientists: 'Mind-Reach', and remote viewing, 'Humanist', May/June, 16-20.
Jammer, M. (1966), 'The Conceptual Development of Quantum Mechanics', New York: McGraw Hill.
Jammer, M. (1974), 'The Philosophy of Quantum Mechanics: The Interpretations of Quantum Mechanics in Historical Perspective', New York: John Wiley.
Jordan, P. (1951), Reflections on parapsychology, psychoanalysis and atomic physics, 'Journal of Parapsychology', 15, 278-81.
Jordan, P. (1955), Atomic physics and parapsychology, 'Newsletter of the Parapsychology Foundation', July-August, 3-7.
Josephson, B.D. (1975), Possible connections between psychic phenomena and quantum mechanics, 'New Horizons', January, 224-6.
Klip, W. (1966), The interpretation of the quantum theory, Letter to the Editor, 'Journal of the Society for Psychical Research', 43, 441.
Klip, W. (1967), An experimental approach to the interpretation of the quantum theory, 'Journal of the Society for Psychical Research', 44, 181-7.
Knight, M. (1950), Theoretical implications of telepathy, 'Science News', 18, 9-20.
Knorr, K.D. (1979), Tinkering toward success: prelude to a theory of scientific practice, 'Theory and Society', 8, 347-76.
Koestler, A. (1975), 'The Midwife Toad', London: Picador.
Krausz, M. (ed.) (1972), 'Critical Essays in the Philosophy of R.G. Collingwood', Oxford: Oxford University Press.
Krausz, M. (1973), Relativism and rationality, 'American Philosophical Quarterly', 10, 307-12.
Kuhn, T.S. (1962), 'The Structure of Scientific Revolutions', Chicago: University of Chicago Press.
Kuhn, T.S. (1970a), Postscript, in 'The Structure of Scientific Revolutions', 2nd edn, Chicago: University of Chicago Press.
Kuhn, T.S. (1970b), Logic of discovery or psychology of research, in Lakatos and Musgrave (1970), 1-24.
Kuhn, T.S. (1977), 'The Essential Tension', Chicago: University of Chicago Press.
Kuhn, T.S. (1978), 'Black-Body Theory and the Quantum Discontinuity, 1894-1912', Oxford: Clarendon Press.
Lakatos, I. and Musgrave, A. (eds) (1970), 'Criticism and the Growth of Knowledge', Cambridge: Cambridge University Press.
LaRue, G.S., Fairbank, W.M. and Hebard, A.F. (1977), Evidence for the existence of fractional charge on matter, 'Physical Review Letters', 38, 1011-4.
Latour, B. and Woolgar, S. (1979), 'Laboratory Life', Beverley Hills: Sage.
Laudan, L. (1977), 'Progress and Its Problems', London: Routledge & Kegan Paul.
McConnell, R.A. (1947), Physical or non-physical?, 'Journal of Parapsychology', 11, 111-17.
MacIntyre, A. (1962), A mistake about causality in social science, in Laslett, P. and Runciman, W.G., (eds), 'Philosophy, Politics and Society', 2nd series, Oxford: Blackwell, 48-70.
McVaugh, M. and Mauskopf, S.H. (1976), J.B. Rhine's extra-sensory perception and its background in psychical research, 'Isis', 67, 161-89.
McVaugh, M. and Mauskopf, S.H. (1980),'The Elusive Science: Origins of Experimental Psychical Research', Baltimore/London: Johns Hopkins University Press.
Mannheim, K. (1936), 'Ideology and Utopia', New York: Harcourt, Brace and World.
Margenau, H. (1956), Physics and psychic research, 'Newsletter of the Parapsychology Foundation', January-February, 14-15.
Margenau, H. (1966), ESP in the framework of modern science, 'Journal of the American Society for Psychical Research', 60, 214-28.

200   *Bibliography*

Marks, D. and Kammann, R. (1980), 'The Psychology of the Psychic', Buffalo: Prometheus Books.
Masterman, M. (1970), The nature of a paradigm, in Lakatos and Musgrave (1970), 59-89.
Mattuck, R.D. (1979), Thermal noise theory of psychokinesis: modified Walker Model with pulsed information rate, 'Psychoenergetic Systems', 3, 301-23.
Mattuck, R.D. and Walker, E.H. (1979), The action of consciousness on matter – a quantum mechanical theory of psychokinesis, in Puharich (1979), 111-60.
Meehl, P.E. and Scriven, M. (1956), Compatibility of science and ESP?, 'Science', 123, 14-15.
Mills, R. (1976), Quantum theory and the mind, unpublished paper, School of Mathematical and Physical Sciences, University of Sussex, November.
Mitchell, E.D. (1974a), Letter to the Editor, 'New Scientist', 28 November, 680-1.
Mitchell, E.D. (ed.) (1974b), 'Psychic Exploration', New York: Putmans.
'Monitor' (1977), The quark: judgement reserved, 'New Scientist', 5 May, 265.
Morris, R.L. (1975), Building experimental models, 'Journal of Communication', 25, 115-25.
Morrison, P. (1976), Uri Geller: international pied piper of the credulous and other matters, 'Scientific American', February, 134-5.
Mulkay, M.J. (1972), 'The Social Processes of Innovation', London: Macmillan.
Mulkay, M.J. (1975), Three models of scientific development, 'Sociological Review', 23, 501-33.
Mulkay, M.J. (1979), 'Science and the Sociology of Knowledge', London: George Allen and Unwin.
Mulkay, M.J. (1980), The study of action and belief or the study of discourse, paper presented to the Philosophy of the Social Sciences Conference, Toronto, 17-19 October.
Mundle, C.W.K. (1950), Contribution to: Symposium: Is psychical research relevant to philosophy?, 'Proceedings of the Aristotelian Society', Supplementary Volume, 24, 207-31.
Mundle, C.W.K. (1952), Some philosophical perspectives for parapsychology, 'Journal of Parapsychology', 16, 257-72.
Mundle, C.W.K. (1967a), ESP phenomena, philosophical implications of, 'The Encyclopedia of Philosophy', vol. 3, New York: Macmillan and Free Press, 49-58.
Mundle, C.W.K. (1967b), The explanation of ESP, in Smythies (1967), 197-208.
Murphy, G. (1953), Psychology and psychical research, 'Proceedings of the Society for Psychical Research', 50, 26-50.
Murphy, G. (1968), Parapsychology: new neighbour or unwelcome guest?, 'Psychology Today', May, 53-5, 65.
'Nature' (1974), Editorial, Science beyond the fringe, vol. 248, 541.
Nilsson, I. (1975), The paradigm of the Rhinean School, Part 1, 'European Journal of Parapsychology', 1, 45-59.
Nilsson, I. (1976), The paradigm of the Rhinean School, Part 2: the concept of science, 'European Journal of Parapsychology', 1, no. 2, 45-56.
'Nous Letter', (1976), Contending modern physics theories in relation to consciousness, vol. 2, no. 2, 23-9 (contributions by S.-P. Sirag, C. Muses and D. Bohm).
O'Regan, B. (1973), Now you see it, now . . .?, 'New Scientist', 12 July, 95-6.
Oteri, L. (ed.) (1975), 'Quantum Physics and Parapsychology', New York: Parapsychology Foundation.
Overington, M. (1979), I'm right and you're wrong; my mummy said so!: a rejoinder, 'American Sociologist', 14, 31-4.
Palfreman, J. (1979), Between scepticism and credulity: a study of Victorian scientific attitudes to modern spiritualism, in Wallis, (1979), 201-36.
Pamplin, B. (1975), Letter to the Editor, 'Assembly News and Views' (University of Bath academics' magazine), 11, 11 October, 36-7.
Pamplin, B. (1976), Are all spoon benders merely twisters?, unpublished manuscript, University of Bath (Excerpt published 'Bath and West Evening Chronicle', March 27).
Pamplin, B. and Collins, H.M. (1975), Correspondence: Spoon bending: an experimental approach, 'Nature', 257, 8.

Panati, C. (ed.) (1976), 'The Geller Papers', Boston: Houghton Mifflin.
Pantell, R.H. and Puthoff, H.E. (1969), 'Fundamentals of Quantum Electronics', New York: John Wiley.
Patterson, D. (1977), Queasy over the quark, 'New Scientist', 30 June, 773-5.
Pinch, T.J. (1976), Hidden Variables, Impossibility Proofs, and Paradoxes: A Sociological Study of Non-Relativistic Quantum Mechanics, M.Sc. dissertation, Manchester University.
Pinch, T.J. (1977), What does a proof do if it does not prove? A study of the social conditions and metaphysical divisions leading to David Bohm and John von Neumann failing to communicate in quantum physics, in Mendelsohn, E., Weingart, P. and Whitley, R.D. (eds), 'The Social Production of Scientific Knowledge', Dordrecht: Reidel, 121-215.
Pinch, T.J. (1979a), Contribution to: Paradigm lost? A review symposium, 'Isis', 70, 437-40.
Pinch, T.J. (1979b), Normal explanations of the paranormal: the demarcation problem and fraud in parapsychology, 'Social Studies of Science', 9, 329-48.
Popper, K.R. (1959), 'The Logic of Scientific Discovery', London: Hutchinson.
Pratt, J.G. (1960), Contribution to: Physicality and psi, a symposium and forum discussion, 'Journal of Parapsychology', 24, 23-7.
Pratt, J.G. (1971), Glimpses of a psi utopia?, 'Journal of the American Society for Psychical Research', 65, 88-102.
Pratt, J.G. (1974), Some notes for the future Einstein for parapsychology, 'Journal of the American Society for Psychical Research', 68, 133-55.
Price, G.R. (1955), Science and the supernatural, 'Science', 122, 359-67.
Price, H.H. (1948-9), Psychical research and human personality, 'Hibbert Journal', 47, 105-13, (Reprinted in Smythies (1967), 33-45.)
Puharich, A. (1974), 'Uri', New York: Anchor Press.
Puharich, A. (ed.) (1979), 'The Iceland Papers', Wisconsin: Essentia Research Associates.
Quine, W.V. (1953), 'From a Logical Point of View', Cambridge, Mass.: Harvard University Press.
Randi, J. (1975), 'The Magic of Uri Geller: As Revealed by the Amazing Randi', New York: Ballantine.
Rush, J.H. (1943), Some considerations as to the physical basis of ESP,'Journal of Parapsychology', 7, 44-9.
Sarfatti, J. (1974a), Implications of meta-physics for psychoenergetic systems, 'Psychoenergetic Systems', 1, 3-10.
Sarfatti, J. (1974b), Geller performs for physicists, 'Science News', 106,46.
Sarfatti, J. (1975), The physical roots of consciousness, in Mishlove, J., 'The Roots of Consciousness', New York: Random House, 279-93.
Sarfatti, J. (1976a), Letter to the Editor, 'Psychoenergetic Systems', 2, 1-8.
Sarfatti, J. (1976b), Reply to Martin Gardner's (M.I.T.) June, 1976. 'Technology Review' article, unpublished letter.
Sarfatti, J. (1977), The case for superluminal transfer, 'Technology Review', March/April, 3.
Scheffler, I. (1967), 'Science and Subjectivity', Indianapolis: Bobs-Merrill.
Schmeidler, G.R. and McConnell, R.A. (1958), 'ESP and Personality Patterns', New Haven: Yale University Press.
Schmidt, H. (1969a), Quantum processes predicted?, 'New Scientist', 16 October, 114-15.
Schmidt, H. (1969b), Precognition of a quantum process, 'Journal of Parapsychology', 33, 99-108.
Schmidt, H. (1970), Quantum-mechanical random-number generator, 'Journal of Applied Physics', 41, 462-8.
Schmidt, H. (1971), Mental influences on random events, 'New Scientist', 24 June, 757-8.
Schmidt, H. (1973), PK test with a high speed random number generator, 'Journal of Parapsychology', 37, 105-18.
Schmidt, H. (1975), A logically consistent model of a world with psi interaction, in Oteri (1975), 205-22.
Schmidt, H. (1976), PK effect on pre-recorded targets, 'Journal of American

Society for Psychical Research', 70, 267-91.
Scott, C. and Haskell, P. (1973), 'Normal' explanation of the Soal-Goldney experiments in extrasensory perception, 'Nature', 245, 52-4.
Scott, C. and Haskell, P. (1974), Fresh light on the Shackleton experiments?, 'Proceedings of the Society for Psychical Research', 56, 43-72.
Scriven, M. (1960a), Contribution to: Responses to the forum on physicality and psi, 'Journal of Parapsychology', 24, 214-5.
Scriven, M. (1960b), Contribution to: Physicality and psi, a symposium and forum discussion, 'Journal of Parapsychology', 24, 14-16.
Scriven, M. (1962), The frontiers of psychology: psychoanalysis and parapsychology, in Colodny, R.G. (ed.), 'Frontiers of Science and Philosophy', Pittsburgh: University of Pittsburgh Press, 79-129.
Sharrock, S. (1977), Quarks out of the bag?, 'Nature', 266, 768.
Shewmaker, K.L. and Berenda, C.W. (1976), Science and the problem of psi, in Wheatley and Edge (1976), 413-24.
Shimony, A. (1963), Role of the observer in quantum theory, 'American Journal of Physics', 31, 755-73.
Silcock, B. (1977), Discreet charm of the quark, 'Sunday Times', 1 May.
Smythies, J.R. (ed.) (1967), 'Science and ESP', London: Routledge & Kegan Paul.
Stapp, H.P. (1968), Mind, matter and quantum mechanics, Lawrence Radiation Laboratory Paper, February 9.
Stapp, H.P. (1975a), Theory of reality, Lawrence Berkeley Laboratory Report no. 3837.
Stapp, H.P. (1975b), Bell's Theorem and world process, 'Nuovo Cimento', 298, 270-6.
Stapp, H.P. (1976), Are superluminal connections necessary?, Lawrence Berkeley Laboratory Report no. 5559.
Stevens, S.S. (1967), The market for miracles, 'Contemporary Psychology', 12, 1-3.
Szasz, T.S. (1957), A critical analysis of the fundamental concepts of psychical research, 'Psychiatric Quarterly', 31, 96-107.
Targ, R. and Hunt, O.B. (1972), Learning clairvoyance and precognition with an extrasensory perception teaching machine, 'Parapsychology Review', July-August, 9-11.
Targ, R. and Puthoff, H. (1974a), Information transmission under conditions of sensory shielding, 'Nature', 251, 602-7.
Targ, R. and Puthoff, H. (1974b), Letter to the Editor, 'New Scientist', 7 November, 443.
Targ, R. and Puthoff, H. (1977), 'Mind-Reach', New York: Delacorte.
Tart, C.T. (1972), States of consciousness and state-specific sciences, 'Science', 176, 1203-10. (Reprinted in Wheatley and Edge (1976), 441-64.)
Taylor, J. (1971), 'The Shape of Minds to Come', New York: Weybright & Talley (Penguin edition, 1974).
Taylor, J. (1973), 'Black Holes: The End of the Universe?', London: Souvenir Press.
Taylor, J. (1975a), 'Superminds: An Enquiry into the Paranormal', London: Macmillan.
Taylor, J. (1975b), Correspondence: Cheating children, 'Nature', 257, 354.
Taylor, J. (1977), New developments in ESP, 'Vogue', November, 84-8.
Taylor, J. (1980), 'Science and the Supernatural', London: Temple Smith.
Taylor, J.G. and Balanovski, E. (1980), Is there any scientific explanation of the paranormal?, 'Nature', 279, 31-3.
'Time', (1973), The magician and the think tank, 12 March, 47-8.
Toben, B. (1975), 'Space, Time and Beyond', New York: Dutton.
Tottle, C.R. (1975), Letter to the Editor, 'Assembly News and Views' (University of Bath academics' magazine), 11, 11 October, 35-6.
Toulmin, S. (1958), 'The Uses of Argument', Cambridge: Cambridge University Press.
Travis, G.D.L. (1980), Creating contradiction, paper presented to the 5th annual meeting of the Society for Social Studies of Science, Toronto, 17-19 October.

Trigg, R. (1973), 'Reason and Commitment', Cambridge: Cambridge University Press.
Truzzi, M. (1975), Editorial, 'Zetetic' (newsletter), 3, no. 2, 1.
Truzzi, M. (1977a), From the Editor, 'Zetetic', 1, no. 2, 3-8.
Truzzi, M. (1977b), Personal communication, October.
von Neumann, J. (1955), 'Mathematical Foundations of Quantum Theory', Princeton: Princeton University Press.
Walker, E.H. (1970), The nature of consciousness, 'Mathematical Biosciences', 7, 131-78.
Walker, E.H. (1971), Consciousness as a hidden variable, 'Physics Today', 39.
Walker, E.H. (1972), Consciousness in the quantum theory of measurement, Parts I and II, 'Journal for the Study of Consciousness', 5, 46-63 and 257-76.
Walker, E.H. (1974a), The complete quantum mechanical anthropologist; paper presented at the Rhine-Swanton Symposium on Parapsychology and Anthropology, 73rd Annual American Anthropological Association Meeting, Mexico City, 19-24 November.
Walker, E.H. (1974b), Consciousness and quantum theory, in Mitchell (1974b), 544-71.
Walker, E.H. (1975), Foundations of paraphysical and parapsychological phenomena, in Oteri (1975), 1-44.
Walker, E.H. (1976), Properties of hidden variables in quantum theory: implications for paraphysics, unpublished paper.
Walker, E.H. (1977), Quantum mechanical tunnelling in synaptic and ephaptic transmission, 'International Journal of Quantum Chemistry', 11, 103-27.
Walker, E.H. (1979), The quantum theory of psi phenomena, 'Psychoenergetic Systems', 3, 259-99.
Wallis, R. (1977), 'The Road to Total Freedom', London: Heinemann Educational.
Wallis, R. (ed.) (1979), 'On the Margins of Science: The Social Construction of Rejected Knowledge', Sociological Review Monograph no. 27, Keele: University of Keele.
Warnock, M. (1967), 'Existentialist Ethics', London: Macmillan.
Watkins, D.S. (1969), Blondlot's N-rays: a history of a notable scientific error, unpublished paper from Department of Liberal Studies in Science, University of Manchester.
Weimer, W.B. (1974), The history of psychology and its retrieval from historiography: I. The problematic nature of history, 'Science Studies', 4, 235-58; II. Some lessons for the methodology of scientific research, Ibid., 367-96.
Weingart, P. (1974), On a sociological theory of scientific change, in Whitley, R.D. (ed.), 'Social Processes of Scientific Development', London: Routledge & Kegan Paul, 44-69.
Werbos, P.J. (1973), An approach to the realistic explanation of quantum mechanics, 'Nuovo Cimento Letters', 8, 105-9.
Werbos, P.J. (1975), Experimental implications of the reinterpretation of quantum mechanics, 'Nuovo Cimento', 298, 169-77.
Werskey, G. (1978), 'The Visible College', London: Allen Lane.
Westrum, R. (1976), Scientists as experts: observation on objections to astrology, 'Zetetic', 1, no. 1, 34-46.
Wheatley, J.M.O. and Edge, H.L. (eds) (1976), 'Philosophical Dimensions of Parapsychology', Illinois: Charles C. Thomas.
Wheeler, J.A. (1979a), Not consciousness but the distinction between the probe and the probed as central to the elemental quantum act of observation, paper presented to the American Association for the Advancement of Science, Houston, January.
Wheeler, J.A. (1979b), Letter to the Editor: Parapsychology - a correction, 'Science', 205, 144.
White, R.A. (1974), Review of Parapsychology Today: A Geographic View, 'Journal of the American Society for Psychical Research', 68, 305-7.
Whiteman, J.H.M. (1973), Quantum theory and parapsychology, 'Journal of the American Society for Psychical Research', 66, 341-60.
Whiteman, J.H.M. (1975), Parapsychology as an analytico-deductive science, in Oteri (1975), 181-204.

Whitley, R.D. (1975), Components of scientific activities, their characteristics and institutionalization in specialties and research areas: a framework for the comparative analysis of scientific specialties, in Knorr, K., Strasser, H. and Zilian, H. (eds), 'Determinants and Controls of Scientific Development', Dordrecht: Reidel, 37-75.

Wigner, E.P. (1963), Remarks on the mind-body question, in Good (1963). (Also published in Wigner (1967).

Wigner, E.P. (1967), 'Symmetries and Reflections', Bloomington: Indiana University Press.

Wilhelm, J.L. (1976), 'The Search for Superman', New York: Pocket Books.

Wilson, B.R. (ed.) (1970), 'Rationality', Oxford: Blackwell.

Winch, P. (1958), 'The Idea of a Social Science', London: Routledge & Kegan Paul.

Winch, P. (1964), Understanding a primitive society, 'American Philosophical Quarterly', 1, 307-24.

Wittgenstein, L. (1953), 'Philosophical Investigations', Oxford: Blackwell.

Wittgenstein, L. (1956), 'Remarks on the Foundations of Mathematics', Oxford: Blackwell.

Wolf, A. (1975), The 'I'-not 'I' process: a physicist's view of parascience, 'Parascience Research Journal', 1, no. 2, 19-28.

Wolf, F.A. (1976), Consciousness, quantum mechanics and the role of the observer Paper presented to the conference on David Bohm's Concept of the Implicate Order, organised by the Center for Process Studies, held on the campus of Harvey Mudd College, Claremont, California, 3 April.

Woolgar, S. (1976), Writing on intellectual history of scientific developments: the use of discovery accounts, 'Social Studies of Science', 6, 395-422.

Wynne, B. (1979), Physics and psychics: science, symbolic action and social control in late Victorian England, in Barnes and Shapin (1979): 168-86.

Zweifel, P.F. (1974), Measurement in quantum mechanics and the EPR paradox, 'International Journal of Theoretical Physics', 10, 67-72.

NAME INDEX

SUBJECT INDEX